Hands-On Linux for Architects

Design and implement Linux-based IT solutions

Denis Salamanca
Esteban Flores

BIRMINGHAM - MUMBAI

Hands-On Linux for Architects

Commissioning Editor: Vijin Boricha
Acquisition Editor: Rohit Rajkumar
Content Development Editor: Jordina Dcunha
Technical Editor: Mamta Yadav
Copy Editor: Safis Editing
Project Coordinator: Nusaiba Ansari
Proofreader: Safis Editing
Indexer: Tejal Daruwale Soni
Graphics: Jisha Chirayil
Production Coordinator: Jyoti Chauhan

First published: April 2019

Production reference: 1270419

Published by Packt Publishing Ltd.
Livery Place
35 Livery Street
Birmingham
B3 2PB, UK.

ISBN 978-1-78953-410-8

www.packtpub.com

`mapt.io`

Mapt is an online digital library that gives you full access to over 5,000 books and videos, as well as industry leading tools to help you plan your personal development and advance your career. For more information, please visit our website.

Why subscribe?

- Spend less time learning and more time coding with practical eBooks and Videos from over 4,000 industry professionals

- Improve your learning with Skill Plans built especially for you

- Get a free eBook or video every month

- Mapt is fully searchable

- Copy and paste, print, and bookmark content

Packt.com

Did you know that Packt offers eBook versions of every book published, with PDF and ePub files available? You can upgrade to the eBook version at `www.packt.com` and as a print book customer, you are entitled to a discount on the eBook copy. Get in touch with us at `customercare@packtpub.com` for more details.

At `www.packt.com`, you can also read a collection of free technical articles, sign up for a range of free newsletters, and receive exclusive discounts and offers on Packt books and eBooks.

Contributors

About the authors

Denis Salamanca is a technology enthusiast living in Costa Rica with his fiancée and step-son. He has been working in IT since he was 20 and has worked for the most influential and leading companies in the industry, including VMware, Microsoft, and Hewlett-Packard Enterprise. He currently holds more than 10 technical certifications across different fields, such as cloud, storage, Linux, Docker, and virtualization. He has also participated in the development of Linux certifications and is part of the CompTIA Linux Subject Matter Experts and Technical Advisory Committee.

His love for technology has driven him to work in different positions and fields across his career, and this has helped him to develop an understanding about the different points of view that a technical solution requires.

Esteban Flores has been meddling with computers since he was 8 years old. His life as an IT expert began when he lost a lot of important data belonging to his family by saying he was "fixing the computer." He's worked for top-tier companies, including Hewlett-Packard Enterprise, VMware, Akamai, and Microsoft. With 10 years' experience, his passion for cutting-edge technology has driven him to work on different roles during his professional career. Storage technologies have always been his forte, focusing mostly on performance tuning and optimization. A photographer during his free time, he's been doing Linux-related things since his first job, finding amazement in its flexibility to run from a small laptop all the way up to the world's fastest supercomputers.

About the reviewer

Donald Tevault—but you can call him "Donnie"—has been working with Linux since way back in 2006. He's a professional Linux trainer, with the LPI Level 3 - Security and the GIAC Incident Handler certifications. Donnie is also a fellow Packt Publishing author, having published *Mastering Linux Security and Hardening* as his first book. He's the brains behind the *BeginLinux Guru* channel on YouTube, and works as a Linux consultant for the VDOO IoT security company.

> *I'd like to thank the good folk at Packt Publishing for giving me this opportunity. I'd also like to thank my cats for finally allowing me to get this done.*

Packt is searching for authors like you

If you're interested in becoming an author for Packt, please visit `authors.packtpub.com` and apply today. We have worked with thousands of developers and tech professionals, just like you, to help them share their insight with the global tech community. You can make a general application, apply for a specific hot topic that we are recruiting an author for, or submit your own idea.

I want to dedicate this book to my parents and my lovely fiancée, who have always supported me and given me their best, so I can not only reach my goals, but also achieve them successfully. Without them, nothing would have been possible. Thank you for always being there for me.

-Denis Salamanca

I would like to dedicate this book to my grandmother, who unfortunately passed away during the development of the book and couldn't see the finished version. Even when she didn't even understand the language or what was being described, she always asked about its progress.

-Esteban Flores

Table of Contents

Section 3: Elastic Stack

Preface

Welcome to *Hands-On Linux For Architects*, an in-depth look at what goes through the mind of an architect when dealing with Linux-based solutions. This book will help you achieve the level of knowledge required to architect and implement different IT solutions.

Additionally, it will show you the flexibility of open source software by demonstrating some of the most widely used products of the industry, presenting you with a solution and analyzing every aspect, from the very beginning of the design phase, all the way up to the implementation stage, where we will build, from the ground up, the infrastructure proposed in our design.

Delve inside the technical aspects of designing a solution, where we dissect every aspect with in-depth details to implement and tune open source Linux-based solutions.

Who this book is for

This book is aimed at Linux system administrators, Linux support engineers, DevOps engineers, Linux consultants, and any other type of open source technology professional looking to learn or expand their knowledge in architecting, designing, and implementing solutions based on Linux and open source software.

What this book covers

Chapter 1, *Introduction to Design Methodology*, kicks off the book by analyzing a proposed problem, as well as what the correct questions are to ask when designing a solution, in order to extract the necessary information to define the correct problem statement.

Chapter 2, *Defining GlusterFS Storage*, goes through what GlusterFS is and defines a storage cluster.

Chapter 3, *Architecting a Storage Cluster*, explores the design aspects of implementing a clustered storage solution using GlusterFS and its various components.

Chapter 4, *Using GlusterFS on the Cloud Infrastructure*, explains the configuration necessary to implement GlusterFS on the cloud.

Chapter 5, *Analyzing Performance in a Gluster System*, details the previously configured solution, explaining the configurations put in place, as well as testing the implementation for performance.

Chapter 6, *Creating a Highly Available Self-Healing Architecture*, talks about how the IT industry has evolved from using monolithic applications into cloud-native, containerized, highly available microservices.

Chapter 7, *Understanding the Core Components of a Kubernetes Cluster*, explores the core Kubernetes components, giving a view of each one and how they can help us solve our customer's problem.

Chapter 8, *Architecting a Kubernetes Cluster*, dives into the requirements and configurations for a Kubernetes cluster.

Chapter 9, *Deploying and Configuring Kubernetes*, goes into the actual installation and configuration of a Kubernetes cluster.

Chapter 10, *Monitoring with the ELK Stack*, explains what each component of the Elastic Stack is and how they're connected.

Chapter 11, *Designing an ELK Stack*, covers the design considerations when deploying an Elastic Stack.

Chapter 12, *Using Elasticsearch, Logstash, and Kibana to Manage Logs*, describes the implementation, installation, and configuration of the Elastic Stack.

Chapter 13, *Solving Management Problems with Salty Solutions*, discusses the business needs to have a centralized management utility for infrastructure, such as Salt.

Chapter 14, *Getting Your Hands Salty*, examines how to install and configure Salt.

Chapter 15, *Design Best Practices*, takes you through some of the different best practices needed to design a resilient and failure-proof solution.

To get the most out of this book

Some basic Linux knowledge is needed, as this book does not explain the basics of Linux management.

The examples given in this book can be implemented either in the cloud or on-premises. Some of the setups were deployed on Microsoft's cloud platform, Azure, so having an account with Azure to follow the examples is recommended. Azure does offer a free trial to evaluate and test deployments before committing—more information can be found at `https://azure.microsoft.com/free/`.

Additionally, more information on Azure's offerings can be found at: `https://azure.microsoft.com`.

Since the book entirely revolves around Linux, having a way to connect to the internet is a requirement. This can be done from a Linux desktop (or laptop), a macOS Terminal, or **Windows Subsystem for Linux** (**WSL**).

All of the examples illustrated in this book make use of open source software that can be easily obtained from either the available repositories or from their respective sources, without the need of a paying license.

Be sure to drop by the projects pages to show some love—a lot of effort goes into developing them:

- `https://github.com/gluster/glusterfs`
- `https://github.com/zfsonlinux/zfs`
- `https://github.com/kubernetes/kubernetes`
- `https://github.com/elastic/elasticsearch`
- `https://github.com/saltstack/salt`

Download the example code files

You can download the example code files for this book from your account at `www.packt.com`. If you purchased this book elsewhere, you can visit `www.packt.com/support` and register to have the files emailed directly to you.

You can download the code files by following these steps:

1. Log in or register at `www.packt.com`.
2. Select the **SUPPORT** tab.
3. Click on **Code Downloads & Errata**.
4. Enter the name of the book in the **Search** box and follow the onscreen instructions.

Once the file is downloaded, please make sure that you unzip or extract the folder using the latest version of:

- WinRAR/7-Zip for Windows
- Zipeg/iZip/UnRarX for Mac
- 7-Zip/PeaZip for Linux

The code bundle for the book is also hosted on GitHub at `https://github.com/PacktPublishing/-Hands-On-Linux-for-Architects`. In case there's an update to the code, it will be updated on the existing GitHub repository.

We also have other code bundles from our rich catalog of books and videos available at `https://github.com/PacktPublishing/`. Check them out!

Download the color images

We also provide a PDF file that has color images of the screenshots/diagrams used in this book. You can download it here: `https://www.packtpub.com/sites/default/files/downloads/9781789534108_ColorImages.pdf`.

Conventions used

There are a number of text conventions used throughout this book.

`CodeInText`: Indicates code words in text, database table names, folder names, filenames, file extensions, pathnames, dummy URLs, user input, and Twitter handles. Here is an example: "The two key points in this command are the `address-prefix` flag and the `subnet-prefix` flag."

A block of code is set as follows:

```
apiVersion: v1
kind: PersistentVolumeClaim
metadata:
 name: gluster-pvc
spec:
 accessModes:
 - ReadWriteMany
 resources:
    requests:
      storage: 1Gi
```

When we wish to draw your attention to a particular part of a code block, the relevant lines or items are set in bold:

```
SHELL ["/bin/bash", "-c"]
RUN echo "Hello I'm using bash"
```

Any command-line input or output is written as follows:

```
yum install -y zfs
```

Bold: Indicates a new term, an important word, or words that you see onscreen. For example, words in menus or dialog boxes appear in the text like this. Here is an example: "To confirm that data is being sent to the cluster, go to **Discover** on the **kibana** screen"

Warnings or important notes appear like this.

Tips and tricks appear like this.

Get in touch

Feedback from our readers is always welcome.

General feedback: If you have questions about any aspect of this book, mention the book title in the subject of your message and email us at customercare@packtpub.com.

Errata: Although we have taken every care to ensure the accuracy of our content, mistakes do happen. If you have found a mistake in this book, we would be grateful if you would report this to us. Please visit www.packt.com/submit-errata, selecting your book, clicking on the Errata Submission Form link, and entering the details.

Piracy: If you come across any illegal copies of our works in any form on the Internet, we would be grateful if you would provide us with the location address or website name. Please contact us at copyright@packt.com with a link to the material.

If you are interested in becoming an author: If there is a topic that you have expertise in and you are interested in either writing or contributing to a book, please visit authors.packtpub.com.

Reviews

Please leave a review. Once you have read and used this book, why not leave a review on the site that you purchased it from? Potential readers can then see and use your unbiased opinion to make purchase decisions, we at Packt can understand what you think about our products, and our authors can see your feedback on their book. Thank you!

For more information about Packt, please visit `packt.com`.

Section 1: High-Performance Storage Solutions with GlusterFS

In this section, the reader will be able to understand the decisions needed to be made when deploying a high-performance storage solution using GlusterFS.

This section contains the following chapters:

- Chapter 1, *Introduction to Design Methodology*
- Chapter 2, *Defining GlusterFS Storage*
- Chapter 3, *Architecting a Storage Cluster*
- Chapter 4, *Using GlusterFS on the Cloud Infrastructure*
- Chapter 5, *Analyzing Performance in a Gluster System*

Introduction to Design Methodology 1

These days, IT solutions require increased performance and data availability, and designing a robust implementation that meets these requirements is a challenge that many IT experts have to go through every day.

In this chapter, you will learn the basics, from a bird's-eye view of architecting IT solutions in any type of environment, to virtualized infrastructure, bare metal, and even the public cloud, as basic concepts of solution design apply to any environment.

You will explore the following subjects:

- Defining the stages of solution design and why they matter
- Analyzing the problem and asking the right questions
- Considering possible solutions
- Implementing the solution

Fully understanding the aspects that you need to consider when architecting a solution is crucial for the success of the project, as this will determine which software, hardware, and configuration will help you achieve the desired state that meets the needs of your customers.

Defining the stages of solution design and why they matter

Like many things, designing solutions is a step-by-step process that not only involves: technical aspects, nor necessarily technical parties. Usually, you will be engaged by an account manager, project manager, or, if you are lucky, a CTO, who understands the technical part of the requirements. They are looking for an expert who can help them deliver a solution to a customer. These requests usually do not contain all the information you will need to deliver your solution, but it's a start to understand what your goal is.

For example, imagine that you receive an email from a project manager with the following statement.

> *We require a solution that can sustain at least 10,000 website hits and will stay available during updates as well as survive outages. Our budget is considerably low, so we need to spend as little as possible, with little to no upfront cost. We're also expecting this to gain momentum during the project's life cycle.*

From the previous statement, you can only get a general idea of what is required, but no specifics have been given. So, you only know basic information: we require a solution that can sustain at least 10,000 website hits, which, for a design, is not good enough, as you require as much information as possible to be able to resolve the problems exposed by your customer. This is where you have to ask for as many details as possible to be able to provide an accurate set of proposals for your customer, which will be the first impression your customer will have of the project. This part is critical, as it will help you understand whether you understand your customer's vision.

It is also important to understand that you need to deliver several different solutions for the customer, as the customer is the one who decides which one fits their business needs the most. Remember that each solution has its own advantages and disadvantages. After the customer decides which way to go, you will have what is necessary to move on to the implementation of your proposal, which can always trigger more challenges. It will require, more often than not, some final customized tuning or changes that were not considered in the initial **Proof of Concept** (**POC**).

From our previous analysis, you can see four well-defined stages of the process that you need to follow in order to reach the final delivery illustrated in the following diagram:

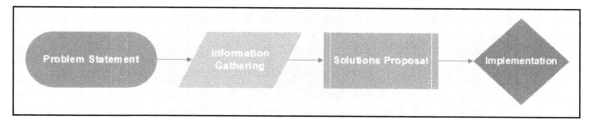

There are many more stages and design methodologies that we could cover, but since they're not in the scope of this book, we will be focusing on these four general stages to help you understand the process in which you will be architecting your solutions.

Analyzing the problem and asking the right questions

After getting the initial premise, you need to break it into smaller pieces in order to understand what is required. Each piece will raise different questions that you will ask your customers later. These questions will help fill in the gaps for your POC, ensuring that your questions cover all business needs from all view standpoints: the business standpoint, the functional standpoint, and, finally, the technical standpoint. One good way to keep track of the questions that arise and which business need they will be resolving is to have a checklist that asks which standpoint the question is being asked from and what is resolved or answered.

It is also important to note that, as questions become answers, they can also come with constraints or other obstacles that will also need to be addressed and mentioned during the POC stage. The customer will have to agree with them and will be decisive when selecting the final solution.

From our previous example, you can analyze the premise by dissecting it into standpoints.

We require a solution that can sustain at least 10,000 website hits and will stay available during updates as well as survive outages. Our budget is considerably low, so we need to spend as little as possible, with little to no upfront cost. We're also expecting this to gain momentum during the project's life cycle.

Technical standpoint

From this perspective, we will analyze all technical aspects of the premise – anything that you will need to provide the initial technical requirements of your solution.

We will analyze it in the following way:

- You can understand, from the premise, that your customer needs some kind of solution that can sustain some amount of website hits, but you can't be certain if the web server is already set up, and whether the customer only needs a load balancing solution. Alternatively, maybe the customer needs both, a web server, that is NGINX, Apache, or something of that sort, and the load balancing solution.
- The customer mentions at least 10,000 hits to their website, but they didn't mention if these hits are concurrent per second, daily, weekly, or even monthly.
- You can also see that they need to stay available during updates and be able to continue serving their website if the company has an outage, but all these statements are very general, since availability is measured in 9s. The more 9s you have, the better (in reality, this is a percentage measurement of the amount of time during the year; a 99% availability means that there can only be 526 minutes of downtime per year). Outages are also very hard to predict, and it's almost impossible to be able to say that you will never have an outage, therefore, you need to plan for it. You have to have a **Recovery point objective** (RPO) and a **Recovery time objective** (RTO) for your solution in case of a disaster. The customer didn't mention this, and it is crucial to understand how much time a business can sustain an outage.
- When it comes to budget, this is usually from a business perspective, but the technical aspects are affected directly by it. It looks like the budget in the project is tight, and the customer wants to spend as little as possible on their solution, but they're not mentioning exact numbers, which you will require in order to fit your proposals to it. Little to no upfront cost? What does this mean? Are we repurposing the existing resources and building a new solution? How can we implement a design with no upfront cost? One way to overcome low budgets, or no upfront costs, at least in software, is to utilize **open source software** (OSS), but this is something that we need to ask the customer.

- Gaining momentum can only mean that they are predicting that their userbase will grow eventually, but you need an estimate of how much they predict this will grow and how fast, as this will imply that you have to leave the solution ready to be scaled vertically or horizontally. Vertically, by leaving space to increase the resources eventually and take into account the business's procurement process if you need to buy more resources such RAM, CPU, or storage. Horizontally will also involve a procurement process and a considerable amount of time to integrate a new node/server/VM/container into the solution. None of these are included in the premise, and it's vital information.

Here, we have a comparison of horizontal and vertical scaling. Horizontal scaling adds more nodes, while vertical scaling adds more resources to the existing nodes:

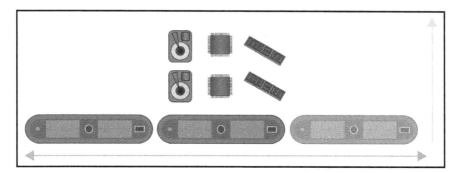

The following is a list of example questions that you could ask to clarify the gray areas:

- Is this solution for a new/existing website or web server?
- When you say 10,000 hits, are these concurrent per second or is it daily/weekly/monthly?
- Do you have any estimates or current data of how large your userbase is?
- Considering that the budget is low, can we use OSS?
- Do you have the technical resources to support the solution in case we use OSS?
- Do you have any sort of update infrastructure in place, or version control software implemented already?
- When you say little to no upfront cost, does this mean that you already have hardware, resources, or infrastructures (virtual or cloud) available that we could recycle and/or reuse for our new solution?

- Are there any disaster recovery sites in place that we could use to provide high availability?
- If your userbase grows, will this generate more storage requirements or only compute resources?
- Do you plan on performing any backups? What is your backup scheme?

From the technical perspective, once you start designing your POCs more questions will arise based on the software or hardware that will be used in the solution. You will need to know how they fit or what is needed for them to adjust to the customer's existing infrastructure, if any.

Business standpoint

Here, we will be analyzing the statement from a business perspective, taking into account all the aspects that can affect our design:

- A main requirement is performance, as this affects how many hits the solution can sustain. Since this is one of the main objectives of the solution, it needs to be sized to meet business expectations.
- Budget seems to be the main constraint that will affect the project's design and scope.
- There is no mention of the actual available budget.
- Availability requirements affect how the business should react in case of an outage. As there's no specific **service level agreement** (**SLA**), this needs to be clarified to adjust to the business needs.
- A main concern is the upfront cost. This can be lowered considerably by utilizing OSS, as there are no licensing fees.
- It has been mentioned that the solution needs to remain up during maintenance operations. This might indicate that the customer is willing to invest in maintenance operation for further upgrades or enhancements.
- The statement—we're also expecting this to gain momentum, indicates that the solution will change in the amount of resources needed, thus directly affecting the amount of money consumed by it.

The following are questions to ask when clarifying doubts from a business standpoint:

- Based on the performance requirements, what is the business impact when performance goes below the expected baseline?
- What is the actual budget for the project?
- Does the budget take into account maintenance operations?
- Considering the possible unplanned outages and maintenance, how much time exactly can your website be down per year? Will this affect business continuity?
- If an outage happens, how much time can the application tolerate not receiving data?
- Do we have data of any sort from which we can estimate how much your userbase will grow?
- Do you have any procurement process in place?
- How much time does it take to approve the acquisition of new hardware or resources?

Functional standpoint

In the functional standpoint, you will be reviewing the functional side of the solution:

- You know that the customer requires 10,000 hits, but what types of user will be using this website?
- You can see that it requires 10,000 hits, but the premise does not specify what the user will be doing with it.
- The premise states that they need the solution to be available during updates. By this, we assume that the application will be updated, but how?

To clarify the gaps in the functional standpoint, we can ask for the following information:

- What type of users will be using your application?
- What will your users be doing in your website?
- How often will this application be updated or maintained?
- Who will be maintaining and supporting this solution?
- Will this website be for internal company users or external users?

It is important to note that functional standpoint overlaps considerably with the business standpoint, as they are both trying to address similar problems.

Once we have gathered all the information, you can build a document summarizing the requirements of your solution; ensure that you go through it with the customer and that they agree to what is required to consider this solution complete.

Considering possible solutions

Once all the doubts that arose during the initial premise have been cleared, you can move on and construct a more elaborate and specific statement that includes all the information gathered. We will continue working with our previous statement and, assuming that our customer responded to all of our previous questions, we can construct a more detailed statement, as follows.

> *We require a new web server for our financial application that can sustain at least 10,000 web hits per second from approximately 2,000 users, alongside another three applications that will consume its data. It will be capable of withstanding maintenance and outages through the use of high-availability implementations with a minimum of four nodes. The budget for the project will be $20,000 for the initial implementation, and the project will utilize OSS, which will lower upfront costs. The solution will be deployed in an existing virtual environment, whose support will be handled by our internal Linux team, and updates will be conducted internally by our own update management solution. The userbase will grow approximately every two months, which is within our procurement process, allowing us to acquire new resources fairly quickly, without creating extensive periods of resource contention. User growth will impact mostly computer resources.*

As you can see, it is a more complete statement on which you can already start working. You know that it will utilize an existing virtual infrastructure. OSS is a go, high availability is also required, and it will be updated via an update and version control infrastructure that it is already in place, so, possibly, only monitoring agents will be needed for your new solution.

A very simplified overview with not many details of the possible design is as follows:

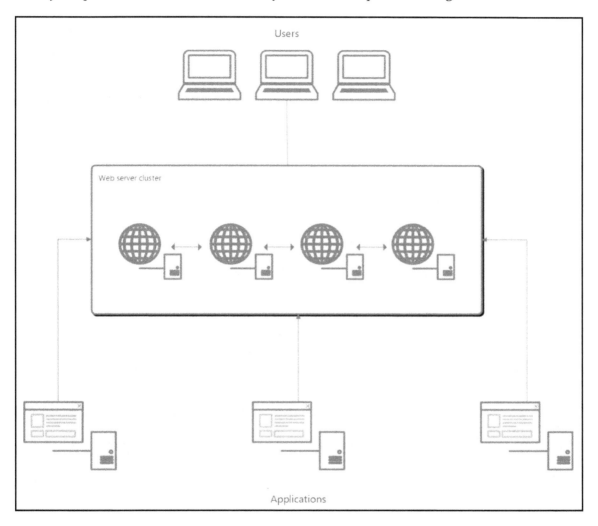

In the diagram, you can see that it's a web server cluster that provides high availability and load balancing to the clients and applications that are consuming the solution.

As you are already utilizing much of the existing infrastructure, there are fewer options for possible POC, so this design will be very straightforward. Nonetheless, there are certain variables that we can play with to provide our customer with several different options. For instance, for the web server we can have one solution with Apache and another with NGINX, or a combination of both, with Apache hosting the website and NGINX providing load balancing.

POC

With a complete statement and several options already defined, we can proceed to provide a POC based on one of the possible routes.

A POC is the process of demonstrating an idea or method, in our case a solution, with the aim of verifying a given functionality. Additionally, it provides a broad overview of how the solution will behave within an environment, allowing further testing to be able to fine-tune for specific workloads and use cases.

Any POC will have its advantages and disadvantages, but the main focus is for customers and architects to explore the different concepts of the solution of an actual working environment. It is important to note that you, as an architect, have a heavy influence in which POC will be used as a final solution, but the customer is the one who chooses which constraints and advantages suit their business better.

With the example of choosing an NGINX as a load balancer to provide high availability and performance improvements to Apache web servers hosting the application files, we can implement a working solution with scaled-down resources. Instead of deploying four nodes for the final solution, we can deploy just two to demonstrate the load-balancing features as well as provide a practical demonstration of high availability by purposely bringing one of them down.

Here's a diagram describing the previous example:

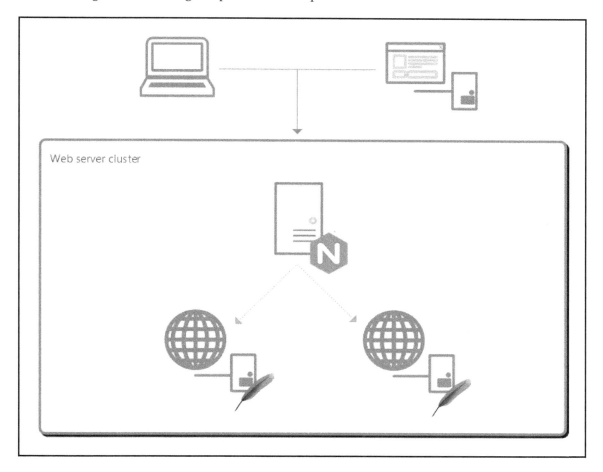

This does not require the full four-node cluster that was envisioned during the design phase, as we're not testing the full performance of the entire solution. For performance or load testing, this can be done by having less concurrent users provide a close to actual workload for the application. While having fewer users will never provide exact performance numbers for the full implementation, it delivers a good baseline with data that can later be extrapolated to provide an approximation of what the actual performance will be.

As an example for performance testing, instead of having 2,000 users load the application, we can have a quarter of the userbase and half of the resources. This will considerably decrease the amount of resources needed, while providing enough data to be able to analyze the performance of the final solution at the same time.

Also, in the information gathering stage, a document that has the different POC documented is a good idea, as it can serve as a starting point if the customer wants to construct a similar solution in the future.

Implementing the solution

Once the customer has selected the optimal route based on their business needs, we can start constructing our design. At this stage, you will be facing different obstacles, as implementing the POC in a development or QA environment might vary from production. Things that worked in QA or development may now fail in production, and different variables might be in place; all these things only arise at the implementation stage, and you need to be aware that, in a worst-case scenario, it might mean changing a large amount of the initial design.

This stage requires hands-on work with the customer and the customer's environment, so it is of utmost importance to ensure that the changes you make won't affect the current production. Working with the customer is also important, because this will familiarize their IT team with the new solution; this way, when the sign-off is done, they will be familiar with it and its configuration.

The creation of an implementation guide is one of the most important parts at this stage, since it will document each step and every minor configuration made to the solution. It will also help in the future in case an issue appears and the support team needs to know how it was configured in order to be able to solve the problem.

Summary

Designing a solution requires different approaches. This chapter went through the basics of the design stages and why each of them matters.

The first stage goes through analyzing the problem the design aims to solve, while at the same time asking the right questions. This will help define the actual requirements and narrow the scope to the real business needs. Working with the initial problem statement will impose problems further down the road, making this stage extremely important, as it will prevent unnecessarily going back and forth.

Then, we considered the possible paths or solutions we can take to solve the already defined problem. With the right questions asked in the previous stage, we should be able to construct several options for the customer to select, and can later implement a POC. POCs help both customers and architects understand how the solution will behave in an actual working environment. Normally, POCs are scaled-down versions of the final solution, making implementation and testing more agile.

Finally, the implementation stage deals with the actual configuration and hands-on aspects of the project. Based on the findings during the POC, changes can be made to accommodate the specifics of each infrastructure. Documentation delivered through this stage will help align parties to ensure that the solution is implemented as expected.

In the next chapter, we will jump into solving a problem that affects every type of implementation, regardless of cloud provider, software, or design, showing the necessity of high-performance redundant storage.

Questions

1. What are the stages of a solution design?
2. Why is it important to ask the right questions when designing a solution?
3. Why should we deliver several design options?
4. What questions can be asked to obtain information that can help design a better solution?
5. What is a POC?
6. What happens in the implementation stage?
7. How does the POC helps with the final implementation?

Further reading

In subsequent chapters, we'll go through the process of creating solutions for specific problems. As these solutions will be implemented in Linux, we recommend reading *Fundamentals of Linux* by *Oliver Pelz* https://www.packtpub.com/networking-and-servers/fundamentals-linux.

Defining GlusterFS Storage 2

Every day, applications require faster storage that can sustain thousands of concurrent I/O requests. GlusterFS is a highly-scalable, redundancy filesystem that can deliver high-performance I/O to many clients simultaneously. We will define the core concept of a cluster and then introduce how GlusterFS plays an important role.

In the preceding chapter, we went through the different aspects of designing solutions to provide high availability and performance to applications that have many requirements. In this chapter, we'll go through solving a very specific problem, that is, storage.

In this chapter, we will cover the following topics:

- Understanding the core concept of a cluster
- The reason for choosing GlusterFS
- Explaining **software-defined storage** (**SDS**)
- Exploring the differences between file, object, and block storage
- Explaining the need for high performance and highly available storage

Technical requirements

This chapter will focus on defining GlusterFS. You can refer to the project's home page at `https://github.com/gluster/glusterfs` or `https://www.gluster.org/`.

Additionally, the project's documentation can be found at `https://docs.gluster.org/en/latest/`.

What is a cluster?

We can leverage the many advantages of SDS, which allows for easy scalability and enhanced fault tolerance. GlusterFS is a piece of software that can create highly scalable storage clusters while providing maximum performance.

Before we go through how we can solve this specific need, we first need to define what a cluster is, why it exists, and what problems a cluster might be able to solve.

Computing a cluster

Put simply, a cluster is a set of computers (often called nodes) that work in tandem on the same workload and can distribute loads across all available members of the cluster to increase performance, while, at the same time, allowing for self-healing and availability. Note that the term **server** wasn't used before as, in reality, any computer can be added to a cluster. Made from a simple Raspberry Pi to multiple CPU servers, clusters can be made from a small two-node configuration to thousands of nodes in a data center.

Here is an example of a cluster:

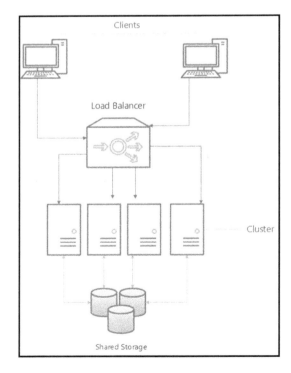

Technically speaking, clustering allows workloads to scale performance by adding servers of the same kind with similar resource characteristics. Ideally, a cluster will have homogeneous hardware to avoid problems where nodes have different performance characteristics and, at the same time, make maintenance reasonably identical—this means hardware with the same CPU family, memory configuration, and software. The idea of adding nodes to a cluster allows you to compute workloads to decrease their processing time. Depending on the application, compute times can sometimes even decrease linearly.

To further understand the concept of a cluster, imagine that you have an application that takes historical financial data. The application then receives such data and creates a forecast based on the stored information. On a single node, the forecast process (processes on a cluster are typically named jobs) takes roughly six days to complete, as we're dealing with several **terabytes** (**TB**) of data. Adding an extra node with the same characteristics decreases the processing time to four days. Adding a third node further decreases the time it takes to complete to three days.

Note that while we added three times the number of compute resources, the compute time only decreased by approximately half. Some applications can scale performance linearly, while others don't have the same scalability, requiring more and more resources for fewer gains, up to the point of diminishing returns. Adding more resources to obtain minimal time gain is not cost-effective.

With all this in mind, we can point out several characteristics that define a cluster:

- It can help reduce processing times by adding compute resources
- It can scale both vertically and horizontally
- It can be redundant, that is, if one node fails, others should take the workload
- It can allow for increased resources to be available for applications
- It is a single pool of resources rather than individual servers
- It has no single point of failure

Storage clusters

Now that we have an understanding of how to compute a cluster, let's move on to another application of clusters.

Instead of aggregating compute resources to decrease processing times, a storage cluster's main functionality is to aggregate available space to provide maximum space utilization while, at the same time, providing some form of redundancy. With the increased need for storing large amounts of data comes the need of being able to do it at a lower cost, while still maintaining increased data availability. Storage clusters help to solve this problem by allowing single monolithic storage nodes to work together as a large pool of available storage space. Thus, it allows storage solutions to reach the petascale mark without the need to deploy specialized proprietary hardware.

For example, say that we have a single node with 500 TB of available space and we need to achieve the 1-**Petabyte** (**PB**) mark while providing redundancy. This individual node becomes a single point of failure because, if it goes down, then there's no way the data can be accessed. Additionally, we've reached the maximum **hard disk drive** (**HDD**) capacity available. In other words, we can't scale horizontally.

To solve this problem, we can add two more nodes with the same configuration, as the already existing one provides a total of 1 PB of available space. Now, let's do some math here, 500 TB times 3 should be approximately 1.5 PB, correct? The answer is most definitely yes. However, since we need to provide high availability to this solution, the third node acts as a backup, making the solution tolerate a single-node failure without interrupting the client's communication. This capability to allow node failures is all thanks to the power of SDS and storage clusters, such as GlusterFS, which we'll explore next.

What is GlusterFS?

GlusterFS is an open source project by Gluster, which was acquired by Red Hat, Inc. in 2011. This acquisition does not mean that you have to acquire a Red Hat subscription or pay Red Hat to use it since, as previously mentioned, it is an open source project; therefore, you can freely install it, look at its source code, and even contribute to the project. Although Red Hat offers paid solutions based on GlusterFS, we will talk about the **open source software** (**OSS**) and project itself in this chapter.

The following diagram is the number of **Contributors** and **Commits** in the Gluster project:

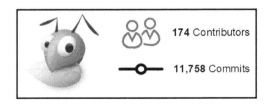

To understand GlusterFS, we must understand how it differs from traditional storage. To do this, we need to understand the concepts behind SDS, including what GlusterFS is.

Traditional storage is an industry-standard storage array with proprietary software in it that is bound to the hardware vendor. All this restricts you to the following set of rules,set by your storage provider:

1. Scalability limitations
2. Hardware compatibility limitations
3. Client-operating system limitations
4. Configuration limitations
5. Vendor lock-in

SDS

With SDS, many, if not all, of the preceding limitations are gone, since it provides impressive scalability by not depending on any hardware. You can fundamentally take an industry-standard server from any vendor that contains the storage you require and add it to your storage pool. By only doing this one simple step, you already overcome four of the preceding limitations.

Cost reduction

The example from *SDS* section, highly reduces the **operating expense** (**OPEX**) costs, as you do not have to buy additional highly-priced expansion shelves for an existing vendor storage array that can take weeks to arrive and be installed. You can quickly grab a server that you have stored in the corner of your data center, and use it to provide storage space for your existing applications. This process is called plugin scalability and is present in most of the open source SDS projects out there. In theory, the sky is the limit when it comes to scalability with SDS.

Scalability

SDS scales when you add new servers to your storage pools and also increases the resilience of your storage cluster. Depending on what configuration you have, data is spread across multiple member nodes providing additional high availability by mirroring or creating parity for your data.

Control

You also need to understand that SDS does not create space out of nothing, nor does it separate the concept of storage from hardware—such as hard drives, **solid state drives (SSD)**, or any hardware device that is designed to store information. These hardware devices will always be where the actual data is stored. SDS adds a logical layer that allows you to control where and how you store this data. It leverages this with its most fundamental components, that is, with an **application programming interface (API)** that allows you to manage and maintain your storage cluster and logical volumes, which provide the storage capacity to your other servers, applications, and even monitoring agents that self-heal the cluster in the event of degradation.

The market is moving toward SDS

SDS is the future, and this is where the storage industry is moving. In fact, it is predicted that, in the next few years, approximately 70% of all current storage arrays will be available as software-only solutions or **virtual storage appliances (VSAs)**. Traditional **network-attached storage (NAS)** solutions are 30% more expensive than current SDS implementations, and mid-range disk arrays are even more costly. Taking all this into account alongside the fact that data consumption is growing approximately 40% in enterprise every year, with a cost decline of only 25%, you can see why we are moving toward an SDS world in the near future.

With the number of applications that are running public, private, and hybrid clouds, consumer and business data consumption is growing exponentially and ceaselessly. This data is usually mission-critical and requires a high level of resiliency. The following is a list of some of these applications:

- E-commerce and online storefronts
- Financial applications
- Enterprise resource planning
- Health care
- Big data
- Customer relationship management

When companies store this type of data (called **bulk data**), they not only need to archive it, but they also need to access it, and with the lowest latency possible. Imagine a scenario where you are sent to take X-rays during your doctor's appointment, and when you arrive, they tell you that you have to wait for a week to get your scans because they have no storage space available to save your images. Naturally, this scenario will not happen because every hospital has a highly efficient procurement process, where they can predict usage based on their storage consumption and decide when to start the purchase and installation of new hardware—but you get the idea. It is much faster and more efficient to install a POSIX-standard server into your SDS layer and be ready to go.

Massive storage

Many other companies also require data lakes as secondary storage, mainly to store data in its raw form for analysis, real-time analytics, machine learning, and more. SDS is excellent for this type of storage, mainly because the maintenance required is minimal and also for the economic reasons that we discussed previously.

We have been talking mainly about how economic and scalable SDS is, but it is also important to mention the high flexibility that it brings to the table. SDS can be used for everything from archiving data and storing reach media to providing storage for **virtual machines** (**VMs**), as an endpoint for object storage in your private cloud, and even in containers. It can be deployed on any of the previously mentioned infrastructures. It can run on your public cloud of choice, in your current on-premises virtual infrastructure, and even in a Docker container or Kubernetes pod. In fact, it's so flexible that you can even integrate Kubernetes with GlusterFS using a RESTful management interface called *heketi* that dynamically provisions volumes every time you require persistent volumes for your pods.

Block, file, and object storage

Now that we have gone through why SDS is the future of next-generation workloads, it is time to dig a little deeper into the types of storage that we can achieve using SDS.

Traditional **storage area network (SAN)** and NAS solutions more commonly serve storage using protocols such as **internet small computer systems interface (iSCSI), fibre channel (FC), fibre channel over ethernet (FCoE), network file system (NFS)**, and **server message block (SMB)/common internet file system (CIFS)**. However, because we are moving more toward the cloud, our storage needs change and this is where object storage comes into play. We will explore what object storage is and how it compares to block and file storage. GlusterFS is also a file storage solution, but it has block and object storage capabilities that can be configured further down the line.

The following diagram displays block, file, and object storage:

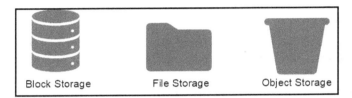

Block storage, file storage, and object storage work in very different ways when it comes to how the client stores data in them—causing their use cases to be completely different.

Block storage

A SAN is where block storage is mainly utilized, using protocols such as FC, or iSCSI, which are essentially mappings of the **Small Computer System Interface (SCSI)** protocol over FC and TCP/IP, respectively.

A typical FC SAN looks like the following diagram:

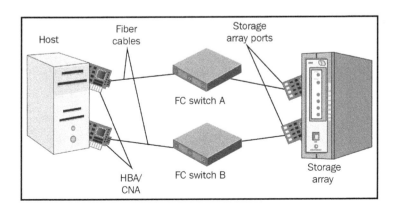

A typical iSCSI SAN looks like the following diagram:

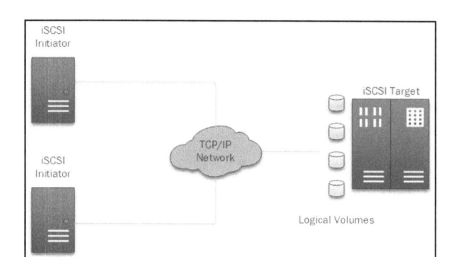

Data is stored in logical block addresses. When retrieving data, the application usually says—*I want X number of blocks from address XXYYZZZZ*. This process tends to be very fast (less than a millisecond), making this type of storage very low on latency, a very transactional-oriented type of storage form, and ideal for random access. However, it also has its disadvantages when it comes to sharing across multiple systems. This is because block storage usually presents itself in its raw form, and you require a filesystem on top of it that can support multiple writes across different systems without corruption—in other words, a clustered filesystem.

This type of storage also has some downsides when it comes to high availability or disaster recovery; because it is presented in its raw form, the storage controllers and managers are, therefore, not aware of how this storage is being used. So, when it comes to replicate its data to a recovery point, it only takes blocks into account, and some filesystems are terrible at reclaiming or zeroing blocks, which leads to unused blocks being replicated as well, thus leading to deficient storage utilization.

Because of its advantages and low latency, block storage is perfect for structured databases, random read/write operations, and to store multiple VM images that query disks with hundreds, if not thousands, of I/O requests. For this, clustered filesystems are designed to support multiple reads and writes from different hosts.

However, due to its advantages and disadvantages, block storage requires quite a lot of care and feeding—you need to take care of the filesystem and partitioning that you are going to put on top of your block devices. Additionally, you have to make sure that the filesystem is kept consistent and secure, with correct permissions, and without corruption across all the systems that are accessing it. VMs have other filesystems stored in their virtual disks that also add another layer of complexity—data can be written to the VM's filesystem and into the hypervisor's filesystem. Both filesystems have files that come and go, and they need to be adequately zeroed for blocks to be reclaimed in a thinly provisioned replication scenario, and, as we mentioned before, most storage arrays are not aware of the actual data being written to them.

File storage

On the other hand, file storage or NAS is far more straightforward. You don't have to worry about partitioning, or about selecting and formatting a filesystem that suits your multi-host environment.

NAS is usually NFS or SMB/CIFS protocols, which are mainly used for storing data in shared folders as unstructured data. These protocols are not very good at scaling or meeting the high media demands that we face in the cloud, such as social media serving and creating/uploading thousands of images or videos each day. This is where object storage saves the day, but we will be covering object storage later in this chapter.

File storage, as the name suggests, works at the file level of storage when you perform a request to NAS; you are requesting a file or a piece of a file from the filesystem, not a series of logical addresses. With NAS, this process is abstracted from the host (where the storage is mounted), and your storage array or SDS is in charge of accessing the disks on the backend and retrieving the file that you are requesting. File storage also comes with native features, such as file-locking, user and group integration (when we are talking about OSS, we are talking about NFS mainly here), security, and encryption.

Even though NAS abstracts and makes things simple for the client, it also has its downsides, as NAS relies heavily, if not entirely, on the network. It also has an additional filesystem layer with much higher latency than block storage. Many factors can cause latency or increase **round-trip time (RTT)**. You need to consider things such as how many hops your NAS is away from your clients, TCP window scaling, or having no jumbo frames enabled on devices accessing your file shares. Also, all these factors not only affect latency but are key players when it comes to the throughput of your NAS solution, which is where file storage excels the most.

The following diagram demonstrates how versatile file storage sharing is:

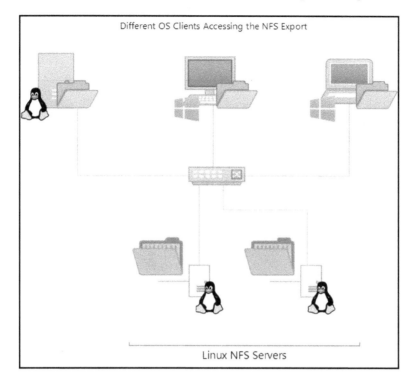

Object storage

Object storage is entirely different from NAS (file storage) and SAN (block storage). Although data is still accessed through the network, the way that data is retrieved is uniquely different. You will not access files through a filesystem, but through RESTful APIs using HTTP methods.

Objects are stored in a flat namespace, which can store millions or billions of them; this is the key to its high scalability, as it is not restrained by the number of nodes as it is in regular filesystems, such as XFS and EXT4. It is important to know that the namespaces can have partitions (often called buckets), but they cannot be nested as regular folders in a filesystem because the namespace is flat:

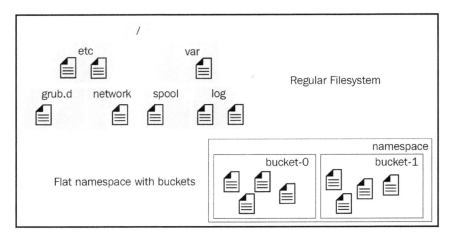

When comparing object storage with traditional storage, the self-parking versus valet-parking analogy is often used. Why is this similar? Well, because, in traditional filesystems, when you store your file you store it in a folder or directory, and it is your responsibility to know where that file was stored, just like parking a car in a parking spot—you need to remember the number and floor of where you left your car. With object storage, on the other hand, when you upload your data or put a file in a bucket, you are granted a unique identifier that you can later use to retrieve it; you don't need to remember where it was stored. Just like a valet, who will go and get the car for you, you simply need to give them the ticket you received when you left your car.

Continuing with the valet-parking reference, you usually give your valet information about the car they need to get to you, not because they need it, but because they can identify your car better in this way—for instance, the color, plate number, or model of the car will help them a lot. With object storage, the process is the same. Each object has its own metadata, its unique ID, and the file itself, which are all part of the stored object.

The following diagram shows what comprises an object in object storage:

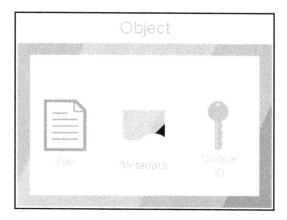

As we have mentioned several times, object storage is accessed through RESTful APIs. So, in theory, any device that supports HTTP protocols can access your object storage buckets via HTTP methods such as PUT or GET. This sounds insecure, but, in fact, most software-defined object storage has some type of authentication method, and you require an authentication token in order to retrieve or upload files. A simple request using the Linux curl tool may look like this:

```
curl -X PUT -T "${path_to_file}" \
    -H "Host: ${bucket_name}.s3.amazonaws.com" \
    -H "Date: ${date}" \
    -H "Content-Type: ${contentType}" \
    -H "Authorization: AWS ${s3Key}:${signature}" \
    https://${bucket}.s3.amazonaws.com/${file}
```

Here, we can see how multiple distinct devices can connect to object storage buckets in the cloud through the HTTP protocol:

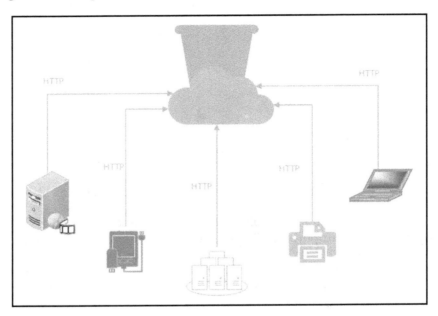

Why choose GlusterFS?

Now that we understand the core concepts of SDS, storage clusters, and the differences between block, file, and object storage, we can go through some of the reasons why enterprise customers choose GlusterFS for their storage needs.

As previously stated, GlusterFS is an SDS, that is, a layer that sits on top of traditional local storage mount points, allowing the aggregation of storage space between multiple nodes into a single storage entity or a storage cluster. GlusterFS can run on shelf-commodity hardware to private, public, or hybrid clouds. Although its primary usage is file storage (NAS), several plugins allow it to be used as a backend for block storage through the gluster-block plugin and for object storage with the gluster-swift plugin.

Some of the main features that define GlusterFS are as follows:

- Commodity hardware
- Can be deployed on a private, public, or hybrid cloud
- No single point of failure

- Scalability
- Asynchronous geo-replication
- Performance
- Self-healing
- Flexibility

GlusterFS features

Let's go through each one of these features to understand why GlusterFS is so attractive to enterprise customers.

Commodity hardware – GlusterFS runs on pretty much anything

From **Advanced RISC Machines (ARM)** on a Raspberry Pi to any variety of x86 hardware, Gluster merely requires local storage used as a brick, which lays the foundation storage for volumes. There is no need for dedicated hardware or specialized storage controllers.

In its most basic configuration, a single disk formatted as XFS can be used with a single node. While not the best configuration, it allows for further growth by adding more bricks or more nodes.

GlusterFS can be deployed on private, public, or hybrid clouds

From a container image to a full VM dedicated to GlusterFS, one of the main points of interest for cloud customers is that since GlusterFS is merely software, it can be deployed on private, public, or hybrid clouds. Because there is no vendor, locking volumes that span different cloud providers is entirely possible. Allowing for multi-cloud provider volumes with high availability setups is done so that when one cloud provider has problems, the volume traffic can be moved to an entirely different provider with minimal-to-no downtime, depending on the configuration.

No single point of failure

Depending on the volume configuration, data is distributed across multiple nodes in the cluster, removing a single point of failure, as no `head` or `master` node controls the cluster.

Scalability

GlusterFS allows for the smooth scaling of resources by vertically adding new bricks, or by horizontally adding new nodes to the cluster.

All this can be done online while the cluster serves data, without any disruption to the client's communication.

Asynchronous geo-replication

GlusterFS takes the no-single-point-of-failure concept, which provides geo-replication, allowing data to be asynchronously replicated to clusters in entirely different geophysical data centers.

The following diagram shows geo-replication across multiple sites:

Performance

Since data is distributed across multiple nodes, we can also have multiple clients accessing the cluster at the same time. This process of accessing data from multiple sources simultaneously is called parallelism, and GlusterFS allows for increased performance by directing clients to different nodes. Additionally, performance can be increased by adding bricks or nodes—effectively, by scaling horizontally or vertically.

Self-healing

In the case of unexpected downtime, the remaining nodes can still serve traffic. If new data is added to the cluster while one of the nodes is down, this data needs to be synchronized once the node is brought back up.

GlusterFS will automatically self-heal these new files once they're accessed, triggering a self-heal operation between the nodes and copying the missing data. This is transparent to the users and clients.

Flexibility

GlusterFS can be deployed on-premises on already existing hardware or existing virtual infrastructure, on the cloud as a VM, or as a container. There is no lock-in as to how it needs to be deployed, and customers can decide what suits their needs best.

Remote direct memory access (RDMA)

RDMA allows for ultra-low latency and extremely high-performance network communication between the Gluster server and the Gluster clients. GlusterFS can leverage RDMA for **high-performance computing** (**HPC**) applications and highly-concurrent workloads.

Gluster volume types

Having gained an understanding of the core features of GlusterFS, we can now define the different types of volumes that GlusterFS provides. This will help in the next chapters as we dive into the actual design of a GlusterFS solution.

GlusterFS provides the flexibility of choosing the type of volume that best suits the needs of the workload; for example, for a high-availability requirement, we can use replicated volume. This type of volume replicates the data between two or more nodes, resulting in exact copies of each of the nodes.

Let's quickly list the types of volumes that are available, and later, we'll discuss each of their advantages and disadvantages:

- Distributed
- Replicated
- Distributed replicated
- Dispersed
- Distributed dispersed

Distributed

As the name implies, data is distributed across the bricks in the volume and across the nodes. This type of volume allows for a seamless and low-cost increase in available space. The main drawback is that there is no data redundancy since files are allocated between bricks that could be on the same node or different nodes. It is mainly used for high-storage-capacity and concurrency applications.

Think of this volume type as **just a bunch of disks (JBOD)** or a linear **logical volume manager (LVM)** where space is just aggregated without any stripping or parity.

The following diagram shows a distributed volume:

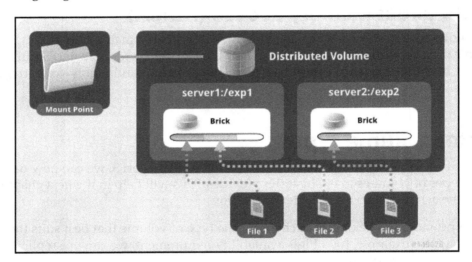

Replicated

In a replicated volume, data is copied across bricks on different nodes. Expanding a replicated volume requires the same number of replicas to be added. For example, if I have a volume with two replicas and I want to expand it, I require a total of four replicas.

A replicated volume can be compared to a RAID1, where data is mirrored between all available nodes. One of its shortcomings is that scalability is relatively limited. On the other hand, its main characteristic is high availability, as data is served even in the event of unexpected downtime.

With this type of volume, mechanisms to avoid split-brain situations must be implemented. A split-brain occurs when new data is written to the volume, and different sets of nodes are allowed to process writes separately. Server quorum is such a mechanism, as it allows for a tiebreaker to exist.

The following diagram shows a replicated volume:

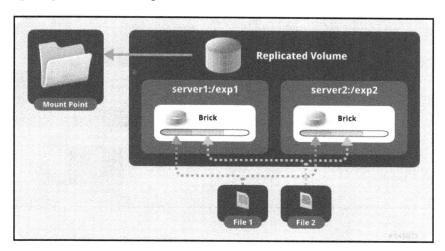

Distributed replicated

A distributed replicated volume is similar to a replicated volume, with the main difference being that replicated volumes are distributed. To explain this, consider having two separate replicated volumes, each with 10 TB of space. When both are distributed, the volume ends up with a total of 20 TB of space.

This type of volume is mainly used when both high availability and redundancy are needed, as the cluster can tolerate node failures.

The following diagram shows a distributed replicated volume:

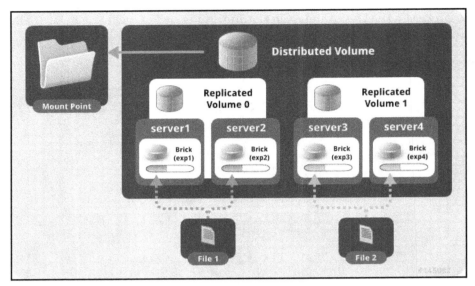

Dispersed

Dispersed volumes take the best of both distributed and replicated volumes by stripping the data across all available bricks and, at the same time, allowing redundancy. Bricks should be of the same size, as the volume suspends all writes once the smallest brick becomes full. For example, imagine a dispersed volume such as a RAID 5 or 6, where data is stripped and parity is created, allowing data to be reconstructed from the parity. While the analogy helps us to understand this type of volume, the actual process is entirely different as it uses erasure codes where data is broken into fragments. Dispersed volumes provide the right balance of performance, space, and high availability.

Distributed dispersed

In a distributed dispersed volume, data is distributed across volumes of a dispersed type. Redundancy is provided at the dispersed volume level, having similar advantages to a distributed replicated volume.

Imagine a JBOD on top of two RAID 5 arrays—growing this type of volume requires an additional dispersed volume. While not necessarily the same size, ideally, it should maintain the same characteristics to avoid complications.

The need for highly redundant storage

With an increase in the available space for applications comes an increased demand on the storage. Applications may require access to their information all of the time without any disruption that could cause the entire business continuity to be at risk. No company wants to have to deal with an outage, let alone an interruption in the central infrastructure that leads to money being lost, customers not being served, and users not being able to log in to their accounts because of bad decisions.

Let's consider storing data on a traditional monolithic storage array—doing this can cause significant risks as everything is in a single place. A single massive storage array containing all of the company's information signifies an operational risk as the array is predisposed to fail. Every single type of hardware—no matter how good—fails at some point.

Monolithic arrays tend to handle failures by providing some form of redundancy through the use of traditional RAID methods used on the disk level. While this is good for small local storage that serves a couple of hundred users, this might not be a good idea when we reach the petascale and storage space and active concurrent users increase drastically. In specific scenarios, a RAID recovery can cause the entire storage system to go down or degrade performance to the point that the application doesn't work as expected. Additionally, with increased disk sizes and single-disk performance being the same over the past couple of years, recovering a single disk now takes a more substantial amount of time; rebuilding 1 TB disks is not the same as rebuilding 10 TB disks.

Storage clusters, such as GlusterFS, handle redundancy differently by providing methods that best fit the workload. For example, when using a replicated volume, data is mirrored from one node to another. If a node goes down, then traffic is seamlessly directed to the remaining nodes, being utterly transparent to the users. Once the problematic node is serviced, it can be quickly put back into the cluster, where it will go through self-healing of the data. In comparison to traditional storage, a storage cluster removes the single point of failure by distributing data to multiple members of the clusters.

Having increased availability means that we can reach the application service-level agreements and maintain the desired uptime.

Disaster recovery

There's no escaping from it—disasters happen, whether it's natural or human error. What counts is how well-prepared we are for them, and how fast and efficiently we can recover.

Implementing disaster recovery protocols is of utmost importance for business continuity. There are two terms that we need to understand before proceeding: **recovery time objective (RTO)** and **recovery point objective (RPO)**. Let's take a quick glance at each. RTO is the time it takes to recover from a failure or event that causes a disruption. Put simply, it refers to how fast we can get the application back up. RPO, on the other hand, refers to how far the data can go back in time without affecting business continuity, that is, how much data you can lose.

The concept of RPO looks something like this:

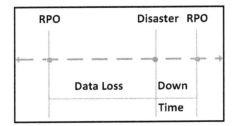

RTO

As previously stated, this is the amount of time it takes to recover a functionality after a failure. Depending on the complexity of the solution, RTO might take a considerable amount of time.

Depending on the business requirements, RTO might be as short as a couple of hours. This is where designing a highly redundant solution comes into play—by decreasing the amount of time that is required to be operational again.

RPO

This is the amount of time data that can be lost and still go back to a recovery point, in other words, this is how often recovery points are taken; in the case of backups, how often a backup is taken (it could be hourly, daily, or weekly), and in the case of a storage cluster, how often changes are replicated.

One thing to take into consideration is the speed at which changes can be replicated, as we want changes to be replicated almost immediately; however, due to bandwidth constraints, the real time replication is not possible most of the time.

Finally, an essential factor to consider is how data is replicated. Generally, there are two types of replication: synchronous and asynchronous.

Synchronous replication

Synchronous replication means that data is replicated immediately after it is written. This is useful for minimizing RPO, as there is no wait or drift between the data from one node to another. A GlusterFS-replicated volume provides this kind of replication. Bandwidth should also be considered, as changes need to be committed immediately.

Asynchronous replication

Asynchronous replication means that the data is replicated into fragments of time, for example, every 10 minutes. During set up, the RPO is chosen based on several factors, including the business need and the bandwidth that is available.

Bandwidth is the primary consideration; this is because, depending on the size of the changes, the real time replication might not fit in the RPO window, requiring a more considerable replication time and directly affecting RPO times. If unlimited bandwidth is available, synchronous replication should be chosen.

In hindsight, we, as IT architects, spend a significant amount of time trying to figure out how to make our systems more resilient. Indeed, successfully decreasing RTO and RPO times can mark the difference between a partially thought out solution and an entirely architected design.

The need for high performance

With more and more users accessing the same resources, response times get slower and applications start taking longer to process. The performance of traditional storage has not changed in the last couple of years—a single HDD yields about 150 MB/s with response times of several milliseconds. With the introduction of flash media and protocols such as **non-volatile memory express** (**NVMe**), a single SSD can easily achieve gigabytes-per-second and sub-millisecond response times; SDS can leverage these new technologies to provide increased performance and significantly reduce response times.

Enterprise storage is designed to handle multiple concurrent requests for hundreds of clients who are trying to get their data as fast as possible, but when the performance limits are reached, traditional monolithic storage starts slowing down, causing applications to fail as requests are not completed in time. Increasing the performance of this type of storage comes at a high price and, in most cases, it can't be done while the storage is still serving data.

The need for increased performance comes from the increased load in storage servers; with the explosion in data consumption, users are storing much more information and require it much faster than before.

Applications also require data to be delivered to them as quickly as possible; for example, consider the stock market, where data is requested multiple times a second by thousands of users. At the same time, another thousand users are continuously writing new data. If a single transaction is not committed in time, people will not be able to make the correct decision when buying or selling stocks because the wrong information is displayed.

The previous problem is something that architects have to face when designing a solution that can deliver the expected performance that is necessary for the application to work as expected. Taking the right amount of time to size storage solutions correctly makes the entire process flow smoother with less back and forth between design and implementation.

Storage systems, such as GlusterFS, can serve thousands of concurrent users simultaneously without a significant decrease in performance, as data is spread across multiple nodes in the cluster. This approach is considerably better than accessing a single storage location, such as with traditional arrays.

Parallel I/O

I/O refers to the process of requesting and writing data to a storage system. The process is done through I/O streams, where data is requested one block, file, or object at a time.

Parallel I/O refers to the process where multiple streams perform operations concurrently on the same storage system. This increases performance and reduces access times, as various files or blocks are read or written at the same time.

In comparison, serial I/O is the process of performing a single stream of I/O, which could lead to reduced performance and increased latency or access times.

Storage clusters, such as GlusterFS, take advantage of parallel I/O, since data is spread through multiple nodes, allowing for numerous clients to access data at the same time without any drop in latency or throughput.

Summary

In this chapter, we went through the core concepts of what a cluster is and defined it as a set of computers called nodes working together in the same type of workload. A compute cluster's primary function is to perform tasks that run CPU-intensive workloads, which are designed to reduce processing time. A storage cluster's function is to aggregate available storage resources into a single storage space that simplifies management and allows you to efficiently reach the petascale or go beyond the 1-PB available space. Then, we explored how SDS is changing the way that data is stored and how GlusterFS is one of the projects that is leading this change. SDS allows for the simplified management of storage resources, while at the same time adding features that were impossible with traditional monolithic storage arrays.

To further understand how applications interact with storage, we defined the core differences between block, file, and object storage. Primarily, block storage deals with logical blocks of data in a storage device, file storage works by reading or writing actual files from a storage space, and object storage provides metadata to each object for further interaction. With these concepts of different interactions with storage in mind, we went on to point out the characteristics of GlusterFS that make it attractive for enterprise customers and how these features tie into what SDS stands for.

Finally, we delved into the main reasons why high availability and high performance are a must for every storage design and how performing parallel, or serial, I/O can affect application performance.

In the next chapter, we will dive into the actual process of architecting a GlusterFS storage cluster.

Questions

1. How can I optimize my storage performance?
2. What type of workload is GlusterFS better suited for?
3. Which cloud providers offer object storage?
4. What types of storage does GlusterFS offer?
5. Does Red Hat own GlusterFS?
6. Do I have to pay to use GlusterFS?
7. Does Gluster offer disaster recovery or replication?

Further reading

- *Ceph Cookbook – Second Edition* by Vikhyat Umrao and Michael Hackett: `https://prod.packtpub.com/in/virtualization-and-cloud/ceph-cookbook-second-edition`
- *Mastering Ceph* by Nick Fisk: `https://prod.packtpub.com/in/big-data-and-business-intelligence/mastering-ceph`
- *Learning Ceph – Second Edition* by Anthony D'Atri and Vaibhav Bhembre: `https://prod.packtpub.com/in/virtualization-and-cloud/learning-ceph-second-edition`

Architecting a Storage Cluster

3

Software-defined storage has changed the way we store our data; with increased functionality comes increased requirements when designing the right solution. A significant amount of variables need to be considered when architecting a storage cluster.

This chapter explores the different design aspects of implementing software-defined storage solutions using GlusterFS and its various components.

In this chapter, we will cover the following topics:

- GlusterFS compute requirements
- Using the right storage size
- Defining performance needs
- Deciding the right approach for high availability
- Establishing how the workload ties everything together

Technical requirements

For this chapter, we'll use the documentation for GlusterFS available on the following URLs:

- https://www.gluster.org/
- https://github.com/gluster/glusterfs

GlusterFS compute requirements

As with any software, GlusterFS has a set of requirements that are defined by the developers to ensure that it works as expected. The actual requirements described in the documentation are relatively low, and pretty much every computer sold in the last 10 years can run GlusterFS. This is probably not at the best possible level of performance, but it still shows the flexibility of being able to run it in mixed conditions.

For compute requirements, we mainly have the following two resources that we need to consider when designing a solution with GlusterFS:

- RAM
- CPU

RAM

With memory, the choice is relatively straightforward—use as much as possible. Unfortunately, there is no such thing as infinite memory, but the statement of using as much as possible couldn't be more real, since GlusterFS uses RAM as a read cache for each of the nodes, and at the same time the Linux kernel uses memory for the read-ahead cache to speedup reads on frequently accessed files.

Depending on the brick layout and filesystem chosen, available memory plays a significant role in read performance. As an example of bricks using the advanced ZFS filesystem, where it uses RAM for its **Adaptive Replacement Cache** (**ARC**). This adds an extra layer of caching sitting on high-speed RAM. The downside is that it consumes as much as it has available, so selecting a server that provides considerable amount of memory helps a lot.

GlusterFS does not require terabytes of RAM—having 32 GB or more per node assures that caches are big enough to allocate frequently accessed files, and if the cluster grows in size by adding more bricks to each node, adding more RAM should be considered in order to increase the available memory for caching.

Why is cache important?

Consider the following: even old RAM technology such as DDR2 can deliver throughput in the GBps and latencies around the several nanoseconds. On the other hand, reading from regular spinning media (hard disk drives) throughput peaks at 150 MBps in most cases, and latency is in the several hundred milliseconds.

Reading from cache is always faster than going to disk—waiting for the disk to move its head, finding the blocks of data requested, then sending it back to the controllers and onto the application.

One thing to keep in mind is that cache needs to be warmed up first; this is the process of allowing the system to determine which files are regularly being accessed and then moving that data to the cache. While it is warming up, requests are slower, as they first have to be fetched from disk.

CPU

Any software requires CPU cycles, and GlusterFS is no exception. CPU requirements are moderately low, and depend on the type of volume used, for example, a **replicated volume** requires far less CPU than a **dispersed volume**.

CPU requirements are also affected by the type of filesystem that the bricks use and what features they have. Going back to the ZFS example, if compression is enabled this adds increased load to the CPU, and not having enough CPU resources decreases performance considerably.

For a simple storage server and no advanced features at the brick level, anything with four CPUs or more is sufficient. When enabling filesystem features, such as compression, eight or more CPUs are required for optimal performance. Additionally, more CPU allows for more concurrent I/O to be done to the cluster. This is of utmost importance when designing a storage cluster for **high-performance compute** (**HPC**) applications, where thousands of users are performing I/O operations at the same time.

Use the following rules as general rules of thumb:

- For highly concurrent workload, go for higher CPU count, above eight CPUs, depending on the concurrency level
- For low-performance requirements and a cost-efficient solution, select a lower number of CPUs, for example, four CPUs

Cloud considerations

Many cloud providers have a fixed set of given resources for their virtual machine sizes that do not allow for custom vCPU to RAM ratios. Finding the right balance depends on which VM size provides the necessary resources.

The concept of GlusterFS in the cloud will be explored in further detail in the upcoming chapters. However, get an overview of the concept, let's explore VM sizes using Microsoft's Azure offering.

Azure VM families range from general-purpose compute to specific workloads, such as GPU. For GlusterFS, we really like the L-series VMs, which are optimized for storage workloads. This VM family has a good ratio of vCPU to RAM, and offers the highest storage performance to cost ratio of any family.

The general idea can be applied to other cloud vendors. A VM size that provides an excellent and cost-effective ratio of vCPU to RAM should be selected.

How much space do you need?

Wouldn't it be nice if we could just use as much space as we need? In reality, storage has a cost, and unlimited storage does not exist.

When it comes to sizing available storage, the following factors have to be taken into consideration:

- GlusterFS volume type
- Required space by the application
- Projected growth

GlusterFS volume type

Let's start with some technical considerations. Each GlusterFS volume has characteristics when it comes to available space. Depending on the volume type, you can end up with less usable space than you initially calculated. We will be exploring the space considerations of each volume type we described in `Chapter 2`, *Defining GlusterFS Storage*.

Distributed

This volume type is reasonably straightforward. The sum of the available space from each node is the total space on the global namespace (another name for the GlusterFS volume mount).

An example is a request of 50 TB volume where the amount of space needed for the bricks is precisely 50 TB. This can be divided into five nodes with 10 TB each or two nodes with 25 TB each.

Replicated

With replica volumes, half of the available raw brick space goes into the mirroring or replication of the data. This means that when sizing this type of volume, you need to at least double the storage capacity of what is requested. This depends on the specific configuration of the volume. A general rule of thumb is that the available capacity is half of the total space on the bricks.

For example, if the request is for 50 TB volume, the node configuration should have at least 100 TB available in brick space between two nodes with 50 TB each.

Dispersed

Dispersed volumes are trickier to size, as they function similar to a RAID 5, where the data is spread across the nodes and a node's worth of capacity is used for parity. This depends on the configuration of the volume, but you could expect space efficiency to increase with the node count.

To further explain, a request for a 50 TB volume can be configured on six nodes with 10 TB each. Note that an extra node was taken into consideration. Selecting five nodes with 10 TB each results in a volume of only 40 TB, which falls short of the requested size.

Space required by the application

Each application has its own set of requirements, and storage requirements are as necessary as any other requirements.

Serving media files require considerably more resources than a website with few users and not many media files. Knowing precisely what the intended usage of the storage system is permits correct sizing of the solution and prevents situations where storage estimates fall short of what was needed from the beginning.

Make sure you go through what minimum requirements the application developers recommend and understand how it interacts with the storage, as this helps prevent headaches.

Projected growth

Your job as an architect is to ask the right questions. When it comes to storage, make sure the growth rate or change rate is taken into account.

Consider that data growth happens no matter what, and thinking ahead avoids complicated situations where there is not enough space, so leaving some margin for future utilization is a good practice. Allowing for 10% or more space should be a good starting point, so if 50 TB spaces are requested then add 5 TB more space to the solution.

Go for the most cost-effective route. While GlusterFS allows for seamless expansion, try to avoid using this feature as an easy solution and make sure that the right size is defined from the start and a buffer is considered for future growth.

Performance considerations

Applications that perform poorly are probably worse than applications that don't work at all. Having something work half of the time is incredibly frustrating and costly to any business.

As an architect, you need to design solutions that perform to the spec or better in order to avoid scenarios where problems arise due to poor performance.

The very first place to start is by defining what the performance requirements are. Most of the time, the application developers mention the performance requirements in their documentation itself. Not meeting these minimum requirements means that the application either doesn't work at all or barely works. Neither is acceptable.

The following are the things to look out for when designing a performance-oriented solution:

- Throughput
- Latency
- IOPS
- I/O size

Throughput

Throughput is a function of a given amount of data over a certain amount of time that is typically described in **megabytes per second** (**MBps**). This means that every second X amount of data is being sent or received from a storage system.

Depending on the workload, the highest throughput might not be possible as the application is unable to perform I/O big enough or fast enough. There is no hard number to recommend here. Try going for the highest possible throughput, and make sure that the storage cluster can sustain the transfer rates necessary for the desired level of concurrency.

Latency

Latency is critical and requires extra care, as some applications are significantly sensitive to high latencies or response times.

Latency is a measurement of the amount of time I/O operations take to complete that is typically measured in milliseconds (1 second is 1,000 milliseconds). High latencies or response times cause applications to take longer to respond and even stop working altogether.

Aim for the lowest latency possible. This is a case where getting the lowest possible number is always the best approach. With latency, there's no such thing as not enough, or, in this case, not too short of response time. Consider the type of storage medium you used. Traditional hard disk drives have response times (or seek times) ranging in the several hundred milliseconds, while newer solid state drives can go past the sub-millisecond mark and into microseconds.

IOPS

Input/output operations per second is a function of a given amount of operations over time, in this case, seconds. This is a measurement of how many operations can be done over a second, and many applications provide a minimum requirement regarding IOPS.

Most applications provide a requirement of the minimum IOPS needed for it to work as expected. Make sure that these are met, as otherwise the application might not behave as intended.

When designing a storage solution, make sure IOPS is considered as a primary deciding factor when taking sizing decisions.

I/O size

I/O size is the amount of data that each operation performs. This is dependent on the workload type, as each application interacts with the storage system differently. The I/O size impacts directly on the previously mentioned aspects of performance.

Smaller I/O results in lower throughput, but, if done fast enough, it results in higher IOPS with lower latencies. Larger I/O, on the other hand, provides a higher throughput, but generally produces lower IOPS as fewer operations are done in the same amount of time.

There is no solid recommendation regarding I/O size. In an ideal, non-realistic world, I/O is done big enough and fast enough, which results in high throughput and high IOPS. In reality, it's either one or the other. Small I/O ends up being slow regarding throughput, but it completes fast enough so that IOPS seem higher. With big I/O, the numbers are inverted, and the throughput becomes high, but since it takes longer to complete, IOPS goes down.

GlusterFS performance

The following aspects need to be taken into consideration when designing a GlusterFS storage cluster when it comes to performance:

- Volume type
- Brick layout
- Number of nodes
- Tuning parameters

Volume type

The volume chosen affects the performance in different ways, since GlusterFS allocates data differently for each type.

For example, a replicated volume mirrors data across nodes, while a dispersed volume tries to maximize node usage and uses them in parallel.

If performance is the primary aim for a dispersed or distributed volume, consider that distributed volumes offer no redundancy, while a dispersed volume does it at the expense of performance degradation.

Brick layout

Having a node with all of its disks in a single large brick does not perform in the same way as having disks grouped in smaller numbers with several bricks. Brick layout is the highest contributing factor to performance, as this directly dictates how disks are used.

If all the disks end up in a single brick, the performance suffers. Generally, having more bricks with fewer disks results in better performance and lower latency.

Consider configuring a software RAID0 for the disks that make up the bricks. For example, you could have 10 disks available and, for simplicity's sake, configure all 10 disks in a RAID0 on a single brick. Alternatively, you could go for a more efficient route and configure five bricks where each brick is made of two disks in a RAID0.

This also allows smoother growth, since adding more bricks with fewer disks is considerably easier than adding a large number of disks. You should aim for more bricks with fewer disks grouped in smaller RAID configurations.

In the following diagram, we can see how each brick is made up of two different disks:

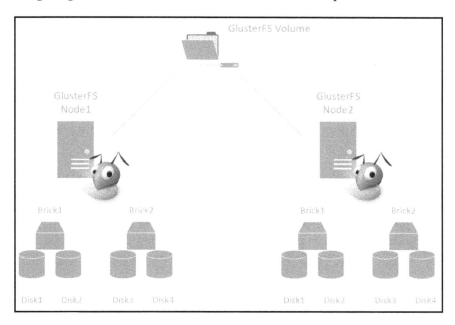

Number of nodes

Increasing the number of nodes in the cluster allows for higher concurrency. While performance gains might not be linear, adding nodes allows for a higher number of users and applications accessing the volumes.

The goal is to have enough nodes for a balance in the available space and concurrency. There is no set number here, but your job as an architect is to define, through testing, what is the right number of nodes for a specific solution. During the POC phase, test with a smaller number of nodes and check whether the performance is acceptable.

Tuning parameters

Filesystem tunables, such as block size can play an important role, and the goal is to match the workload I/O size, the GlusterFS volume block size, and the filesystem block size to the same amount.

Typically, 4 K is the most used block size that works for general workloads. For a large number of small files, go for a smaller block size. For big files, aim for a bigger block size, such as 1 M.

The best approach for high availability

With GlusterFS, high availability can be delivered through the volume configuration; deciding how this is done depends on the application needs, available space, and required performance.

Since GlusterFS handles high availability, there is no need to configure any form of redundancy at the brick level. This is especially true with cloud instances and virtual machines, where there are no physical disks that can go bad. For physical installations, it is always better to have an extra layer of redundancy by configuring the local disks with RAID5 or RAID6 for a balance in performance and resiliency. For now, let's stick to cloud deployments.

With GlusterFS, only two volume types offer high availability: replicated and dispersed. Replicated volumes are reasonably straightforward since data is just replicated from one node to another. These offer lower performance, but are considerably easier to configure, deploy, and maintain.

Replicated

Choose a replicated volume when there is no need for extreme performance. Select the number of replicas based on how many nodes or bricks the volume should tolerate. Consider that using a higher replica number will decrease the amount of available space, but increase the availability of the volume.

The following example shows that losing a node in a replicated volume does not disrupt volume operations:

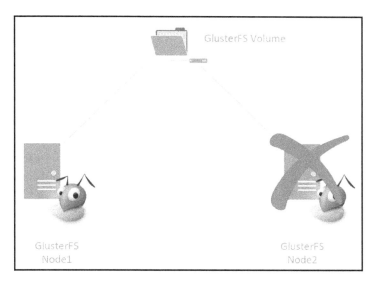

Dispersed

Dispersed volumes offer a good balance between high availability and performance; this should be the go-to volume when both are a requirement. Configuring a dispersed volume is a more complicated process since the redundancy is handled as in a RAID5 setup, where a node is used as parity. The redundancy value can be chosen at the time of volume creation which allows for greater flexibility.

In the following diagram, you can see that losing one node does not disrupt the volume:

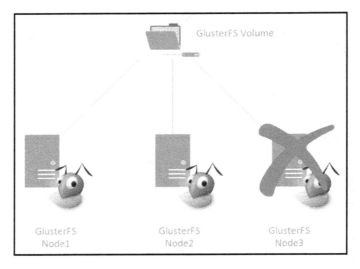

Plan for high availability when there is a specific requirement. Remember that volume types can be mixed and matched. For example, a distributed replicated volume will have a good mix of available space and redundancy.

Geo-replication

Geo-replication allows for asynchronous replication of data between different sites through local networks or the internet. This provides high availability by having a copy of the data in a different geo-location, and ensures disaster recovery in case of failures.

Consider going the geo-replication route when there is a specific use case where the added layer of redundancy is needed. Remember that this is asynchronous replication, so, in the case of a disaster, consider the RPO and RTO times explained in the previous chapters.

The following diagram gives you a general understanding of how geo-replication works—**Site A** replicates to **Site B** through the WAN:

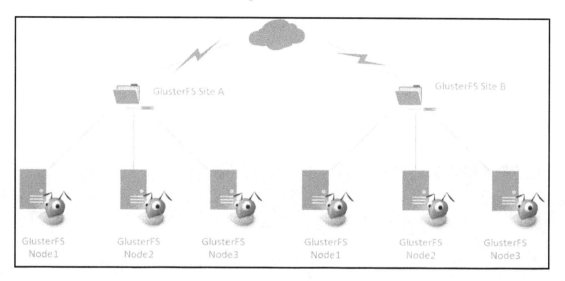

How the workload defines requirements

Delivering video files to streaming web servers is not the same as hosting a large database. I/O is done in an entirely different way, and knowing exactly how the workload interacts with the storage system is crucial to successfully size and design a robust storage solution.

Documentation

The application documentation is your best friend when trying to figure out what the storage requirements are. When there's an existing implementation of the application, ask the administrators what the software expects for performance and how it reacts when it doesn't meet the minimum requirements.

System tools

Using tools such as `iostat` gives a good understanding of how the application interacts with the storage, for example, by using the following command:

```
iostat -dxctm 1
```

The previous code shows per block device usage, the `areq-sz` column (previously known as `avgrq-sz`) shows the average request size in kilobytes, making this a good starting point to understand the I/O size the application typically uses.

The output looks similar to the following screenshot:

In the preceding image, we could appreciate the block devices and their respective performance.

File type and size

As an example, designing a storage solution for a media streaming server requires the use of large block sizes, as media files tend to be bigger than small text files. If you use a larger block size for the bricks, the GlusterFS volume will not only make more efficient use of the space but will also allow for faster operations, as the transaction size matches the file size.

On the other hand, a storage server for sensor logging that usually creates a large number of small files containing text requires a smaller block size to match the size of the files being created. Using a smaller block size avoids allocating an entire block, say 4 K, for a file that is only 1 K in size.

Ask the right questions

Your goal as an architect is to make sure the workload is very clear. The intended use for the storage server defines how many resources need to be allocated. Failing to do so could result in resources being wasted that in turn means money being wasted, or, in a worst case scenario, could lead to a solution that does not perform to spec, which leads to applications failing and users not able to work.

Remember from the `Chapter 1`, *Introduction to Design Methodology*: ask the right questions. When sizing a storage solution, you can ask the following questions:

- How much space does the current implementation consume (if there's one already in place)?
- What are the performance requirements of the application?
- How many users interact with the application?
- Is high availability required?
- How does the application store its data?
- Does it create large files and append data to them?
- Does it create a large number of small files?

Possible answers to these questions could be the following:

- Right now, the application consumes 20 TB, but we expect it to increase 5% each month and stabilize at 80 TB.
- The application requires at least 100 MB/s of throughput and a latency no higher than 10 ms.
- Currently, about 300 users have access to the application; concurrently, we've seen peaks of 150 users, but we expect the user count to increase significantly.
- We can sustain not being able to access the storage for some time, but we do need to be able to recover from a failure reasonably quickly, and could possibly have a copy of the data off-site.
- The application primarily saves its information in small files.
- It does not append data, and if more space is needed, it merely creates more small files.
- Yes, we've seen several thousands of files created no bigger than 4 KB.

From the previous example, you can surmise that the application creates a lot of small files, and it can tolerate being down for some time but requires off-site replication for smooth disaster recovery. Performance requirements seem to be relatively high, so we could opt for a dispersed or distributed volume with geo-replication enabled.

Summary

The process of architecting a storage solution requires many variables to be known. In this chapter, we defined that deciding how much space is needed depends on the GlusterFS volume type, the application requirements, and the estimated growth in data utilization.

Depending on the volume type, the available space is affected, a distributed volume aggregates all of the available space making it the most space efficient, while a replicated volume uses half of the available raw space for mirroring.

The application and user base dictate how much space is required. This is because, depending on the type of data being served, the storage requirements change. Thinking ahead and planning for storage growth avoids the potential to run out of resources, and allows for at least a 10% buffer when sizing should fit most situations.

With the performance requirements, we defined the concepts of throughput, latency, IOPS, and I/O size and how these interact with each other. We defined what variables come into play when configuring GlusterFS for optimal performance, how each volume has its performance characteristics, and how the brick layout plays an important role when trying to optimize a GlusterFS volume.

We also defined how high availability requirements affect sizing and how each volume provides different levels of HA. When disaster recovery is needed, GlusterFS geo-replication adds the required level of availability by replicating data to another physical region, which allows the smooth recovery of services in case of a disaster.

Finally, we went through how the workload defines how the solution is designed and how using tools to verify how the application interacts with the storage allows for the correct configuration of the storage cluster. We also found out how file types and sizes define performance behavior and space utilization, and how asking the right questions allows for a better understanding of the workload, which results in a more efficient and optimized solution.

The main takeaway is to always ask how the application and workload interact with its resources. This allows for the most efficient design possible.

In the next chapter, we'll go through the actual configuration needed for GlusterFS.

Questions

1. What are the compute requirements for GlusterFS?
2. How does GlusterFS use RAM?
3. What is a cache?
4. How does concurrency affect CPU sizing?
5. How do GlusterFS volumes affect available space?
6. How much space does the application need?
7. What is projected growth?
8. What is throughput, latency IOPS, and I/O size?
9. What is brick layout?
10. What is geo-replication?

Further reading

- *Architecting Data-Intensive Applications* by Anuj Kumar
- *Microsoft Azure Storage Essentials* by Chukri Soueidi
- *Azure for Architects* by Ritesh Modi

4
Using GlusterFS on the Cloud Infrastructure

With a good understanding of the core concepts of GlusterFS, we can now dive into the installation, configuration, and optimization of a storage cluster.

We will be installing GlusterFS on a three-node cluster using Azure as the cloud provider for this example. However, the concepts can also be applied to other cloud providers.

In this chapter, we will cover the following topics:

- Configuring GlusterFS backend storage
- Installing and configuring GlusterFS
- Setting up volumes
- Optimizing performance

Technical requirements

Here's the list of technical resources for this chapter:

- A detailed view of Azure **virtual machine** (**VM**) sizes:
  https://docs.microsoft.com/en-us/azure/virtual-machines/linux/sizes-storage
- A detailed view of Azure disk sizes and types:
  https://azure.microsoft.com/en-us/pricing/details/managed-disks/
- The main page for the ZFS on Linux project:
  https://github.com/zfsonlinux/zfs/wiki/RHEL-and-CentOS
- GlusterFS installation guide for CentOS:
  https://wiki.centos.org/HowTos/GlusterFSonCentOS
- GlusterFS quick start guide on the Gluster website:
  https://docs.gluster.org/en/latest/Quick-Start-Guide/Quickstart/

- GlusterFS setting up volumes on the administrators guide:
  `https://docs.gluster.org/en/latest/Administrator%20Guide/`
  `Setting%20Up%20Volumes/`
- GlusterFS tuning volumes for better performance:
  `https://docs.gluster.org/en/latest/Administrator%20Guide/`
  `Managing%20Volumes/#tuning-options`

Setting up the bricks used for backend storage

The following is the list of components that we'll be using:

- Azure L4s VM with 4vCPUs and 32 GB of RAM
- Four S10 128 GB Disks per VM
- CentOS 7.5
- ZFS on Linux as the filesystem for the bricks
- A single RAID 0 group with four disks
- GlusterFS 4.1

Azure deployment

Before going into the details of how to configure the bricks, we first need to deploy the nodes in Azure. For this example, we are using the storage optimized VM series, or L-series. One thing that is worth mentioning is that Azure has a 30-day free trial that can be used for testing before committing to any deployment.

In Azure, performance is defined on several levels. The first level is the VM limit, which is the maximum performance that the VM allows. The L-series family provides the correct balance of price versus performance as these VMs are optimized to deliver higher **input/output operations per second** (IOPS) and throughput rather than delivering high compute or memory resources. The second level on which performance is defined is through the disks that are attached to the VM. For this example, we will be using standard **hard disk drives** (HDD) for a cost-effective solution. If more performance is needed, the disks can always be migrated to premium **solid-state drives** (SSD) storage.

The exact VM size for this example will be L4s, which provides four vCPUs and 32 GB of RAM, and is enough for a small storage cluster for general purposes. With a maximum of 125 MB/s and 5k IOPS, it still retains respectable performance when correctly configured.

 A new generation of storage optimized VMs has been recently released, offering a locally-accessible NVMe SSD of 2 TB. Additionally, it provides increased core count and memory, making these new VMs ideal for a GlusterFS setup with **Z file system** (**ZFS**). The new L8s_v2 VM can be used for this specific setup, and the sizes and specifications can be seen on the product page (`https://docs.microsoft.com/en-us/azure/virtual-machines/linux/sizes-storage#lsv2-series`).

The following screenshot shows the **Availability set**, **Current fault domain**, and **Current update domain** settings:

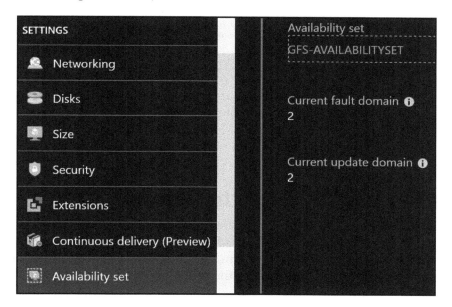

 When deploying a GlusterFS setup in Azure, make sure that each node lands on a different update and fault domain. This is done through the use of availability sets (refer to the preceding screenshot). Doing so ensures that if the platform restarts a node, the others remain up and serving data.

Finally, for the Azure setup, we need **512 GB** per node for a total of 1.5 TB raw, or 1 TB usable space. The most cost-effective way to achieve this is by using a single **S20 512 GB** disk, since the price per gigabyte per month is approximately **$0.04**. Going down the route of a single disk will impact on performance, as a single standard disk only provides a maximum of 500 IOPS and 60 MB/s. Considering performance and accepting the fact that we will lose a bit of efficiency in the cost department, we will be using four **S10 128** GB disks in a single RAID0 group. The price per month per gigabyte of an **S10** disk is **$0.05**, compared to **$0.04** per month for an **S20** disk. You can refer to the following table, where the calculation is done based on the cost of the managed disk divided by its respective size:

Disk	Size GB	Price/month	Price/GB/month
S4	32	$1.54	$0.05
S6	64	$3.01	$0.05
S10	128	$5.89	$0.05
S15	256	$11.33	$0.04
S20	512	$21.76	$0.04
S30	1024	$40.96	$0.04
S40	2048	$81.92	$0.04
S50	4096	$163.84	$0.04

Make sure that all three nodes are deployed on the same region and the same resource group for consistency.

ZFS as the backend for the bricks

We spoke about ZFS in a Chapter 3, *Architecting a Storage Cluster*. ZFS is a filesystem that was developed by Sun Microsystems and was later acquired by Oracle. The project was later made open source and was ported to Linux. Although the project is still in beta, most of the features work fine and the majority of the problems have been ruled out—the project is now focused on adding new features.

ZFS is a software layer that combines disk management, logical volumes, and a filesystem all in one. Advanced features such as compression, **adaptive replacement cache** (**ARC**), deduplication, and snapshots make it ideal to work with GlusterFS as the backend for the bricks.

Installing ZFS

Let's start by installing ZFS; there are some dependencies, such as **dynamic kernel modules** (**DKMS**), that live in the EPEL repository.

 Note that most of the commands that run here are assumed to be running as root; the commands can be run as the non-root account by prefacing `sudo` before each.

To install the required components, we can use the following commands:

```
yum install -y epel-release
yum install -y
http://download.zfsonlinux.org/epel/zfs-release.el7_5.noarch.rpm
```

Next, we will use the following command:

```
yum install -y zfs
```

The following commands are used to enable the ZFS components:

```
systemctl enable zfs.target
systemctl enable --now zfs-import-scan.service
```

Configuring the zpools

With ZFS installed and enabled, we can now create the zpools. Zpool is the name given to volumes that are created within ZFS.

Since we will be using a single RAID 0 group consisting of four disks, we can create a zpool named `brick1`; this needs to be done on all three nodes. Additionally, let's create a directory named `bricks` that lives under the root (/); this directory houses the bricks under a directory with the brick name. The command required to do this is as follows:

```
mkdir -p /bricks/brick1
```

This creates the directory tree, as follows:

```
zpool create brick1 /dev/disk/by-id/scsi-360022480f0da979b536cde32a4a17406
\
 /dev/disk/by-id/scsi-360022480fb9d18bbdfb9175fd3e0bbf2 \
/dev/disk/by-id/scsi-360022480fb9d18bbdfb9175fd3e0bae4 \
/dev/disk/by-id/scsi-360022480fb9d18bbdfb9175fd3e049f2
```

To further explain the command, `brick1` is the name of the zpool. Then, we indicate the path to the disks. In this example, we are using the ID of the disks since this avoids problems if the disks change order. While ZFS is not affected for disks in a different order, it is better to avoid problems by using an ID that will never change.

> ZFS can use the entire disk because it creates the required partitions automatically.

With the `zpool` instance created, we can check whether it has completed correctly by using the `zpool status` command:

```
[root@gfs1 /]# zpool status
  pool: brick1
 state: ONLINE
  scan: none requested
config:

        NAME                                        STATE     READ WRITE CKSUM
        brick1                                      ONLINE       0     0     0
          scsi-360022480b73cfc2c8ec934cab5ddc3cf    ONLINE       0     0     0
          scsi-36002248035a747697e238a3c1143b742    ONLINE       0     0     0
          scsi-360022480f0da979b536cde32a4a17406    ONLINE       0     0     0
          scsi-360022480fb9d18bbdfb9175fd3e0bbf2    ONLINE       0     0     0

errors: No known data errors
```

Let's enable compression and change the mount point of the pool to the previously created directory. To do this, run the following command:

```
zfs set compression=lz4 brick1
```

You will also need to run the following command:

```
zfs set mountpoint=/bricks/brick1 brick1
```

The first command enables compression with the `lz4` algorithm, which has a low CPU overhead. The second command changes the mount point of the zpool. Make sure that you use the correct name of the pool when changing the settings.

After doing this, we should have the ZFS volume mounted under `/bricks/brick1`, as shown in the `df` command:

```
[root@gfs1 /]# df -h
Filesystem      Size  Used Avail Use% Mounted on
/dev/sda2        30G  1.8G   28G   6% /
devtmpfs         16G     0   16G   0% /dev
tmpfs            16G     0   16G   0% /dev/shm
tmpfs            16G  9.1M   16G   1% /run
tmpfs            16G     0   16G   0% /sys/fs/cgroup
/dev/sda1       497M  105M  393M  22% /boot
tmpfs           3.2G     0  3.2G   0% /run/user/1000
brick1          493G   33G  461G   7% /bricks/brick1
[root@gfs1 /]#
```

We need to create a directory on the recently added mount point to use as the brick; the consensus is to use the name of the volume. In this case, we'll name the volume `gvol1`, and simply create the directory:

```
mkdir -p /bricks/brick1/gvol1
```

This needs to be done on all the nodes.

Adding the ZFS cache to the pool (optional)

With Azure, every single VM has a temporary resource drive. The performance of this temporary resource drive is considerably higher than the data disks that are added to it. This drive is ephemeral, meaning the data is wiped once the VM is deallocated; this should work very well as a read cache drive since there is no need to persistently keep the data across reboots.

Since the drive is wiped with every `stop/deallocate/start` cycle, we need to tweak some things with the unit files for ZFS to allow the disk to be added on every reboot. The drive will always be `/dev/sdb`, and since there is no need to create a partition on it, we can simply tell ZFS to add it as a new disk each time the system boots.

This can be achieved by editing the `systemd` unit for `zfs-mount.service`, which is located under `/usr/lib/systemd/system/zfs-mount.service`. The problem with this approach is that the ZFS updates will overwrite the changes made to the preceding unit. One solution to this problem is to run `sudo systemctl edit zfs-mount` and add the following code:

```
[Service]
ExecStart=/sbin/zpool remove brick1 /dev/sdb
ExecStart=/sbin/zpool add brick1 cache /dev/sdb
```

To apply the changes, run the following command:

```
systemctl daemon-reload
```

Now that we have ensured that the cache drive will be added after every reboot, we need to change an Azure-specific configuration with the Linux agent that runs on Azure VMs. This agent is in charge of creating the temporary resource drive, and since we'll be using it for another purpose, we need to tell the agent not to create the ephemeral disk. To achieve this, we need to edit the file located in `/etc/waagent.conf` and look for the following line:

```
ResourceDisk.Format=y
```

You will then need to change it to the following line:

```
ResourceDisk.Format=n
```

After doing this, we can add the cache drive to the pool by running the following command:

```
zpool add brick1 cache /dev/sdb -f
```

The `-f` option must only be used the first time because it removes the previously created filesystem. Note that the `stop/deallocate/start` cycle of the VM is required to stop the agent from formatting the resource disk, as it gets an `ext4` filesystem by default.

The previous process can also be applied to the newer Ls_v2 VMs, which use the much faster NVMe drives, such as the L8s_v2; simply replace `/dev /sdb` with `/dev/nvme0n1`.

You can verify that the cache disk was added as follows:

```
[root@gfs1 /]# zpool status
  pool: brick1
 state: ONLINE
  scan: none requested
config:

        NAME                                        STATE    READ WRITE CKSUM
        brick1                                      ONLINE     0     0     0
          scsi-360022480b73cfc2c8ec934cab5ddc3cf    ONLINE     0     0     0
          scsi-36002248035a747697e238a3c1143b742    ONLINE     0     0     0
          scsi-360022480f0da979b536cde32a4a17406    ONLINE     0     0     0
          scsi-360022480fb9d18bbdfb9175fd3e0bbf2    ONLINE     0     0     0
        cache
          sdb                                       ONLINE     0     0     0

errors: No known data errors
[root@gfs1 /]#
```

As we'll be using a single RAID group, this will be used as a read cache for the entire brick, allowing better performance when reading the files of the GlusterFS volume.

Installing GlusterFS on the nodes

With each node having the bricks already configured, we can finally install GlusterFS. The installation is relatively straightforward and requires just a couple of commands.

Installing the packages

We'll be using the packages provided by CentOS. To install GlusterFS, we first install the repository as follows:

```
yum install -y centos-release-gluster41
```

Then, we install the `glusterfs-server` package:

```
yum install -y glusterfs-server
```

We then make sure the `glusterd` service is enabled and started:

```
[root@gfs1 /]# systemctl enable glusterd
[root@gfs1 /]# systemctl start glusterd.service
[root@gfs1 /]# systemctl status glusterd
• glusterd.service - GlusterFS, a clustered file-system server
   Loaded: loaded (/usr/lib/systemd/system/glusterd.service; enabled; vendor preset: disabled)
   Active: active (running) since Wed 2018-08-15 04:09:14 UTC; 4s ago
  Process: 4276 ExecStart=/usr/sbin/glusterd -p /var/run/glusterd.pid --log-level $LOG_LEVEL $GLUSTERD_OPTIONS
de=exited, status=0/SUCCESS)
 Main PID: 4277 (glusterd)
   CGroup: /system.slice/glusterd.service
           └─4277 /usr/sbin/glusterd -p /var/run/glusterd.pid --log-level INFO

Aug 15 04:09:14 gfs1 systemd[1]: Starting GlusterFS, a clustered file-system server...
Aug 15 04:09:14 gfs1 systemd[1]: Started GlusterFS, a clustered file-system server.
[root@gfs1 /]#
```

These commands need to be run on each of the nodes that will be part of the cluster; this is because each node requires the packages and services to be enabled.

Creating the trusted pool

Finally, we need to create a trusted pool. A trusted pool is a list of nodes that will be part of the cluster, where each Gluster node trusts the other, thus allowing for the creation of volumes.

To create the trusted pool, run the following code from the first node:

```
gluster peer probe gfs2
gluster peer probe gfs3
```

You can verify that the nodes show up as follows:

```
[root@gfs1 /]# gluster peer probe gfs2
peer probe: success.
[root@gfs1 /]# gluster peer probe gfs3
peer probe: success.
[root@gfs1 /]# gluster peer status
Number of Peers: 2

Hostname: gfs2
Uuid: 2d0ee0b9-3a6f-449e-8945-64f1aa35b962
State: Peer in Cluster (Connected)

Hostname: gfs3
Uuid: 80a06eae-fb2a-4a65-a7d4-91ed9a91c050
State: Peer in Cluster (Connected)
[root@gfs1 /]#
```

The command can be run from any node, and the hostnames or IPs need to be modified to include the others. In this case, I have added the IP addresses of each of the nodes onto the `/etc/hosts` file to allow for easy configuration. Ideally, the hostnames should be registered with the DNS server for the name resolution within the network.

After the installation, the `gluster` nodes should allow volumes to be created.

Creating the volumes

We have now reached the point where we can create the volumes; this is because we have the bricks configured and the necessary packages for GlusterFS to work.

Creating a dispersed volume

We'll be using a dispersed volume type across three nodes, giving a good balance of high availability and performance. The raw space of all of the nodes combined will be around 1.5 TB; however, the distributed volume will have a usable space of approximately 1 TB.

To create a dispersed volume, use the following code:

```
gluster volume create gvol1 disperse 3 gfs{1..3}:/bricks/brick1/gvol1
```

Then, start the volume using the following code:

```
gluster volume start gvol1
```

Make sure that it starts correctly by using the following code:

```
gluster volume status gvol1
```

The volume should show up now as follows:

```
[root@gfs1 /]# gluster volume create gvol1 disperse 3 gfs{1..3}:/bricks/brick1/gvol1
volume create: gvol1: success: please start the volume to access data
[root@gfs1 /]# gluster volume start gvol1
volume start: gvol1: success
[root@gfs1 /]# gluster volume status gvol1
Status of volume: gvol1
Gluster process                        TCP Port  RDMA Port  Online  Pid
------------------------------------------------------------------------------
Brick gfs1:/bricks/brick1/gvol1        49152     0          Y       7541
Brick gfs2:/bricks/brick1/gvol1        49152     0          Y       5694
Brick gfs3:/bricks/brick1/gvol1        49152     0          Y       5145
Self-heal Daemon on localhost          N/A       N/A        Y       7625
Self-heal Daemon on gfs2               N/A       N/A        Y       5768
Self-heal Daemon on gfs3               N/A       N/A        Y       5216

Task Status of Volume gvol1
------------------------------------------------------------------------------
There are no active volume tasks

[root@gfs1 /]#
```

Mounting the volume

The volume is now created and can be mounted on the clients; the preferred method for doing this is by using the native `glusterfs-fuse` client, which allows for automatic failovers in the event that one of the nodes goes down.

To install the `gluster-fuse` client, use the following code:

```
yum install -y glusterfs-fuse
```

Then, let's create a directory under root called `gvol1`:

```
mkdir /gvol1
```

Finally, we can mount the GlusterFS volume on the client as follows:

```
mount -t glusterfs gfs1:/gvol1 /gvol1
```

It doesn't matter which node you specify, as the volume can be accessed from any of them. In the event that one of the nodes goes down, the client will automatically redirect I/O requests to the remaining nodes.

Optimizing performance

With the volume created and mounted, we can tweak some parameters to get the best performance. Mainly, performance tuning can be done on the filesystem level (in this case, ZFS), and on the GlusterFS volume level.

GlusterFS tuning

Here, the main variable is `performance.cache-size`. This setting specifies the amount of RAM to be allocated as a read cache for the GlusterFS volume. By default, it is set to 32 MB, which is fairly low. Given that the selected VM has enough RAM, this can be bumped to 4 GB using the following command:

```
gluster volume set gvol1 performance.cache-size 4GB
```

Another essential parameter once the cluster starts growing is `performance.io-thread-count`. This controls how many I/O threads are spawned by the volume. The default is `16` threads, which are enough for small-to-medium clusters. However, once the cluster size starts growing, this can be doubled. To change the setting, use the following command:

```
gluster volume set gvol1 performance.io-thread-count 16
```

This setting should be tested to check whether increasing the count improves the performance or not.

ZFS

We'll be primarily changing two settings: ARC and the L2ARC feed performance.

ARC

The primary setting for ZFS is its read cache, called ARC. Allowing more RAM to be allocated to ZFS increases read performance substantially. Since we have already allocated 4 GB to the Gluster volume read cache and the VM has 32 GB available, we can allocate 26 GB of RAM to ZFS, which will leave approximately 2 GB for the OS.

To change the maximum size that is allowed for ARC, use the following code:

```
echo 27917287424 > /sys/module/zfs/parameters/zfs_arc_max
```

Here, the number is the amount of RAM in bytes, in this case, 26 GB. Doing this changes the setting on the fly but does not make it boot persistent. To have the settings applied on boot, create a file named /etc/modprobe.d/zfs.conf and add the following values:

```
options zfs zfs_arc_max=27917287424
```

By doing this, you can make the changes persist across boots.

L2ARC

L2ARC refers to a second level of read cache; this is the cache disk that was previously added to the zpools. Changing the speed in which data is fed to the cache helps by decreasing the amount of time it takes to warm or fill up the cache with constantly accessed files. The setting is specified in bytes per second. To change it you can use the following command:

```
echo 2621440000 > /sys/module/zfs/parameters/l2arc_max_write
```

As with the previous setting, this is applied to the running kernel. To make it boot-persistent, add the following line to the /etc/modprobe.d/zfs.conf file:

```
options zfs l2arc_write_max=2621440000
```

This setting allows a maximum of 256 MB/s of L2ARC feed; the setting should be increased to at least double if the VM size is changed to a higher tier.

In the end, you should end up with a file on each node that looks like this:

```
options zfs zfs_arc_max=27917287424
options zfs l2arc_write_max=2621440000
```

Regarding ZFS, on other types of filesystems, changing the block size helps to gain some performance. ZFS has a variable block size, allowing for small and big files to achieve similar results, so there is no need to change this setting.

Summary

After installing ZFS, creating the zpools, installing GlusterFS, and creating the volumes, we have ended up with a solution with respectable performance that can sustain a node failure and still serve data to its clients.

For the setup, we used Azure as the cloud provider. While each provider has their own set of configuration challenges, the core concepts can be used on other cloud providers as well.

However, this design has a disadvantage. When adding new disks to the zpools, the stripes don't align, causing new reads and writes to yield lower performance. This problem can be avoided by adding an entire set of disks at once; lower read performance is mostly covered by the read cache on RAM (ARC) and the cache disk (L2ARC).

For GlusterFS, we used a dispersed layout that balances performance with high availability. In this three-node cluster setup, we can sustain a node failure without holding I/O from the clients.

The main takeaway is to have a critical mindset when designing a solution. In this example, we worked with the resources that we had available to achieve a configuration that would perform to specification and utilize what we provided. Make sure that you always ask yourself how this setting will impact the result, and how you can change it to be more efficient.

In the next chapter, we'll go through testing and validating the performance of the setup.

Questions

- What are GlusterFS bricks?
- What is ZFS?
- What is a zpool?
- What is a cache disk?
- How is GlusterFS installed?
- What is a trusted pool?
- How is a GlusterFS volume created?
- What is performance.cache-size?
- What is ARC?

Further reading

- *Learning Microsoft Azure* by Geoff Webber-Cross: `https://www.packtpub.com/networking-and-servers/learning-microsoft-azure`
- *Implementing Azure Solutions* by Florian Klaffenbach, Jan-Henrik Damaschke, and Oliver Michalski: `https://www.packtpub.com/virtualization-and-cloud/implementing-azure-solutions`
- *Azure for Architects* by Ritesh Modi: `https://www.packtpub.com/virtualization-and-cloud/azure-architects`

Analyzing Performance in a Gluster System

5

In the Chapter 4, *Using GlusterFS on the Cloud Infrastructure*, we have completed a working implementation of GlusterFS, we can focus on the testing aspect of the solution. We will look at a high-level overview of what was deployed and explain the reasoning behind the chosen components.

Once the configuration is defined, we can go through testing the performance to verify that we are achieving the expected results. We can then conduct availability testing by deliberately bringing down nodes while performing I/O.

Finally, we will see how we can scale the solution both vertically and horizontally.

In this chapter, we will cover the following topics:

- A high-level overview of the implementation
- Going through Performance testing
- Performance availability testing
- Scaling the solution vertically and horizontally

Technical requirements

Here's the list of technical resources for this chapter:

- Zpool iostat—used for performance monitoring on ZFS: `https://docs.oracle.com/cd/E19253-01/819-5461/gammt/index.html`
- Sysstat—used for live block performance statistics: `https://github.com/sysstat/sysstat`
- The iostat man page containing the different options for the command: `http://sebastien.godard.pagesperso-orange.fr/man_iostat.html`
- FIO documentation to provide configuration parameters and usage: `https://media.readthedocs.org/pdf/fio/latest/fio.pdf`
- GlusterFS monitoring workload documentation on how to view statistics: `https://gluster.readthedocs.io/en/latest/Administrator%20Guide/Monitoring%20Workload/`

An overview of the implementation

After having the solution deployed and configured in `Chapter 4`, *Using GlusterFS on the Cloud Infrastructure*, we can validate the performance of the implementation. The primary goal is to understand how this can be done and the tools that are available.

Let's first take a step back and see what we implemented.

An overview of the cluster

In `Chapter 4`, *Using GlusterFS on the Cloud Infrastructure*, we deployed GlusterFS version 4.1 on an Azure **virtual machine** (**VM**). We used ZFS as the storage backend for the bricks by using four disks per node on a three-node setup. The following diagram offers a high-level overview of how this is distributed:

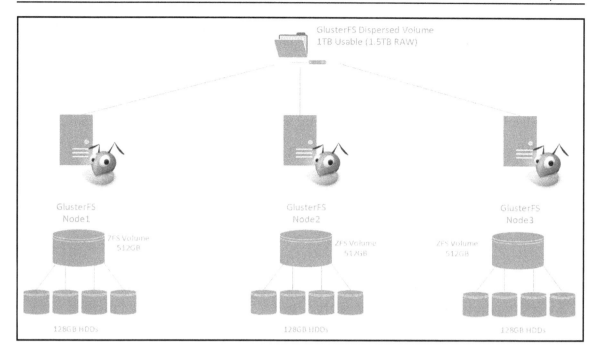

This setup gives 1 TB of usable space. The volume can tolerate an entire node going down while still serving data to the clients.

This setup should be able to deliver approximately 375 **megabytes per second (MB/s)**, handle several hundred clients at once, and should be reasonably straightforward to scale both horizontally and vertically.

Performance testing

We now need to validate that the theoretical performance can be achieved through actual implementation. Let's break this down into several parts.

Performance theory

Let's figure out how much performance we should be getting based on the specifications of the setup. Consider that each of the nodes should provide a maximum of 125 MB/s. The disk subsystem is more than capable of delivering performance since each disk yields 60 MB/s.

The total achievable performance should be around 375 MB/s, assuming that the client or clients can keep up by sending or requesting enough data to the volume.

Performance tools

We'll be using three main tools to validate and test the performance of the solution:

- `zpool iostat`
- `iostat`
- **Flexible I/O tester (FIO)**

Each of these tools works at a different level. Let's now detail what each one does and how to understand the information that they provide.

The ZFS zpool iostat command

ZFS works on the backend volume level; the `zpool iostat -v` command gives performance statistics for each of the members in the ZFS volume and statistics for the ZFS volume as a whole.

The command can provide real-time data by passing a number in seconds that it will iterate after that period of time has passed. For example, `zpool iostat -v 1` reports disk statistics each second. Here, the `-v` option shows each of the members of the pool and their respective data.

This tool helps to present the performance at the lowest level possible because it shows data from each of the disks, from each of the nodes:

```
[root@gfs1 /]# zpool iostat -vLP 1
                 capacity      operations     bandwidth
pool           alloc   free   read  write   read  write
----------     -----  -----   ----  -----   ----  -----
brick1         62.3G   446G      0      1  11.3K  26.0K
   /dev/sdf1   15.4G   112G      0      0  2.61K  6.18K
   /dev/sdd1   15.9G   111G      0      0  2.33K  6.73K
   /dev/sdc1   15.6G   111G      0      0  2.70K  6.20K
   /dev/sde1   15.4G   112G      0      0  3.65K  6.92K
cache              -      -      -      -      -      -
   /dev/sdb1      8K   678G      0      0    303     98
----------     -----  -----   ----  -----   ----  -----
```

Note that we used the extra −L and −P options so that the absolute paths of the device's files or the **Universally Unique Identifier** (**UUID**) are printed; this is because we created the pool using the unique identifier of each of the disks.

From the preceding screenshot, we can see four main groups, as follows:

- pool: This is created with each of the members.
- capacity: This is the amount of space that is allocated to each device.
- operations: This is the number of IOPSes that are done on each of the devices.
- bandwidth: This is the throughput of each device.

In the first line, the command prints the statistics since the last boot. Remember that this tool helps to present the performance from a ZFS-pool level.

iostat

As part of the sysstat package, iostat provides low-level performance statistics from each of the devices. iostat bypasses filesystems and volumes and presents the RAW performance data from each of the block devices in the system.

The iostat tool can be run with options to alter the information that is printed onscreen, for example, iostat −dxctm 1. Let's explore what each part does:

- iostat: This is the primary command.
- d: This prints the device utilization.
- x: This displays the extended device statistics.
- c: This displays the CPU utilization.
- t: This displays the time for each report printed.
- m: This ensures that the statistics will be displayed in MB/s.
- 1: This is the amount of time in seconds in which iostat prints data.

In the following screenshot, you can see that `iostat` displays information in different columns:

08/29/2018 01:16:57 AM										
avg-cpu: %user	%nice	%system	%iowait	%steal	%idle					
0.17		1.61	0.22		98.00					

Device	r/s	w/s	rMB/s	wMB/s	rrqm/s	wrqm/s	%rrqm	%wrqm	r_await	w_await
sda	0.77	19.07	0.01	0.14		0.01	0.61	0.08	37.69	0.49
sdb	2.30	5.49	0.01	0.31	0.01	0.47	0.46	7.86	0.59	0.50
sdc	0.78	19.06	0.01	0.14		0.01	0.55	0.08	37.61	0.49
sdd	0.78	19.05	0.01	0.14		0.01	0.56	0.07	37.43	0.49
sde	0.77	18.59	0.01	0.14		0.02	0.59	0.09	39.46	0.70
sdf	0.78	18.53	0.01	0.14		0.02	0.60	0.08	38.07	0.70

There's no need to go through all of the columns, but the most important ones are as follows:

- `Device`: This shows the block devices that are present on the system.
- `r/s`: These are the read operations per second.
- `w/s`: These are the write operations per second.
- `rMB/s`: These are the MB/s read from the device.
- `wMB/s`: These are the MB/s written to the device.
- `r_await`: This is the average time in milliseconds for read requests.
- `w_await`: This is the average time in milliseconds for write requests.

The `r_await` and `w_await` columns in conjunction with the `avg-cpu %iowait` time are essential; this is because these metrics can help determine whether one of the devices has increased latency over the others. A high CPU `iowait` time means that the CPU is continuously waiting for I/O to complete, which, in turn, might mean that the block devices have high latency.

The `iostat` tool can be run on each of the nodes in the cluster, providing low-level statistics for each of the disks that make up the GlusterFS volume.

 Details on the rest of the columns can be found on the man page for `iostat`.

The FIO tester

FIO is a benchmarking tool that is used to conduct performance testing by generating synthetic workloads and presenting a summary of the I/O metrics.

 Note that `fio` does not come by default on CentOS, but it is available in the base repository and can be installed by running `sudo yum install -y fio`.

This tool is exceptionally helpful as it allows us to perform tests that are close to what the real workload of the system will be—by allowing the user to change parameters such as the block size, file size, and thread count. FIO can deliver data that is close to real-world performance. This level of customization can be potentially confusing as it provides many options for workload simulation, and some of these are not very intuitive at first.

The easiest way to perform testing with FIO is by creating a configuration file, which tells the software how to behave; a configuration file looks like this:

```
[global]
name=rw-nocache-random
rw=randrw
rwmixread=50
rwmixwrite=50
group_reporting=1
bs=1M
direct=1
numjobs=4
time_based=1
runtime=180
ioengine=libaio
iodepth=64

[file1]
size=10G
filename=rw-nocache-random.1
```

Let's break it down so that we can understand how each part of the configuration file works:

- `[global]`: This denotes the configuration parameters that affect the entire test (parameters for individual files can be set).
- `name=`: This is the name of the test; it can be anything meaningful.
- `rw=randrw`: This tells FIO what type of I/O to perform; in this case, it does random reads and writes.

- `rwmixread` and `rwmixwrite`: These tell FIO what percentage or mix of reads and writes to perform—in this case, it is a 50-50 mix.
- `group_reporting=1`: This is used to give statistics for the entire test rather than for each of the jobs.
- `bs=1M`: This is the block size that FIO uses when performing the test; it can be changed to a value that mimics the workload intended.
- `numjobs=4`: This controls how many threads are opened per file. Ideally, this can be used to match the number of users or threads that will be using the storage.
- `runtime=180`: This controls, in seconds, how long the test will run for.
- `ioengine=libaio`: This controls the type of I/O engine to be used. The most common is `libaio` as it resembles most workloads.
- `iodepth=64`: This controls the I/O depth of the test; a higher number allows the storage device to be used at its fullest.

Finally, the file group controls how many files are created for the test and what their size will be. Certain settings, such as `iodepth`, can be added to this group that only affect the file where the parameter is defined. Another consideration is that `fio` opens a thread based on the `numjobs` parameter for each of the files. In the preceding configuration, it will open a total of 16 threads.

To run FIO, simply move into the directory where the mount point is located and point it to the configuration file, as follows:

```
cd /gvol1
fio /root/test.fio
```

 Note that FIO requires root privileges, so make sure that FIO is run with `sudo`.

While FIO is running, it displays statistics such as throughput and IOPS:

```
fio-3.1
Starting 16 processes
Jobs: 16 (f=16): [m(16)][12.2%][r=134MiB/s,w=145MiB/s][r=134,w=145 IOPS][eta 02m:38s]
```

Once done, FIO reports the test statistics on screen. The main things to look for are the IOPS and **bandwidth** (**BW**) for both read and write operations:

```
file1: (groupid=0, jobs=16): err= 0: pid=2747: Wed Aug 29 05:18:42 2018
  read: IOPS=141, BW=141MiB/s (148MB/s)(8482MiB/60155msec)
    slat (msec): min=7, max=387, avg=91.82, stdev=55.91
    clat (usec): min=7, max=4742.4k, avg=3422222.67, stdev=595136.99
     lat (msec): min=44, max=4790, avg=3514.04, stdev=596.21
    clat percentiles (msec):
     |  1.00th=[  584],  5.00th=[ 2702], 10.00th=[ 2937], 20.00th=[ 3138],
     | 30.00th=[ 3272], 40.00th=[ 3373], 50.00th=[ 3473], 60.00th=[ 3574],
     | 70.00th=[ 3708], 80.00th=[ 3842], 90.00th=[ 4010], 95.00th=[ 4144],
     | 99.00th=[ 4396], 99.50th=[ 4463], 99.90th=[ 4597], 99.95th=[ 4665],
     | 99.99th=[ 4732]
   bw (  KiB/s): min= 2043, max=22894, per=6.32%, avg=9125.00, stdev=3924.97, samples=1799
   iops        : min=    1, max=   22, avg= 8.83, stdev= 3.82, samples=1799
  write: IOPS=143, BW=144MiB/s (151MB/s)(8649MiB/60155msec)
    slat (usec): min=1515, max=211350, avg=20973.18, stdev=21320.17
    clat (usec): min=9, max=4742.2k, avg=3442255.32, stdev=599417.47
     lat (msec): min=28, max=4760, avg=3463.23, stdev=599.80
    clat percentiles (msec):
     |  1.00th=[  676],  5.00th=[ 2702], 10.00th=[ 2970], 20.00th=[ 3171],
     | 30.00th=[ 3272], 40.00th=[ 3406], 50.00th=[ 3507], 60.00th=[ 3608],
     | 70.00th=[ 3708], 80.00th=[ 3842], 90.00th=[ 4044], 95.00th=[ 4178],
     | 99.00th=[ 4396], 99.50th=[ 4463], 99.90th=[ 4665], 99.95th=[ 4665],
     | 99.99th=[ 4732]
   bw (  KiB/s): min= 1865, max=25026, per=6.31%, avg=9295.26, stdev=3981.09, samples=1798
   iops        : min=    1, max=   24, avg= 9.00, stdev= 3.87, samples=1798
  lat (usec)   : 10=0.06%, 20=0.02%, 50=0.01%
  lat (msec)   : 50=0.03%, 100=0.06%, 250=0.23%, 500=0.39%, 750=0.39%
  lat (msec)   : 1000=0.40%, 2000=1.55%, >=2000=96.86%
  cpu          : usr=0.08%, sys=1.46%, ctx=185112, majf=0, minf=470
  IO depths    : 1=0.1%, 2=0.2%, 4=0.4%, 8=0.7%, 16=1.5%, 32=3.0%, >=64=94.1%
     submit    : 0=0.0%, 4=100.0%, 8=0.0%, 16=0.0%, 32=0.0%, 64=0.0%, >=64=0.0%
     complete  : 0=0.0%, 4=99.9%, 8=0.0%, 16=0.0%, 32=0.0%, 64=0.1%, >=64=0.0%
     issued rwt: total=8482,8649,0, short=0,0,0, dropped=0,0,0
     latency   : target=0, window=0, percentile=100.00%, depth=64

Run status group 0 (all jobs):
   READ: bw=141MiB/s (148MB/s), 141MiB/s-141MiB/s (148MB/s-148MB/s), io=8482MiB (8894MB), run=60155-60155msec
  WRITE: bw=144MiB/s (151MB/s), 144MiB/s-144MiB/s (151MB/s-151MB/s), io=8649MiB (9069MB), run=60155-60155msec
```

From the test results, we can see that the GlusterFS volume can sustain about 150 MB/s of both read and write operations simultaneously. We're off by 75 MB/s from the theoretical maximum performance of the cluster; in this specific case, we're hitting a network limit.

FIO can be extremely effective at validating performance and detecting problems; `fio` can be run on clients mounting the Gluster volume or directly on the bricks of each of the nodes. You can use FIO for testing existing solutions in order to validate performance needs; just make sure the settings in the FIO configuration are changed based on what needs to be tested.

TIP

GlusterFS provides some tools to monitor performance from the perspective of volume. These can be found in the GlusterFS documentation page, under *Monitoring Workload*.

Availability testing

Making sure that the cluster is able to tolerate a node going down is crucial because we can confirm that no downtime occurs if a node is lost.

This can be done by forcibly shutting down one of the nodes while the others continue to serve data. To function as a synthetic workload, we can use FIO to perform a continuous test while one of the nodes is being shut down.

In the following screenshot, we can see that the `gfs2` node was not present, but the FIO test continued serving data as expected:

Scaling

Scaling this setup is relatively straightforward. As previously mentioned, we can either scale vertically, by adding more disks to each of the nodes, or scale horizontally, by adding more nodes to the cluster.

Scaling vertically is considerably simpler than horizontally as it requires fewer resources. For example, a single disk can be added to the ZFS pool on each of the nodes—effectively increasing the available space by 256 GB if three 128 GB disks are added.

Adding disks to the ZFS pool can be done with the following command:

```
zpool add brick1 /dev/disk/by-id/<disk-id>
```

From the previous command, `brick1` is the name of the pool and `disk-id` is the UUID of the recently added disk or disks.

Scaling horizontally requires the exact setup to be mirrored on a new node and then added to the cluster. This requires a new set of disks. The advantage is that the available space and performance will grow accordingly.

Summary

In this chapter, we looked at an overview of the implementation done in the previous `Chapter 4`, *Using GlusterFS on the Cloud Infrastructure*, so that we could have a fresh understanding of what was implemented in order to understand how we could test performance. Given the previous setup, the implementation should be capable of a theoretical 375 MB/s of throughput. We can validate this number with several tools that work at different levels.

For ZFS volumes, we can use the `zpool iostat` command, which provides data for each of the block devices that are part of the ZFS volume. `iostat` can be used to determine performance for all of the block devices present in the system. These commands can only be run on each of the nodes of the cluster. To be able to verify the actual performance of the implementation, we used the FIO tool, which can simulate specific workloads by changing the parameters of how I/O is performed. This tool can be used on each of the nodes on the brick level or on each of the Gluster clients on the GlusterFS volume to get a general overview of the performance that is achievable by the cluster.

We went through how we can perform availability testing by purposely shutting down one of the nodes while performing a test through FIO. Finally, scaling the solution can be done either vertically, by adding disks to each of the volumes in each of the nodes, or horizontally, by adding an entirely new node to the cluster. Your main takeaway from this chapter is to consider how the configuration that was implemented can be validated using widely available tools. These are just a set of tools. Many other tools might be available, which could be better for the solution that you're implementing.

In the next chapter, we'll jump into creating a highly-available self-healing architecture.

Questions

1. What is MB/s?
2. What is `zpool iostat`?
3. Where can I run `zpool iostat`?
4. What is `iostat`?
5. What does `r_await` mean?
6. What is CPU IOWAIT time?
7. What is FIO?
8. How can I run FIO?
9. What is an FIO configuration file?
10. How can I validate availability in a Gluster cluster?
11. How can I scale vertically?

Further reading

- *Learning Microsoft Azure Storage* by Mohamed Waly: `https://www.packtpub.com/big-data-and-business-intelligence/learning-microsoft-azure-storage`

2
Section 2: High-Availablility Nginx Web Application Using Kubernetes

In this section, the reader will learn to understand the advantages of using Kubernetes as an orchestrator for deploying and managing containerized applications, and how to deploy such a solution.

This section contains the following chapters:

- Chapter 6, *Creating a Highly Available Self-Healing Architecture*
- Chapter 7, *Understanding the Core Components of a Kubernetes Cluster*
- Chapter 8, *Architecting a Kubernetes Cluster*
- Chapter 9, *Deploying and Configuring Kubernetes*

6
Creating a Highly Available Self-Healing Architecture

In this chapter, we will go through how the IT industry has evolved from using monolithic applications to cloud-native, containerized, and highly available microservices.

With open source, we can provide solutions that will enable us to create highly available and on-demand scales of our applications based on our user consumption.

We will cover the following topics in this chapter:

- Describing microservices
- Why containers are the home of microservices
- How we can orchestrate our containers
- Exploring the most commonly-used orchestrator in Open Source, Kubernetes.

Microservices

Microservices are used to design applications in a modular way, where each module is deployed independently, and they communicate with each other through APIs. All these modules work together to deliver a single application where each function has its own purpose.

For example, let's take a look at an online store. All we can see is the main website; however, on the backend there are several microservices that come into play, one service to take orders, another to suggest items for you based on your previous browsing, payment processing, review and comment handlers, and more.

The following diagram is an example of a microservice application:

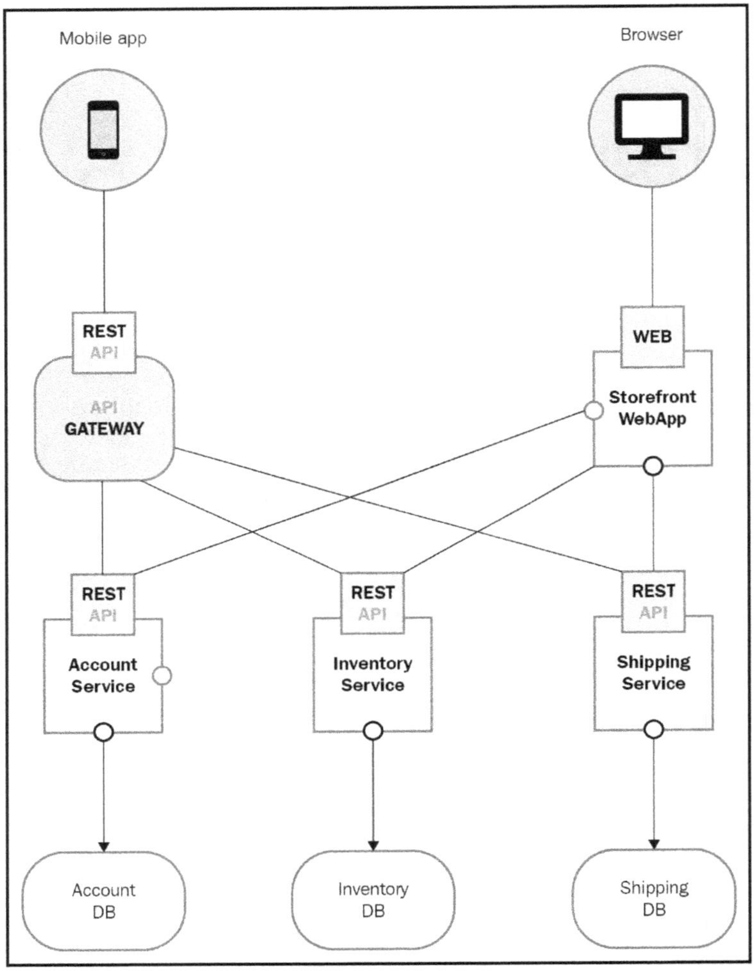

By nature, microservice applications do not require a huge team to support the application as a whole. One single team supports only one or two modules in the big picture, creating a more granular approach in terms of support and expertise of each moving part of the final product. Support and development are not only granular, but there are also failures. In the case of a single microservice failure, only that portion of the application will fail.

Continuing with our online store example, let's say that the microservice that handles the reviews and comments fails. This is due to the fact that our website is constructed using microservices, so only that component of our site will be unavailable to our customers.

They will, however, still be able to continue purchasing and using the website with no issues, and while users will not be able to see the reviews for the products they are interested in, this does not mean that our entire website usability is compromised. Depending on what caused the issue, you can either patch the microservice or restart it. Bringing down the entire website for a patch or restart is no longer necessary.

As an infrastructure engineer you might think, why do I have to know what a microservice is or what its benefits are? Well, the reason is simple. As an architect or infrastructure engineer, you are building the underlying infrastructure for this type of application. Whether they are monolithic applications running on a single host or microservices spread out across multiple containers, it will certainly impact the way you design your customer's architecture.

Linux will be your best friend here, as you will find multiple open source tools that will help you to maintain high availability, load balancing, and **continuous integration** (**CI**)/**continuous delivery** (**CD**) with tools such as Docker, Kubernetes, Jenkins, Salt, and Puppet. So whenever a customer asks you for which OS environment he should start designing his microserviced applications, Linux will be your answer.

Currently, Docker Swarm and Kubernetes are leaders when it comes to container orchestration. When it comes to microservices, containers will be also your go-to when designing an infrastructure for a customer.

We will be diving into Kubernetes in `Chapter 7`, *Understanding the Core Components of a Kubernetes Cluster*, and showing how it will help you orchestrate and deliver an elegant but complex solution for hosting microservices and other types of applications.

However, before talking about Kubernetes or container orchestration, we need to explain the concept of a container in order to understand why they are perfect for housing microservice apps.

Containers in Linux have been available for some time now, but it was not until a few years ago (with the release of the Docker Engine) that they gained momentum and admiration across all the tech communities. Containers came into play at the right time, and with the rise of microservices architecture they came to stay, and are shaping the way that we design and perform it.

Let's take a step back so that you can understand the benefits of such technology. Imagine that you have a simple monolith application that is running an API from which you can consult a list of users and what they have bought from a website that you are hosting on the same application bundle.

After a while, your customer sees that their API is becoming really popular among other applications, who are now making thousands of HTTP GET requests during peak hours. The current infrastructure is not able to handle so many requests, so your customer asks you to scale their infrastructure in a way that can handle more requests. The problem here is that because this is a monolithic application, you will not only need to calculate the resources required for the API, but you will have to also take into account the web-store frontend that is hosted alongside the API—even though the API is the only thing that you actually need to scale.

This will be a waste of resources as you are taking the web-store frontend as well, which does not require any additional replicas or resources. You are wasting precious, and sometimes expensive (if you are in the public cloud) storage, memory, and CPU resources on something that doesn't really require it.

So, this is where microservices, and also containers for hosting such types of applications, come into play. With microservices in container images, you don't have to provision a new server every time you need to scale up your services due to demand, nor do you have to restart the server, or struggle with package dependencies every time you perform an update of the app or the OS. With a simple single command (docker container run companyreg.io/storeapi:latest), your application is up and ready to serve requests. Similarly, if your application fails, just restart your container or provision a new one, and you are ready to go. What if an update that was made to the microservice had a bug? Just go ahead and revert to the previous image version and you can be up and running again; there is no need to start uninstalling updated libraries or dealing with dependency issues.

Containers also allow consistency across application deployments because, as you may know, there are multiple ways of installing a package. You can do so through a package manager such as apt, yum, and apk, or through git, /curl/wget, pip, and juju, and depending on how you install it, it will also define the way you maintain it.

Imagine a production environment where the developers send their package to the **open profiling standard (OPS)** team for deployment, and every OPS engineer deploys the app in a different way! This will become unsupportable and very hard to track. A container image with your app on it will create consistency because, no matter where you deploy it as a container, it will have the same location for all the configuration files, binaries, libraries, and dependencies everywhere you deploy it. Everything will be isolated into a container running with its own **process namespace (PID namespace)**, network namespace, and **mount namespace (MNT namespace)**.

The point of having an app architected in microservices is to provide isolation to each of the microservices in the app so that they can be easily managed and maintained—and a container achieves exactly that. You can even define how you want to start your application every time the container comes up—again, consistency plays a leading role here.

Creating container images

The way you build a container is through something called a **Dockerfile**. A Dockerfile is basically a set of instructions on how to build your container image; a typical Dockerfile is as follows:

```
FROM ubuntu:latest
LABEL maintainer="WebAdmin@company.com"

RUN apt update
RUN apt install -y apache2
RUN mkdir /var/log/my_site

ENV APACHE_LOG_DIR /var/log/my_site
ENV APACHE_RUN_DIR /var/run/apache2
ENV APACHE_RUN_USER www-data
ENV APACHE_RUN_GROUP www-data

COPY /my_site/ /var/www/html/

EXPOSE 80

CMD ["/usr/sbin/apache2", "-D", "FOREGROUND"]
```

As you can see, it is a very readable set of instructions. Without even knowing what each instruction does, we can assume its function because it's very similar to English. This Dockerfile is just an example and by far the most efficient way to do it.

An image is essentially like a template in the **virtual machine** (**VM**) world; it is a set of read-only layers that contain all the information that you need to deploy your containers—from a single image you can deploy multiple containers as they all work on their own writable layer.

For example, whenever you pull an image you will see the following output:

```
[dsala@redfedora ~]# docker pull httpd:latest
latest: Pulling from library/httpd
d660b1f15b9b: Pull complete
aa1c79a2fa37: Pull complete
```

```
f5f6514c0aff: Pull complete
676d3dd26040: Pull complete
4fdddf845a1b: Pull complete
520c4b04fe88: Pull complete
5387b1b7893c: Pull complete
Digest:
sha256:8c84e065bdf72b4909bd55a348d5e91fe265e08d6b28ed9104bfdcac9206dcc8
Status: Downloaded newer image for httpd:latest
```

Each `Pull complete` instance that you see corresponds to a layer of the image. So, what are these layers and where do they come from?

When we perform the build of the image, some of the instructions that we define in the Dockerfile will create a new layer. Each instruction in the file is executed in a read-write layer in a container that, at the end of the build, will be committed to the final layer stack that shapes the final image. One thing to note is that even if each instruction during the build is executed in a container, not all commands will create data that will make the image larger in terms of size and layers—some of them will only write to something called the **image manifest**, which is essentially a file that contains all the images' metadata.

Let's explore each command a little bit more.

FROM

The `FROM` instruction indicates what your initial image will be and, essentially, the grounds on which you will start building your own image.

What you put here will depend on your needs, for instance, which image has the libraries preinstalled that my application needs, which image already has the compiler that I need to compile my application, or which image has the least impact on our final size. For example, your application is built on Python 2. Instead of using CentOS or Ubuntu as the initial image and then installing Python manually, you can just use the `python:2.7` image, and it will already come with Python preinstalled for you.

Clearly, there are more things to consider here, but we will be going through them later in this chapter when we look at the best practices of image building.

Since this instruction takes another image and uses it as its basis, your final image will inherit the layers of your base; so, the total number of final layers will be as follows:

Final image layers = base image layers + the layers you create

LABEL

The LABEL instruction is very self-explanatory—it labels your images with key-value pairs as metadata that you will later be able to retrieve through the docker inspect command. You can use this to add data that you would like the user of your image to know. Usually, it is used to add the information about the author of the image, such as their email or company:

```
LABEL maintener="john.doe@company.com"
```

Because this instruction is just metadata, no extra layers will be added to your image.

RUN

With RUN, you will run the commands that you need to prepare your container to run your application; for example, to install packages, compile your code, and create users or directories. RUN has two ways of running commands.

The shell form is as follows:

```
RUN <command>
```

In this form, all your commands will be run with the /bin/sh -c shell by default, although you can change the shell by using the SHELL instruction, as follows:

```
SHELL ["/bin/bash", "-c"]
RUN echo "Hello I'm using bash"
```

The SHELL keyword can only be run in the JSON array format, which leads us to the second form that you can use to run the RUN instruction.

The exec form is as follows:

```
RUN ["echo","hello world"]
```

The main difference here, besides the formatting, is that in the exec form the shell is not invoked, so normal variable substitution will not happen—instead, you will have to invoke the shell as a command for the shell to be able to provide variable expansion:

```
RUN ["/bin/bash","-c","echo $HOME"]
```

Due to the nature of the RUN keyword, each instance of it will be executed on a new layer and committed to the final image, therefore, every time you use RUN it will add a new layer to your image.

ENV

For ENV, there is not much to say—this instruction sets variables for the environment. They will be used during build time and will be available during container runtime. ENV does not generate extra layers to the container as it stores the environment variables on the image manifest as metadata:

```
ENV <key>=<value>
```

The parameters for ENV are treated in <key> /<value> pairs, where the <key> parameter is the variable name and the <value> parameter is its contents or value. You can either declare them by using the = sign or without it. Quote marks and backslashes can be used to escape spaces in the value field.

All the following variations are valid:

```
ENV USER="Jane Doe"

ENV USER=Jane\ Doe

ENV USER Jane Doe
```

COPY

With COPY, we can copy files or directories from our local host (where you are executing the Docker build) to our image. This is very useful as you are actually moving content to the image, so that you can copy your applications, files, or anything that you might need for your container to work. As we previously mentioned, any instructions that add actual data to the container will create a new layer, therefore, increasing the storage footprint of your final image.

This instruction shares the same forms as RUN; you can either use JSON formatting or just space the <src> source separately from the <dst> destination:

```
COPY <src>   <dst>
COPY ["<src1>","<src2>","<dst>"]
```

There are several catches that we need to go through. First, if any of the filenames or directories has a space on its name, you have to use the JSON array format.

Second, by default, all files and directories will be copied with **user identifier (UID)** and **group identifier (GID)** 0 (root). To override this, you can use the `--chown=<UID>:<GID>` flag as follows:

```
COPY --chown=JANE:GROUP <src> <dst>
```

`chown` accepts either the numerical ID or the name of the user or group. If there is only one of them, then it is defined as follows:

```
COPY --chown=JANE <src> <dst>
```

`COPY` will assume that both the user and the group are the same.

If you are copying similarly-named files, then you can always use wildcards—`COPY` will use the Go `filepath.Match` rule, which can be found at `http://golang.org/pkg/path/filepath#Match`.

How you define the `<src>` and `<dst>` entries is very important because they follow these three rules:

- The path that you define in `<src>` must be inside the context of the build, essentially, all files and directories that are located in the directory that you specified when running the Docker build `PATH` command.
- If you are copying directories, then always end them with `/`. In this way, Docker knows that this is a directory and not a single file that you are copying. Additionally, if it's a directory, all of the files inside of it will be copied as well.
- The path defined in `<dst>` will always have to be an absolute path, unless you specify a working directory to be relative to with the `WORKDIR` instruction.

Finishing with the `COPY` instruction, I must add that `COPY` only supports copying locally-located files. If you want to copy files from a remote server using URLs, you must use the `ADD` instruction, which follows the same rules that `COPY` does but with some other caveats for URLs. This is beyond the scope of this chapter, but you can learn more about it at `https://docs.docker.com`.

EXPOSE

With the `EXPOSE` keyword, we are not actually publishing the container port that we specify here; instead, we are creating a guideline for the container's user to know which ports to publish when they start the container.

Therefore, this is only metadata that is again created in the image's manifest, which can later be retrieved with `docker inspect`. No additional layers are created with this keyword.

Ports defined in the `EXPOSE` instruction can be either **user datagram protocol (UDP)** or **transmission control protocol (TCP)**, but, by default, TCP is assumed if no protocol is specified.

Here are some examples of the `EXPOSE` instruction:

```
EXPOSE 80
EXPOSE 53/udp
EXPOSE 80/tcp
```

CMD and ENTRYPOINT

These are probably the most important instructions in a Dockerfile, since they tell the container what to run when it's started. We will go through both of them and explore how they interact with one another and how they differ from one another.

Let's start with `ENTRYPOINT` first. This instruction, as we mentioned before, allows you to define the executable that you want to run when starting the container. You can add multiple `ENTRYPOINT` definitions in a Dockerfile, but only the last one will be executed on `docker container run`.

When you run a container with the `run` argument, you can usually add command-line arguments. These arguments will be appended to the `ENTRYPOINT` parameter unless you use the `--entrypoint` flag while using `docker container run` to overwrite the `ENTRYPOINT` executable.

Let's look at some examples. Let's say that we are using a container with the following Dockerfile:

```
FROM alpine
ENTRYPOINT ["echo","Hello from Entrypoint"]
```

Now, let's assume that we built the image and tagged it `entrypointexample`. When we run this container without extra command-line arguments, it will appear as follows:

```
[dsala@redfedora]# docker container run entrypointexample
Hello from Entrypoint
```

If we add command-line arguments to the `run` command, we will see something like this:

```
[dsala@redfedora]# docker container run entrypointexample /bin/bash
Hello from Entrypoint /bin/bash
```

As you can see, it is not actually executing a BASH shell, but it's taking `/bin/bash` as though it was a string for the `echo` command that we defined in our Dockerfile. Let's consider a more explicit example as, with the previous one, I only wanted to demonstrate that even if you pass an actual command or try to execute a shell, it will still take it and pass it as arguments for ENTRYPOINT. Here is a more clear example with a simple string:

```
[dsala@redfedora]# docker container run entrypointexample I AM AN ARGUMENT
Hello from Entrypoint I AM AN ARGUMENT
```

Now, if we pass the `--entrypoint` flag, we will overwrite the ENTRYPOINT executable:

```
[dsala@redfedora]# docker container run --entrypoint /bin/ls
entrypointexample -lath /var
total 0
drwxr-xr-x    1 root root            6 Aug 8 01:22 ..
drwxr-xr-x   11 root root          125 Jul 5 14:47 .
dr-xr-xr-x    2 root root            6 Jul 5 14:47 empty
drwxr-xr-x    5 root root           43 Jul 5 14:47 lib
drwxr-xr-x    2 root root            6 Jul 5 14:47 local
drwxr-xr-x    3 root root           20 Jul 5 14:47 lock
drwxr-xr-x    2 root root            6 Jul 5 14:47 log
drwxr-xr-x    2 root root            6 Jul 5 14:47 opt
lrwxrwxrwx    1 root root            4 Jul 5 14:47 run -> /run
drwxr-xr-x    3 root root           18 Jul 5 14:47 spool
drwxrwxrwt    2 root root            6 Jul 5 14:47 tmp
drwxr-xr-x    4 root root           29 Jul 5 14:47 cache
```

Okay, so why is the formatting of this command this way? As we saw earlier, the `--entrypoint` flag only replaces the executable—all additional parameters have to be passed as arguments. This is the reason why our `ls` has its `-lath /var` arguments at the very end. There are some additional things that we need to see here, and they correspond to the forms that the ENTRYPOINT instruction has.

As with the other Dockerfile instruction, ENTRYPOINT has two forms, shell and exec:

```
ENTRYPOINT command argument1 argument2
ENTRYPOINT ["executable", "param1", "param2"]
```

For the exec form, the same rules that apply to the previous Dockerfile instructions apply here as well.

No shell is invoked in exec form, therefore, the $PATH variable is not present, and you will not be able to use the executables without providing their full path—this is why we used /bin/ls instead of just ls. Also, you can see that you first define the executable in the JSON array and then its parameters, this first field is what the --entrypoint flag will replace. Any additional parameters when using the flag will have to be passed to the docker container run command arguments as we did in our example.

Shell form, on the other hand, will load /bin/sh so that environment variables are available. Let's take a look at an example; here is a container with the following Dockerfile using the exec form:

```
FROM alpine
ENTRYPOINT ["echo", "$PATH"]
```

Let's assume that we built the image and tagged it pathexampleexec. When we run the container, we will see the following:

```
[dsala@redfedora]#docker container run pathexampleexec
$PATH
```

Here is a container with the following Dockerfile using the shell form:

```
FROM alpine
ENTRYPOINT echo $PATH
```

When we run the container, we will see the following:

```
[dsala@redfedora]# docker container run pathexampleshell
/usr/local/sbin:/usr/local/bin:/usr/sbin:/usr/bin:/sbin:/bin
```

Now, let's say that you want to have some default arguments for your application, but you want your user to be able to overwrite and use different arguments if they require. This is where CMD comes in; with CMD, you can specify default parameters for your executable, but they will be overwritten if a user runs the container with command arguments on docker container run. You have to be careful of how you declare ENTRYPOINT, because if ENTRYPOINT is declared using the shell form, all CMD definitions will be ignored.

Let's take a look at a couple of examples; the following is a Dockerfile of the container to run:

```
FROM alpine
ENTRYPOINT echo Hello
CMD ["I'm Ignored"]
```

Here is the running of the previously mentioned container, assuming that it was built and tagged as `cmdexample`:

```
[dsala@redfedora]# docker container run cmdexample
Hello
```

Now, if we use the exec form for `ENTRYPOINT`, the CMD parameters will be appended to the `ENTRYPOINT`. Dockerfile for reference:

```
FROM alpine
ENTRYPOINT ["echo", "hello from ENTRY"]
CMD ["hello", "from CMD"]
```

Here is the output, assuming that the image was built and tagged as `execcmdexample`:

```
[dsala@redfedora]# docker container run execcmdexmple
hello from ENTRY hello from CMD
```

Notice that this time the `CMD` entries were appended to `ENTRYPOINT` as arguments. However, remember that the contents of `CMD` are just defaults; if we specify the arguments on `docker container run`, these will overwrite those in `CMD`.
Using the same Dockerfile as the preceding example, we will something similar to the following:

```
[dsala@redfedora]# docker container run execcmdexmple "hello" "from" "run"
 hello from ENTRY hello from run
```

There are several combinations between `CMD` and `ENTRYPOINT`, and you can see all of them in the following chart taken from `https://docs.docker.com`:

	No ENTRYPOINT	ENTRYPOINT exec_entry p1_entry	ENTRYPOINT ["exec_entry", "p1_entry"]
No CMD	*error, not allowed*	/bin/sh -c exec_entry p1_entry	exec_entry p1_entry
CMD ["exec_cmd", "p1_cmd"]	exec_cmd p1_cmd	/bin/sh -c exec_entry p1_entry	exec_entry p1_entry exec_cmd p1_cmd
CMD ["p1_cmd", "p2_cmd"]	p1_cmd p2_cmd	/bin/sh -c exec_entry p1_entry	exec_entry p1_entry p1_cmd p2_cmd
CMD exec_cmd p1_cmd	/bin/sh -c exec_cmd p1_cmd	/bin/sh -c exec_entry p1_entry	exec_entry p1_entry /bin/sh -c exec_cmd p1_cmd

Building container images using best practices

Dockerfiles are like recipes for your applications, but you can't just throw in the ingredients and hope for the best. Creating an efficient image requires you to be careful about how you utilize the tools at your disposal.

The whole point of containers is to have a small footprint—having a 1 GB+ image for a 100 MB application is not indicative of a small footprint, nor is it efficient at all. Microservices are all about this as well; having small container images for your microservices not only improves performance, but storage utilization decreases security vulnerabilities and points of failure, and it also saves you money.

Container images are stored locally in your host and remotely in a container registry. Public cloud providers charge you for the storage utilization of your registry and not by the image quantity that you have stored there. Think of a registry as the GitHub of containers. Let's say that you have to pull an image from your cloud provider's registry; which image do you think it will be faster to pull? A 1 GB image or a 100 MB image? The image size is essential.

The first thing to consider when building an image is the base image that you are going to use. Instead of using large images (such as full Linux distributions, Ubuntu, Debian, or CentOS) that have a lot of tools and executables that you will not need for your application to run, use smaller ones such as Alpine:

REPOSITORY	SIZE
centos	200 MB
ubuntu	83.5 MB
debian	101 MB
alpine	4.41 MB

You will find that most of the images have a slimmer version of themselves, for example, httpd and nginx:

REPOSITORY	TAG	SIZE
httpd	alpine	91.4 MB
httpd	latest	178 MB
nginx	alpine	18.6 MB
nginx	latest	109 MB

As you can see, `httpd:alpine` is almost 50% smaller than `httpd:latest`, while `nginx:alpine` is 80% smaller!

Smaller images will not only reduce your storage consumption, but they will also reduce your attack surface. This is because a smaller container has a lower attack surface; let's take a look at the latest Ubuntu image versus the latest Alpine.

For Ubuntu, we can see an increased count for vulnerabilities as per the Docker Hub page for the latest tag; this is captured in the following screenshot:

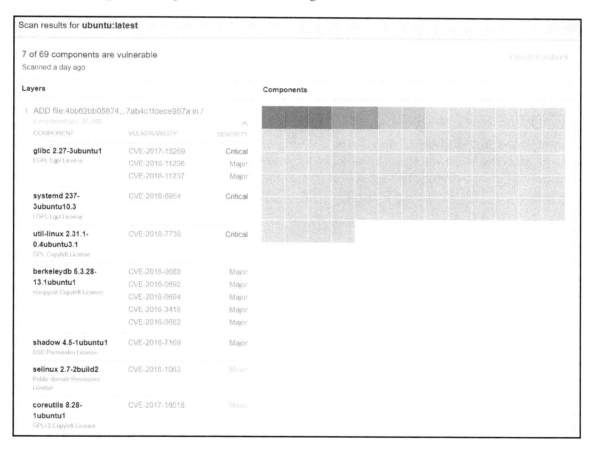

For Alpine Linux, the count goes down to zero, as demonstrated in the following screenshot:

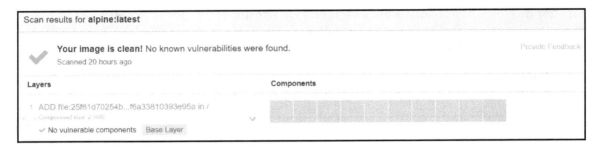

In the preceding screenshot, we can see the vulnerability count when compared to Ubuntu. Even today, the latest Alpine image has no vulnerabilities whatsoever. In comparison, Ubuntu has seven vulnerable components that are not even needed for our application to run.

Another thing to take into account is the layering of your image; each time you run a RUN statement in the build it will add one more layer and size to your final image. Reducing the number of RUN statements and what you run on them will dramatically decrease your image size.

Let's take our first Dockerfile, as follows:

```
FROM ubuntu:latest
LABEL maintainer="WebAdmin@company.com"

RUN apt update
RUN apt install -y apache2
RUN mkdir /var/log/my_site

ENV APACHE_LOG_DIR /var/log/my_site
ENV APACHE_RUN_DIR /var/run/apache2
ENV APACHE_RUN_USER www-data
ENV APACHE_RUN_GROUP www-data

COPY /my_site/ /var/www/html/

EXPOSE 80

CMD ["/usr/sbin/apache2","-D","FOREGROUND"]
```

We can modify the RUN instruction into the following way:

```
RUN apt update && \
    apt install -y apache2 --no-install-recommends && \
    apt clean && \
    mkdir /var/my_site/ /var/log/my_site
```

Now instead of creating three layers, we will be producing only one, by running all our commands in a single statement.

Remember that everything you do in RUN is executed with /bin/sh -c or any other shell that you specified with SHELL, so &, ;, and \ are accepted as they would be in a regular shell.

However, we didn't only remove the extra RUN instructions; we also added apt clean to clean the cache of our container before it commits, and used the --no-install-recommend flag to avoid installing any unnecessary packages, thus reducing both storage space and the attack surface:

Here are the details of the original image:

REPOSITORY	SIZE
bigimage	221 MB

Here are the details of the smaller image:

REPOSITORY	SIZE
smallerimage	214 MB

Of course, this is not a huge difference, but this is only an example and no real application was being installed. In a production image, you will have to do more than just install apache2.

Now let's use both of the techniques that we have learned and slim our image down:

```
FROM alpine

RUN apk update && \
    apk add mini_httpd && \
     mkdir /var/log/my_site

COPY /my_site/ /var/www/localhost/htdocs/
EXPOSE 80

CMD ["/usr/sbin/mini_httpd", "-D", "-d", "/var/www/localhost/htdocs/"]
```

Here is the final size of the image:

REPOSITORY	SIZE
finalimage	5.79 MB

Now, you can see there is a great difference in sizes—we passed from 221 MB to 217 MB, and finally ended up with a 5.79-MB image! Both images did the exact same thing, which was to serve a web page, but with an entirely different footprint.

Container orchestration

Now that we know how to create our images, we need a way to maintain the desired state of our applications. Here's where container orchestrators come in. Container orchestrators answer questions such as the following:

- How do I maintain my applications so that they are highly available?
- How do I scale each microservice on demand?
- How do I load balance my application across multiple hosts?
- How do I limit my application's resource consumption on my hosts?
- How do I easily deploy multiple services?

With container orchestrators, administrating your containers has never been as easy or efficient as it is now. There are several orchestrators available, but the most widely used are Docker Swarm and Kubernetes. We will discuss Kubernetes later on in this chapter and take a more in-depth look at it in the Chapter 7, *Understanding the Core Components of a Kubernetes Cluster*.

What all orchestrators have in common is that their basic architecture is a cluster that is composed of some master nodes watching for your desired state, which will be saved in a database. Masters will then start or stop your containers depending on the state of the worker nodes that are in charge of the container workloads. Each master node will also be in charge of dictating which container has to run on which node, based on your predefined requirements, and to scale or restart any failed instances.

However, orchestrators not only provide high availability by restarting and bringing up containers on demand, both Kubernetes and Docker Swarm also have mechanisms to control traffic to the backend containers, in order to provide load balancing for incoming requests to your application services.

The following diagram demonstrates the traffic going to an orchestrated cluster:

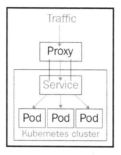

Let's explore Kubernetes a little bit more.

Kubernetes

Kubernetes is by far the most popular container orchestrator out there. Many public cloud providers are now adopting it as the de facto container orchestrator; for instance, Azure with its **Azure Kubernetes Services** (**AKS**), Amazon Web Services with **elastic container service for Kubernetes** (**EKS**), and Google Cloud with **Google Kubernetes Engine** (**GKE**). Most of these solutions are managed, abstracting the management plane for the user for ease of use, and adopting cloud-native solutions such as integration with public cloud load balancers and DNS services.

Kubernetes sits in the middle of a **platform as a service** (**PaaS**) solution and an **infrastructure as a service** (**IaaS**) solution because it provides you with a platform to run your containers and manage your data, but it still lets you provision software-defined infrastructures such as load balancers, network management, ingress controls, and resource allocation.

With Kubernetes, we can automate the process of deploying our containers and maintaining our desired state while controlling the resource consumption of our applications and providing high availability and isolation across our different applications.

Kubernetes has the basic orchestrator components that we mentioned before; it has worker nodes, master nodes, and a database that saves the status of our cluster. We will start exploring Kubernetes concepts in depth in Chapter 7, *Understanding the Core Components of a Kubernetes Cluster*.

The following diagram shows the basic architecture of Kubernetes:

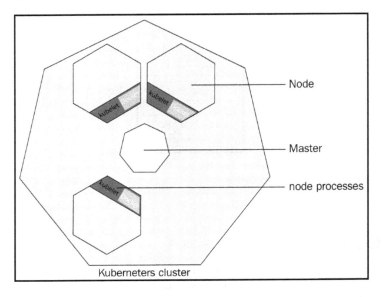

Kuberneters cluster

Summary

In this chapter, we discussed how IT is evolving from a monolithic design to microservices, and how containers are helping us achieve this type of architecture by allowing a modularized infrastructure. We used the example of an online store to demonstrate how microservices allow for the scalability of specific components without the need to bring down the entire application. Additionally, we explored how the same example has a highly available design by discussing how the microservices approach allows for just a portion of the application to fail without impacting the entire solution (that is, how only the reviews part failed without bringing down the entire online store).

Later, we learned how containers are created from images through the use of a Dockerfile, which uses a readable set of instructions to create the base image. An image can be seen as the counterpart of a template in the context of VMs.

From this Dockerfile, we learned that a FROM statement indicates what will be the initial image, how the LABEL instruction adds metadata to the container, how RUN executes the commands that you need to prepare your container to run your application, and how ENV sets variables for the environment used for container building.

Furthermore, we discussed some of the best practices when building container images, such as the use of smaller images (such as Alpine), and how choosing a smaller image helps to reduce the number of vulnerabilities present in the built containers.

Finally, we quickly glanced over some of the more popular orchestration tools that are available, these being Docker Swarm and Kubernetes.

In the next chapter, we will jump into exploring the core components of a Kubernetes cluster.

Questions

1. What are the components of Kubernetes?
2. What is the difference between GKE, EKS, and AKS?
3. How secure are containers from exploits?
4. How easy is to deploy an application in a container?
5. Are Docker containers and Kubernetes exclusive to Linux?

Further reading

- *Mastering Kubernetes* by Gigi Sayfan: https://www.packtpub.com/virtualization-and-cloud/mastering-kubernetes
- *Kubernetes for Developers* by Joseph Heck: https://www.packtpub.com/virtualization-and-cloud/kubernetes-developers
- *Hands-On Microservices with Kubernetes* by Gigi Sayfan: https://www.packtpub.com/virtualization-and-cloud/hands-microservices-kubernetes
- *Getting Started with Kubernetes – Third Edition* by Jonathan Baier, Jesse White: https://www.packtpub.com/virtualization-and-cloud/getting-started-kubernetes-third-edition
- *Mastering Docker - Second Edition* by Russ McKendrick, Scott Gallagher: https://www.packtpub.com/virtualization-and-cloud/mastering-docker-second-edition
- *Docker Bootcamp* by Russ McKendrick et al: https://www.packtpub.com/virtualization-and-cloud/docker-bootcamp

Bibliography/sources

- What are microservices?: http://microservices.io/
- Docker Hub: https://hub.docker.com/
- Production-Grade Container Orchestration: http://kubernetes.io/

7
Understanding the Core Components of a Kubernetes Cluster

In this chapter, we will be going through a 10,000-foot view of the main Kubernetes components, from what each controller is composed of to how a container in a pod is deployed and scheduled across each of the workers. It is crucial to understand the ins and outs of the Kubernetes cluster in order to be able to deploy and design a solution based on Kubernetes as an orchestrator for your containerized applications:

- Control plane components
- The Kubernetes workers' components
- Pods as basic building blocks
- Kubernetes services, load balancers, and Ingress controllers
- Kubernetes deployments and DaemonSets
- Persistent storage in Kubernetes

The Kubernetes control plane

The Kubernetes master nodes are where the core control plane services live; not all services have to reside on the same node; however, for centralization and practicality, they are often deployed this way. This obviously raises services availability questions; however, they can easily be overcome by having several nodes and providing load balancing requests to achieve a highly available set of **master nodes**.

The master nodes are composed of four basic services:

- The kube-apiserver
- The kube-scheduler
- The kube-controller-manager
- The etcd database

Master nodes can either run on bare metal servers, virtual machines, or a private or public cloud, but it is not recommended to run container workloads on them. We will see more on this later.

The following diagram shows the Kubernetes master nodes components:

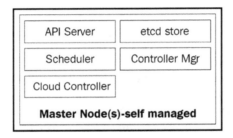

The kube-apiserver

The API server is what ties everything together. It is the frontend REST API of the cluster that receives manifests to create, update, and delete API objects such as services, pods, Ingress, and others.

The **kube-apiserver** is the only service that we should be talking to; it is also the only one that writes and talks to the etcd database for registering the cluster state. With the kubectl command, we will send commands to interact with it. This will be our Swiss Army knife when it comes to Kubernetes.

The kube-controller-manager

The **kube-controller-manager** daemon, in a nutshell, is a set of infinite control loops that is shipped for simplicity in a single binary. It watches for the defined desired state of the cluster and it makes sure that it is accomplished and satisfied by moving all the bits and pieces necessary to achieve it. The kube-controller-manager is not just one controller; it contains several different loops that watch different components in the cluster. Some of them are the service controller, the namespace controller, the service account controller, and many others. You can find each controller and its definition in the Kubernetes GitHub repository:

```
https://github.com/kubernetes/kubernetes/tree/master/pkg/controller.
```

The kube-scheduler

The **kube-scheduler** schedules your newly created pods to nodes with enough space to satisfy the pods' resource needs. It basically listens to the kube-apiserver and the kube-controller-manager for newly created pods that are put into a queue and then scheduled to an available node by the scheduler. The kube-scheduler definition can be found here:

```
https://github.com/kubernetes/kubernetes/blob/master/pkg/scheduler.
```

Besides compute resources, the kube-scheduler also reads the nodes' affinity and anti-affinity rules to find out whether a node can or cannot run that pod.

The etcd database

The **etcd database** is a very reliable consistent key-value store that's used to store the state of the Kubernetes cluster. It contains the current status of the pods in which the node is running on, how many nodes the cluster currently has, what the state of those nodes is, how many replicas of a deployment are running, services names, and others.

As we mentioned before, only the kube-apiserver talks to the `etcd` database. If the kube-controller-manager needs to check the state of the cluster, it will go through the API server in order to get the state from the `etcd` database, instead of querying the `etcd` store directly. The same happens with the kube-scheduler, if the scheduler needs to make it known that a pod has been stopped or allocated to another node; it will inform the API server, and the API server will store the current state in the etcd database.

With etcd, we have covered all the main components for our Kubernetes master nodes so that we are ready to manage our cluster. But a cluster is not only composed of masters; we still require the nodes that will be performing the heavy lifting by running our applications.

Kubernetes worker nodes

The worker nodes that do this task in Kubernetes are simply called nodes. Previously, around 2014, they were called **minions**, but this term was later replaced with just nodes, as the name was confusing with Salt's terminologies and made people think that Salt was playing a major role in Kubernetes.

These nodes are the only place that you will be running workloads, as it is not recommended to have containers or loads on the master nodes, as they need to be available to manage the entire cluster.

The nodes are very simple in terms of components; they only require three services to fulfill their task:

- Kubelet
- Kube-proxy
- Container runtime

Let's explore these three components in a little bit more depth.

Container runtime

To be able to spin up containers, we require a **container runtime**. This is the base engine that will create the containers in the nodes kernel for our pods to run. The kubelet will be talking to this runtime and will spin up or stop our containers on demand.

Currently, Kubernetes supports any OCI-compliant container runtime, such as Docker, rkt, runc, runsc, and so on.

 You can learn more about all the specifications from the OCI GitHub page: https://github.com/opencontainers/runtime-spec.

The kubelet

The **kubelet** is a low-level Kubernetes component and one of the most important ones after the kube-apiserver; both of these components are essential for the provisioning of pods/containers in the cluster. The kubelet is a service that runs on the Kubernetes nodes and listens to the API server for pod creation. The kubelet is only in charge of starting/stopping and making sure that containers in pods are healthy; the kubelet will not be able to manage any containers that were not created by it.

The kubelet achieves the goals by talking to the container runtime via something called the **container runtime interface** (**CRI**). The CRI provides pluggability to the kubelet via a gRPC client, which is able to talk to different container runtimes. As we mentioned earlier, Kubernetes supports multiple container runtimes to deploy containers, and this is how it achieves such diverse support for different engines.

 You can check the kubelet's source code via the following GitHub link: `https://github.com/kubernetes/kubernetes/tree/master/pkg/kubelet`.

The kube-proxy

The **kube-proxy** is a service that resides on each node of the cluster, and is the one that makes communications between pods, containers, and nodes possible. This service watches the kube-apiserver for changes on defined services (a service is a sort of logical load balancer in Kubernetes; we will dive deeper into services later on in this chapter) and keeps the network up to date via `iptables` rules that forward traffic to the correct endpoints. Kube-proxy also sets up rules in `iptables` that do random load balancing across pods behind a service.

Here is an example of an `iptables` rule that was made by the kube-proxy:

```
-A KUBE-SERVICES -d 10.0.162.61/32 -p tcp -m comment --comment
"default/example: has no endpoints" -m tcp --dport 80 -j REJECT --reject-
with icmp-port-unreachable
```

 This is a service with no endpoints (no pods behind it).

Now that we have gone through all the core components that form a cluster, we can talk about what we can do with them and how Kubernetes is going to help us orchestrate and manage our containerized applications.

Kubernetes objects

Kubernetes objects are exactly that: they are logical persistent objects or abstractions that will represent the state of your cluster. You are the one in charge of telling Kubernetes what your desired state of that object is so that it can work to maintain it and make sure that the object exists.

To create an object, there are two things that it needs to have: a status and its spec. The status is provided by Kubernetes, and it is the current state of the object. Kubernetes will manage and update that status as needed to be in accordance to your desired state. The spec field, on the other hand, is what you provide to Kubernetes, and is what you tell it to describe the object you desire, for example, the image that you want the container to be running, the number of containers of that image that you want to run, and so on. Each object has specific spec fields for the type of task that they perform, and you will be providing these specifications on a YAML file that is sent to the kube-apiserver with kubectl, which that transforms it into JSON and sends it as an API request. We will dive deeper into each object and its spec fields later in this chapter.

Here is an example of a YAML that was sent to kubectl:

```
cat << EOF | kubectl create -f -
kind: Service
apiVersion: v1
metadata:
 Name: frontend-service
spec:
 selector:
   web: frontend
 ports:
 - protocol: TCP
   port: 80
   targetPort: 9256
EOF
```

The basic fields of the object definition are the very first ones, and these ones will not vary from object to object and are very self-explanatory. Let's take a quick look at them:

- `kind`: The `kind` field tells Kubernetes what type of object you are defining: a pod, a service, a deployment, and so on
- `apiVersion`: Because Kubernetes supports multiple API versions, we need to specify a REST API path that we want to send our definition to
- `metadata`: This is a nested field, which means that you have several more subfields to metadata, where you will write basic definitions such as the name of your object, assigning it to a specific namespace, and also tag a label to it to relate your object to other Kubernetes objects

So, we have now been through the most-used fields and their contents; you can learn more about the Kuberntes API conventions at the following GitHub page:

`https://github.com/kubernetes/community/blob/master/contributors/devel/api-conventions.md`.

Some of the fields of the object can later be modified after the object has been created, but that will depend on the object and the field that you want to modify.

The following is a short list of the various Kubernetes objects that you can create:

- Pod
- Volume
- Service
- Deployment
- Ingress
- Secret
- ConfigMap

And there are many more.

Let's take a closer look at each one of these items.

Pods – the basis of Kubernetes

Pods are the most basic objects in Kubernetes and also the most important ones. Everything revolves around them; we can say that Kubernetes is for the pods! All of the other objects are here to serve them, and all the tasks that they do are to make the pods achieve your desired state.

So, what is a pod and why are pods so important?

A pod is a logical object that runs one or more containers together on the same network namespace, the same **inter-process communication** (**IPC**) and, sometimes, depending on the version of Kubernetes, the same **process ID** (**PID**) namespace. This is because they are the ones that are going to run our containers and hence will be the center of attention. The whole point of Kubernetes is to be a container orchestrator, and with pods, we make orchestration possible.

As we mentioned before, containers on the same pod live in a "bubble" where they can talk to one another via localhost, as they are local to one another. One container in a pod has the same IP address as the other container because they are sharing a network namespace, but in most cases, you will be running on a one-on-one basis, that is to say, a single container per pod. Multiple containers per pod are only used on very specific scenarios, such as when an application requires a helper such as a data pusher or a proxy that needs to communicate in a fast and resilient way with the primary application.

The way you define a pod is the same way you would do so for any other Kubernetes object: via a YAML that contains all the pod specs and definitions:

```
kind: Pod
apiVersion: v1
metadata:
name: hello-pod
labels:
  hello: pod
spec:
  containers:
    - name: hello-container
      image: alpine
      args:
      - echo
      - "Hello World"
```

Let's go through the basic pod definitions needed under the `spec` field to create our pod:

- **Containers:** Containers is an array; therefore, we have a set of several subfields under it. Basically, it's what defines the containers that are going to be running on the pod. We can specify a name for the container, the image that is going to be spin-off from, and the arguments or command that we need it to run. The difference between arguments and commands is the same as the difference between `CMD` and `ENTRYPOINT` that we went through in `Chapter 6`, *Creating a Highly Available Self-Healing Architecture,* when we talked about creating Docker images. Take note that all the fields that we just went through are for the `containers` array. They are not directly part of the `spec` of the pod.
- **restartPolicy:** This field is exactly that: it tells Kubernetes what to do with a container, and it applies to all the containers in the pod in the case of a zero or non-zero exit code. You can choose from either option, Never, OnFailure or Always. Always will be the default in case a restartPolicy is not defined.

These are the most basic specs that you are going to declare on a pod; other specs will require that you have a little bit more background knowledge on how to use them and how they interact with various other Kubernetes objects. We will revisit them later on this chapter, some of them are as follows:

- Volume
- Env
- Ports
- dnsPolicy
- initContainers
- nodeSelector
- Resource limits and requests

To view the pods that are currently running in your cluster, you can run `kubectl get pods`:

```
dsala@MININT-IB3HUA8:~$ kubectl get pods
NAME       READY STATUS    RESTARTS AGE
busybox    1/1 Running    120 5d
```

Alternatively, you can run `kubectl describe pods` without specifying any pod. This will print out a description of every pod running in the cluster. In this case, it will be only the `busybox` pod, as it is the only one that's currently running:

```
dsala@MININT-IB3HUA8:~$ kubectl describe pods
Name:              busybox
Namespace:         default
Priority:          0
PriorityClassName: <none>
Node:              aks-agentpool-10515745-2/10.240.0.6
Start Time:        Wed, 19 Sep 2018 14:23:30 -0600
Labels:            <none>
Annotations:       <none>
Status:            Running
IP:                10.244.1.7
Containers:
 busybox:
[...] (Output truncated for readability)
Events:
Type     Reason Age                     From           Message
----     ------ ----                    ----           -------
Normal   Pulled 45s (x121 over 5d)  kubelet, aks-agentpool-10515745-2
Container image "busybox" already present on machine
Normal   Created 44s (x121 over 5d)  kubelet, aks-agentpool-10515745-2
Created container
Normal   Started 44s (x121 over 5d)  kubelet, aks-agentpool-10515745-2
Started container
```

Pods are mortal, and this is the clue in knowing how to manage your application. You have to understand that once a pod dies or is deleted, there is no way to bring it back. Its IP and the containers that were running on it will be gone; they are totally ephemeral. The data on the pods that is mounted as a volume may or may not survive, depending on how you set it up; however, this is a discussion that we will have later in this chapter. If our pods die and we lose them, how do we ensure that all our microservices are running? Well, deployments are the answer.

Deployments

Pods by themselves are not very useful, since it is not very efficient to have more than a single instance of our application running in a single pod. Provisioning hundreds of copies of our application on different pods without having a method to look for them all will get out of hand really quickly.

This is where deployments come into play. With deployments, we can manage our pods with a controller. This allows us to not only decide how many we want to run, but we can also manage updates by changing the image version or the image itself that our containers are running. Deployments are what you will be working with most of the time. With deployments as well as pods and any other objects that we mentioned before, they have their own definition inside a YAML file:

```yaml
apiVersion: apps/v1
kind: Deployment
metadata:
 name: nginx-deployment
 labels:
   deployment: nginx
spec:
 replicas: 3
 selector:
   matchLabels:
     app: nginx
 template:
   metadata:
     labels:
       app: nginx
   spec:
     containers:
     - name: nginx
       image: nginx:1.7.9
       ports:
       - containerPort: 80
```

Let's start exploring their definition.

At the beginning of the YAML, we have more general fields, such as `apiVersion`, `kind`, and `metadata`. But under `spec` is where we will find the specific options for this API Object.

Under `spec`, we can add the following fields:

- **Selector**: With the Selector field, the deployment will know which pods to target when changes are applied. There are two fields that you will be using under the selector: `matchLabels` and `matchExpressions`. With `matchLabels`, the selector will use the labels of the pods (key/value pairs). It is important to note that all the labels that you specify here will be ANDed. This means that the pod will require that it has all the labels that you specify under `matchLabels`. `matchExpressions` is rarely used, but you can learn more about by reading our recommended books in the *Further reading* section.

- **Replicas**: This will state the number of pods that the deployment needs to keep running via the replication controller; for example, if you specify three replicas, and one of the pods dies, the replication controller will watch the replicas spec as the desired state and inform the scheduler to schedule a new pod, as the current status is now 2 since the pod died.

- **RevisionHistoryLimit**: Every time you make a change to a deployment, this change is saved as a revision of the deployment, which you can later either revert to that previous state or keep a record of what was changed. You can consult your history with `kubectl` rollout history deployment/<name of deployment>. With `revisionHistoryLimit`, you can set up a number stating how many records you want to save.

- **Strategy**: This will let you decide how you want to handle any update or horizontal pod scale. To overwrite the default, which is `rollingUpdate`, you need to write the `type` key, where you can choose between two values: `recreate` or `rollingUpdate`. While `recreate` is a fast way to update your deployment, it will delete all the pods and replace them with new ones, but it will imply that you will have to take into consideration that a system downtime will be in place for this type of strategy. The `rollingUpdate`, on the other hand, is smoother and slower, and is ideal for stateful applications that can rebalance their data. The `rollingUpdate` opens the door for two more fields, which are `maxSurge` and `maxUnavailable`. The first one will be how many pods above your total amount you want when performing an update; for example, a deployment with 100 pods and a 20% `maxSurge` will grow up to a maximum of 120 pods while updating. The next option will let you select how many pods in the percentage you are willing to kill in order to replace them with new ones in a 100 pod scenario. In cases where there is 20% `maxUnavailable`, only 20 pods will be killed and replaced with new ones before continuing to replace the rest of the deployment.

- **Template**: This is just a nested pod spec field where you will include all the specs and metadata of the pods that the deployment is going to manage.

We have seen that, with deployments, we manage our pods, and they help us maintain them in a state that we desire. All these pods are still in something called the **cluster network**, which is a closed network in which only the Kubernetes cluster components can talk to one another, even having their own set of IP ranges. How do we talk to our pods from the outside? How do we reach our application? This is where services come into play.

Services

The name *service* doesn't fully describe what services actually do in Kubernetes. Kubernetes services are what route traffic to our pods. We can say that services are what tie pods together.

Let's imagine that we have a typical frontend/backend type of application where we have our frontend pods talking to our backend ones via the IP addresses of the pods. If a pod in the backend dies, we know that pods are ephemeral and therefore we lose communication with our backend, and so now we are in a world of hurt. This is not only because the new pod will not have the same IP address of the pod that died, but now we also have to reconfigure our app to use the new IP address. This issue and similar issues are solved with services.

A service is a logical object that tells the kube-proxy to create iptables rules based on which pods are behind the service. Services configure their endpoints, which is how the pods behind a service are called, the same way as deployments know which pods to control, the selector field, and the pods' labels.

This diagram shows you how services use labels to manage traffic:

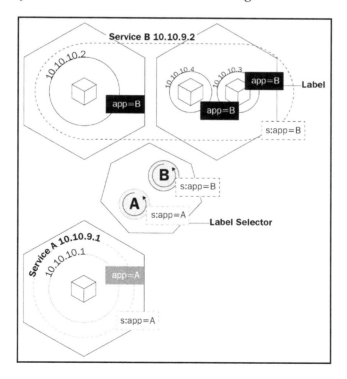

Services will not only make kube-proxy create rules to route traffic; it will also trigger something called **kube-dns**.

Kube-dns is a set of pods with SkyDNS containers that run on the cluster that provides a DNS server and forwarder, which will create records for services and sometimes pods for ease of use. Whenever you create a service, a DNS record pointing to the service's internal cluster ipaddress will be created with the form service-name.namespace.svc.cluster.local. You can learn more about the Kubernetes DNS specifications on the Kubernetes GitHub page: https://github.com/kubernetes/dns/blob/master/docs/specification.md.

Going back to our example, we will now only have to configure our application to talk to the service **fully qualified domain name (FQDN)** in order to talk to our backend pods. This way, it will not matter what IP address the pods and services have. If a pod behind the service dies, the service will take care of everything by using the A record, as we will be able to tell our frontend to route all traffic to my-svc. The logic of the service will take care of everything else.

There are several types of service that you can create whenever you are declaring the object to be created in Kubernetes. Let's go through them to see which one will be best suited for the type of work we need:

- **ClusterIP**: This is the default service. Whenever you create a ClusterIP service, it will create a service with a cluster-internal IP address that will only be routable inside the Kubernetes cluster. This type is ideal for pods that only need to talk to one another and not go outside the cluster.
- **NodePort**: When you create this type of service, by default a random port from 30000 to 32767 will be allocated to forward traffic to the endpoint pods of the service. You can override this behavior by specifying a node port in the ports array. Once this is defined you will be able to access your pods via <Nodes-IP>:<Node-Port>. This is useful to access your pods from outside the cluster via the Node IP address.
- **LoadBalancer**: Most of the time, you will be running Kubernetes on a cloud provider. The LoadBalancer type is ideal for these situations, as you will be able to allocate public IP addresses to your service via your cloud provider's API. This is the ideal service for when you want to communicate with your pods from outside your cluster. With LoadBalancer, you will be able to not only allocate a publicIP address but also, using Azure, allocate a private IP address from your virtual private network. So, you can talk to your pods from the internet or internally on your private subnet.

Let's review YAML's definition of a service:

```
apiVersion: v1
kind: Service
metadata:
 name: my-service
spec:
 selector:
   app: front-end
 type: NodePort
 ports:
 - name: http
   port: 80
   targetPort: 8080
   nodePort: 30024
   protocol: TCP
```

A service's YAML is very simple, and the specs will vary, depending on the type of service that you are creating. But the most important thing you have to take into account is port definitions. Let's take a look at these:

- port: This is the service port that is exposed
- targetPort: This is the port on the pods to where the service is sending traffic
- nodePort: This is the port that will be exposed

Although we now understand how we can communicate with the pods in our cluster, we still need to understand how we are going to manage the problem of losing our data every time a pod is terminated. This is where **Persistent Volumes** (**PV**) comes into play.

Kubernetes and persistent storage

Persistent storage in the container world is a serious issue. When we studied Docker images, we learned that the only storage that is persistent across container runs are the layers of the image, and they are read-only. The layer where the container runs is read/write, but all data in this layer is deleted when the container stops. With pods, this is the same. When a container dies, the data written to it is gone.

Kubernetes has a set of objects to handle storage across pods. The first one that we will discuss is volumes.

Volumes

Volumes solve one of the biggest problems when it comes to persistent storage. First of all, volumes are not actually objects, but a definition of a pod's spec. When you create a pod, you can define a volume under the pod's spec field. Containers in this pod will be able to mount the volume on their mount namespace, and the volume will be available across container restarts or crashes. Volumes are tied to the pods, though, and if the pod is deleted, the volume will be gone as well. The data on the volume is another story; data persistence will depend on the backend of that volume.

Kubernetes supports several types of volumes or volume sources and how they are called in the API specifications, which range from filesystem maps from the local node, cloud providers' virtual disks, and software-defined storage-backed volumes. Local filesystem mounts are the most common ones that you will see when it comes to regular volumes. It's important to note that the disadvantage of using local node filesystems is that the data will not be available across all the nodes of the cluster, and just on that node where the pod was scheduled.

Let's examine how a pod with a volume is defined in YAML:

```
apiVersion: v1
kind: Pod
metadata:
 name: test-pd
spec:
 containers:
 - image: k8s.gcr.io/test-webserver
   name: test-container
   volumeMounts:
   - mountPath: /test-pd
     name: test-volume
 volumes:
 - name: test-volume
   hostPath:
     path: /data
     type: Directory
```

Note how there is a field called `volumes` under `spec` and then there is another one called `volumeMounts`.

The first field (`volumes`) is where you define the volume you want to create for that pod. This field will always require a name and then a volume source. Depending on the source, the requirements will be different. In this example, the source would be `hostPath`, which is a node's local filesystem. `hostPath` supports several types of mappings, ranging from directories, files, block devices, and even Unix sockets.

Under the second field, `volumeMounts`, we have `mountPath`, which is where you define the path inside the container where you want to mount your volume to. The `name` parameter is how you specify to the pod which volume to use. This is important because you can have several types of volumes defined under `volumes`, and the name will be the only way for the pod to know which volumes mount to which container.

We will not be going through all the different types of volumes because it is irrelevant to know about them unless you are going to use a specific one. The important part is to know that they exist and what type of sources we can have.

You can learn more about the different types of volumes in the volume definitions in the Kubernetes website (`https://kubernetes.io/docs/concepts/storage/volumes/#types-of-volumes`) and in the Kubernetes API reference document (`https://kubernetes.io/docs/reference/generated/kubernetes-api/v1.11/#volume-v1-core`).

Having volumes die with the pods is not ideal. We require storage that persists, and this is how the need for PVs came to be.

Persistent Volumes, Persistent Volume Claims, and Storage Classes

The main difference between volumes and PVs is that, unlike volumes, PVs are actually Kubernetes API objects, so you can manage them individually like separate entities, and therefore they persist even after a pod is deleted.

You might be wondering why this subsection has PV, **persistent volume claims** (**PVCs**), and storage classes all mixed in. This is because we can't talk about one without talking about the others; all of them depend on one another, and it is crucial to understand how they interact among one another to provision storage for our pods.

Let's begin with PVs and PVCs. Like volumes, PVs have a storage source, so the same mechanism that volumes have applies here. You will either have a software-defined storage cluster providing **logical unit number** (**LUNs**), a cloud provider giving virtual disks, or even a local filesystem to the Kubernetes node, but here, instead of being called volume sources, they are called **persistent volume types** instead.

PVs are pretty much like LUNs in a storage array: you create them, but without a mapping; they are just a bunch of allocated storage waiting to be used. Here is where PVCs come into play. PVCs are like LUN mappings: they are backed or bound to a PV and also are what you actually define, relate, and make available to the pod that it can then use for its containers.

The way you use PVCs on pods is exactly the same as with normal volumes. You have two fields: one to specify which PVC you want to use, and the other one to tell the pod on which container to use that PVC.

The YAML for a PVC API object definition should have the following code:

```
apiVersion: v1
kind: PersistentVolumeClaim
metadata:
 name: gluster-pvc
spec:
 accessModes:
 - ReadWriteMany
 resources:
    requests:
      storage: 1Gi
```

The YAML for pod should have the following code:

```
kind: Pod
apiVersion: v1
metadata:
 name: mypod
spec:
 containers:
    - name: myfrontend
      image: nginx
      volumeMounts:
      - mountPath: "/mnt/gluster"
        name: volume
 volumes:
    - name: volume
      persistentVolumeClaim:
        claimName: gluster-pvc
```

When a Kubernetes administrator creates a PVC, there are two ways that this request is satisfied:

- **Static**: Several PVs have already been created, and then when a user creates a PVC, any available PV that can satisfy the requirements will be bound to that PVC.
- **Dynamic**: Some PV types can create PVs based on PVC definitions. When a PVC is created, the PV type will dynamically create a PV object and allocate the storage in the backend; this is dynamic provisioning. The catch with dynamic provisioning is that you require a third type of Kubernetes storage object, called a **storage class**.

Storage classes are like a way of **tiering** your storage. You can create a class that provisions slow storage volumes, or another one with hyper-fast SSD drives. However, storage classes are a little bit more complex than just tiering. As we mentioned in the two ways of creating a PVC, storage classes are what make dynamic provisioning possible. When working on a cloud environment, you don't want to be manually creating every backend disk for every PV. Storage classes will set up something called a **provisioner**, which invokes the volume plugin that's necessary to talk to your cloud provider's API. Every provisioner has its own settings so that it can talk to the specified cloud provider or storage provider.

You can provision storage classes in the following way; this is an example of a storage class using Azure-disk as a disk provisioner:

```
kind: StorageClass
apiVersion: storage.k8s.io/v1
metadata:
  name: my-storage-class
provisioner: kubernetes.io/azure-disk
parameters:
  storageaccounttype: Standard_LRS
  kind: Shared
```

Each storage class provisioner and PV type will have different requirements and parameters, as well as volumes, and we have already had a general overview of how they work and what we can use them for. Learning about specific storage classes and PV types will depend on your environment; you can learn more about each one of them by clicking on the following links:

- https://kubernetes.io/docs/concepts/storage/storage-classes/#provisioner
- https://kubernetes.io/docs/concepts/storage/persistent-volumes/#types-of-persistent-volumes

Summary

In this chapter, we learned about what Kubernetes is, its components, and what the advantages of using orchestration are.

You should now be able to identify each of the Kubernetes API objects, their purpose, and their use cases. You should be able to understand how the master nodes control the cluster and the scheduling of the containers in the worker nodes.

Questions

1. What is Kubernetes?
2. What are the components of Kubernetes?
3. What are Kubernetes's API objects?
4. What can we do with Kubernetes?
5. What is a container orchestrator?
6. What is a pod?
7. What is a deployment?

Further reading

- *Mastering Kubernetes*, by Packt Publishing: `https://prod.packtpub.com/in/virtualization-and-cloud/mastering-kubernetes`
- *Kubernetes for Developers*, by Packt Publishing: `https://prod.packtpub.com/in/virtualization-and-cloud/kubernetes-developers`
- *Getting Started with Kubernetes*, by Packt Publishing: `https://prod.packtpub.com/in/virtualization-and-cloud/getting-started-kubernetes-third-edition`

8
Architecting a Kubernetes Cluster

Now that we understand the basics of what composes a Kubernetes cluster, we still need to understand how to place all the Kubernetes components together, and how to suit their requirements to provision a production-ready Kubernetes cluster.

In this chapter, we will examine how to determine these requirements and how they will help us maintain steady workloads and achieve a successful deployment.

We will explore the following topics in this chapter:

- Kube-sizing
- Determining storage considerations
- Determining network requirements
- Customizing kube objects

Kube-sizing

When designing a Kubernetes cluster, we don't just need to worry about how we are going to configure our deployment objects to host our applications, or how we are going to configure our service objects to provide communication across our pods—where all this is hosted is also important. Therefore, we also need to take into account the resources that are required to bring balance to our application workloads and our control plane.

etcd considerations

We will require at least a three-node etcd cluster in order for it to be able to support itself in case one node fails. Because etcd uses a distributed census algorithm called **Raft**, odd-numbered clusters are recommended. This is because, in order for an action to be allowed, more than 50% of the members of the cluster have to agree on it. In a scenario with a two-node cluster, for example, if one of the nodes fails, the other node's vote is only 50% of the cluster, and therefore, the cluster loses quorum. Now, when we have a three-node cluster, a single node failure represents only a 33.33% vote loss and the two remaining nodes' votes still 66.66% for the action to be allowed.

 The following link is for a great website where you can learn exactly how the Raft algorithm works: http://thesecretlivesofdata.com/raft/.

For etcd, we can choose from two deployment models for our cluster. We can either run it on the same node as our kube-apiserver, or we can have a separate set of clusters running our key-value store. Either way, this will not change how etcd reaches quorum, so you will still have to install etcd in odd numbers across your control-plane manager nodes.

For a Kubernetes use case, etcd won't consume lots of compute resources such as CPU or memory. Although etcd does aggressively cache key-value data and uses most of its memory-tracking watchers, two cores and 8 GB of RAM will be more than enough.

When it comes to the disk, this is where you need to be more critical. The etcd cluster relies heavily on disk latency, because of the way the consensus protocol persistently stores metadata in the log. Every member of the etcd cluster has to store every request, and any major spike in latency can trigger a cluster leader election, which will cause instability for the cluster. A **hard disk drive (HDD)** for etcd is out of the question unless you are running 15k RPM disks in a Raid 0 disk to squeeze the highest performance possible out of a magnetic drive. A **solid state drive (SSD)** is the way to go and, with extremely low latency and higher **input/output operations per second (IOPS)**, they are the perfect candidate to host your key-value store. Thankfully, all major cloud providers offer SSD solutions to satisfy this need.

kube-apiserver sizing

The remaining resources that are required for the control-plane components will depend on the number of nodes that they will be managing and which add-ons you will be running on them. One additional thing to take into account is the fact that you can put these master nodes behind a load balancer to ease the load and provide high availability. In addition to this, you can always horizontally scale your master nodes in periods of contention.

Taking all this into consideration, and taking into account that etcd will be hosted alongside our master nodes, we can say that a three-master node cluster with **virtual machines (VMs)** with 2 to 4 vCPUs, and between 8 and 16 GB of RAM will be more than enough to handle greater than or equal to 100 worker nodes.

Worker nodes

The worker nodes, on the other hand, are the ones that'll be doing the heavy lifting—these guys are the ones that will be running our application workloads. Standardizing the size of these nodes will be impossible as they fall into a *What if?* scenario. We are required to know exactly what type of applications we will be running on our nodes, and what their resource requirements are, for us to be able to size them correctly. Nodes will not only be sized on the application resource requirements, but we will also have to consider periods where we will have more than our planned pods running on them. For instance, you can perform a rolling update on a deployment to use a newer image depending on how you have configured your maxSurge; this node will have to handle 10% to 25% more load.

Containers are really lightweight, but when orchestrators come into play, you can have 30, 40, or even 100 containers running on a single node! This exponentially increases your resource consumption per host. While pods come with resource-limiting functionalities and specifications to limit the container's resource consumption, you still need to account for the required resources of those containers.

Nodes can always be scaled horizontally during periods of contention and high-resource demand. However, it's always good to have those extra resources available to avoid any undesirable **out of memory (OOMs)** killers. So, plan for the future and for the *What if?* scenario by having a pool of extra resources.

Load balancer considerations

Our nodes still need to talk to our API server and, as we mentioned before, having several master nodes requires a load balancer. When it comes to load balancing requests from our nodes to the masters, we have several options to pick from, depending on where you are running your cluster. If you are running Kubernetes in a public cloud, you can go ahead with your cloud provider's load balancer option, as they are usually elastic. This means that they autoscale as needed and offer more features than you actually require. Essentially, load balancing requests to the API server will be the only task that your load balancer will perform. This leads us to the on-premises scenario—as we are sticking to open source solutions here, then you can configure a Linux box running either HAProxy or NGINX to satisfy your load balancing needs. There is no wrong answer in choosing between HAProxy and NGINX, as they provide you with exactly what you need.

So far, the basic architecture will look like the following screenshot:

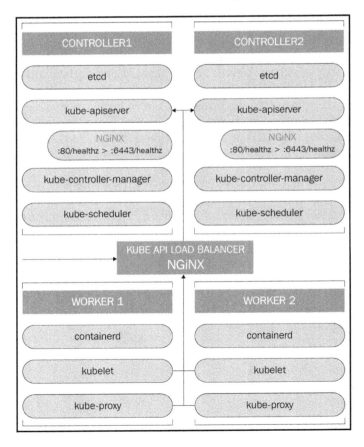

Storage considerations

Storage needs are not as straightforward as they are for a regular host or hypervisor. There are several types of storage that our nodes and pods will be consuming, and we need to tier them properly. Because you are running Linux, tiering the storage into different filesystems and storage backends will be extremely easy—nothing that **logical volume manager** (**LVM**) or different mount points can't solve.

The basic Kubernetes binaries, such as `kubelet` and `kube-proxy`, can run on basic storage alongside the OS files; nothing very high-end is required, as any SSD will be enough to satisfy their needs.

Now, on the other hand, we have the storage in which our container images will be stored and run from. Going back to the `Chapter 6`, *Creating a Highly Available Self-Healing Architecture*, we learned that containers are composed of read-only layers. This means that when the disks are running tens or even hundreds of containers in a single node, they will be hit very hard on read requests. The storage backend for this will have to serve read requests with very low latency. Specific numbers in terms of IOPS and latency will vary across each environment, but the basis will be the same. This is because of the nature of containers—disks that provide a higher read performance over writes will be preferable.

Storage performance is not the only factor to take into account. Storage space is also very important. Calculating how much space you require will depend on the following two things:

1. How big are the images that you are going to be running?
2. How many different images will you be running and what are their sizes?

This will directly consume the space in `/var/lib/docker` or `/var/lib/containerd`. With this in mind, a separate mount point for `/var/lib/docker` or `containerd/` with enough space to store all the images that you are going to be running on the pods will be a good option. Take into account that these images are ephemeral and will not live on your node forever. Kubernetes does have garbage collection strategies embedded in kubelet, which will delete old images that are no longer in use if you reach a specified threshold for disk usage. These options are `HighThresholdPercent` and `LowThresholdPercent`. You can set them with a kubelet flag: `--eviction-hard=imagefs.available` or `--eviction-soft=imagefs.available`. These flags are already configured by default to garbage collect when free storage reaches less than 15%, however, you can adjust them to your needs. `eviction-hard` is the threshold that it needs to reach in order to start deleting images, while `eviction-soft` is the percentage or amount that it needs to reach to stop deleting images.

Some containers will still require some sort of read/write volume for persistent data. As discussed in `Chapter 7`, *Understanding the Core Components of a Kubernetes Cluster*, there are several storage provisioners, and all of them will suit different scenarios. All you need to know is that you have a series of options available to you, thanks to the Kubernetes storage classes. Some of the open source software-defined storage solutions that are worth mentioning are as follows:

- Ceph
- GlusterFS
- OpenStack Cinder
- **Network File System** (NFS)

Each storage provisioner will have its benefits and downsides, but it is beyond the scope of this book to go through each one in detail. We have offered a good overview of Gluster in previous chapters, as it is what we are going to use in later chapters for our example deployment.

Network requirements

In order to understand the network requirements of our cluster, we first need to understand the Kubernetes networking model and what problems it aims to solve. Container networking can be very hard to grasp; however, it has three essential problems:

1. How do containers talk to each other (on the same host and on different hosts)?
2. How do containers talk to the outside world, and how does the outside world talk to the containers?
3. Who allocates and configures each container's unique IP address?

Containers on the same host can talk to each other through a virtual bridge that you can see with the `brctl` utility from the `bridge-utils` package. This is handled by the Docker engine and it's called the Docker networking model. Containers are attached to the virtual bridge named `docker0` through a `veth` virtual interface that is allocated an IP from a private subnet address. In this way, all containers can talk to each other through their `veth` virtual interface. The problem with the Docker model arises when containers are allocated on different hosts, or when external services want to communicate with them. To solve this, Docker provides a method where containers are exposed to the outside world through the host's ports. Requests come into a certain port in the host's IP address and are then proxied to the container behind that port.

This method is useful but not ideal. You can't configure services to specific ports or in a dynamic port allocation scenario—our services will require flags to connect to the correct ports each time we deploy them. This can get really messy very quickly.

To avoid this, Kubernetes have implemented their own networking model that has to comply with the following rules:

1. All pods can communicate with all other pods without **network address translation (NAT)**
2. All nodes can communicate with all pods without NAT
3. The IP that the pod sees itself as is the same IP that others see it as

There are several open source projects out there that can help us to reach this goal, and the one that suits you best will depend on your circumstances. Here are some of them:

- Project Calico
- Weave Net
- Flannel
- Kube-router

Assigning IPs to pods and making them talk between them is not the only issue to be aware of. Kubernetes also provides DNS-based service discovery, because applications that talk through DNS records rather than IPs are far more efficient and scalable.

Kubernetes DNS-based service discovery

Kubernetes has a deployment in its kube-system namespace and we will revisit namespaces later in this chapter. The deployment is composed of a pod with a set of containers that forms a DNS server that is in charge of creating all DNS records in the cluster and serving DNS requests for service discovery.

Kubernetes will also create a service pointing to the mentioned deployment, and will tell the kubelet to configure each pod's container to use the service's IP as the DNS resolver by default. This is the default behavior, but you can overwrite this by setting a DNS policy on your pod's specification. You can choose from the following specifications:

- **Default**: This one is counter-intuitive as it is not the default one in reality. With this policy, pods will inherit the name resolution from the node that runs that pod. For example, if a node is configured to use `8.8.8.8` as its DNS server, the `resolv.conf` pods will also be configured to use that same DNS server.

- **ClusterFirst**: This is actually the default policy and, as we mentioned before, any pod running with ClusterFirst will have `resolv.conf` configured with the IP of the `kube-dns` service. Any requests that are not local to the cluster will be forwarded to the node's configured DNS server.

Not all Kubernetes objects have DNS records. Only services and, in some specific cases, pods have records created for them. There are two types of records in the DNS server: **A records** and **service records** (**SRVs**). A records are created depending on the type of service created; and we are not referring to `spec.type` here. There are two types of services: **normal services**, which we revised in `Chapter 7`, *Understanding the Core Components of a Kubernetes Cluster*, and correspond to the ones under the `type` specification; and **headless services**. Before explaining headless services, let's explore how normal services behave.

For each normal service, an A record that points to the service's cluster IP address is created; these records are in the following structure:

```
<service-name>.<namespace>.svc.cluster.local
```

Any pod that is running on the same namespace as the service can resolve the service through only its `shortname: <service-name>` field. This is because any other pod outside of the namespace has to specify the namespace after the shortname instance:

```
<service-name>.<namespace>
```

For headless services, records work a little bit different. First of all, a headless service is a service with no cluster IP assigned to it. Therefore, an A record that points to the service's IP is impossible to create. To create a headless service, you define the `.spec.clusterIP` namespace with `none` in this way, so that no IP is assigned to it. Kubernetes will then create A records based on the endpoints of this service. Essentially, the pods are selected through the `selector` field, although this is not the only requirement. Because of the format in which the A record is created, pods require several new fields in order for the DNS server to create records for them.

Pods will require two new specification fields: `hostname` and `subdomain`. The `hostname` field will be the `hostname` field of the pod, while `subdomain` will be the name of the headless service that you are creating for these pods. The A records for this will point to each pod's IP in the following way:

```
<pod hostname>.<subdomian/headless service
name>.<namespace>.svc.cluster.local
```

Additionally, another record will be created with only the headless service, as follows:

```
<headless service>.<namespace>.svc.cluster.local
```

This record will return all the IP addresses of the pods behind the service.

We now have what's necessary to start building our cluster. However, there are still some design features that do not only include the Kubernetes binaries and their configuration, Kubernetes API objects can also be tuned. We will go through some of the adjustments that you can perform in the next section.

Customizing kube objects

When it comes to Kubernetes objects, everything will depend on the type of workload or application that you are trying to build the infrastructure for. Therefore, rather than designing or architecting any particular customization, we will go through how to configure the most commonly used and helpful specifications on each object.

Namespacing

Kubernetes offers namespaces as a way of segmenting your cluster into multiple **virtual clusters**. Think of it as a way of segmenting your cluster's resources and objects and putting them in logical isolation from each other.

Namespaces will only be used in very specific scenarios, but Kubernetes comes with some predefined namespaces:

- **Default**: This is the default namespace that all objects without a namespace definition will be placed into.
- **kube-system**: Any object that is created by and for the Kubernetes cluster will be placed on this namespace. Objects that are required for the basic functionality of the cluster will be placed here. For example, you will find `kube-dns`, `kubernetes-dashboard`, `kube-proxy`, or any additional component or agent for external applications, such as `fluentd`, `logstash`, `traefik`, and ingress controllers.
- **kube-public**: A namespace that is reserved for objects that can be visible to anyone, including non-authenticated users.

Creating a namespace is very simple and straightforward; you can do so by running the following command:

```
kubectl create namespace <name>
```

That's it—you now have your own namespace. To place objects in this namespace, you will be using the `metadata` field and adding the `namespace` key-value pair; for example, consider this excerpt from a YAML pod:

```
apiVersion: v1
kind: Pod
metadata:
    namespace: mynamespace
    name: pod1
```

You will find yourself creating custom namespaces for clusters that are usually very large and have a considerable number of users or different teams that are consuming their resources. For these types of scenarios, namespaces are perfect. Namespaces will let you segregate all the objects of a team from the rest. Names can even be repeated on the same class objects as long as they are on different namespaces.

Namespaces will not only provide isolation for objects, but you can also set resource quotas for each namespace. Let's say that you have a couple of development teams working on your cluster—one team is developing a very lightweight application, and the other one is developing a very resource-intensive app. In this scenario, you don't want the first development team consuming any additional compute resources from the resource-intensive app team—this is where resource quotas come into play.

Limiting namespace resources

Resource quotas are also Kubernetes API objects; however, they are designed to work specifically on namespaces by creating limits on compute resources and even limiting the number of objects on each assigned space.

The `ResourceQuota` API object is declared like any other object in Kubernetes, through a `YAML` file passed to the `kubectl` command.

A basic resource quota definition is as follows:

```
apiVersion: v1
kind: ResourceQuota
Metadata:
  Namespace: devteam1
  name: compute-resources
```

```
spec:
  hard:
    pods: "4"
    requests.cpu: "1"
    requests.memory: 1Gi
    limits.cpu: "2"
    limits.memory: 2Gi
```

There are two types of basic quotas that we can set: compute resource quotas and object resource quotas. As seen in the previous example, `pods` is an object quota and the rest are compute quotas.

In each of these fields, you will specify the total sum of the provided resource, which the namespace cannot exceed. For example, in this namespace, the total number of running `pods` cannot exceed `4`, and the sum of their resources can't exceed `1` CPU and `2Gi` of RAM memory.

The maximum number of objects per namespace can be assigned to any kube API object that can be put in a namespace; here is a list of the objects that can be limited with namespaces:

- **Persistent Volume Claims (PVCs)**
- Services
- Secrets
- ConfigMaps
- Replication controllers
- Deployments
- ReplicaSets
- StatefulSets
- Jobs
- Cron jobs

When it comes to compute resources, it is not only memory and CPU that can be limited, but you can also assign quotas to storage space—these quotas will apply only to PVCs, however.

In order to understand compute quotas better, we need to dive deeper and explore how these resources are managed and assigned on a pod basis. This will also be a good time to understand how to architect pods better.

Customizing pods

Pods without resource limitations on non-limited namespaces can consume all of a node's resources without warning; however, you have a set of tools in the pod's specification to handle their compute allocation better.

When you allocate resources to a pod, you are not actually allocating them to the pod. Instead, you are doing it on a container basis. Therefore, a pod with multiple containers will have multiple resource constraints for each of its containers; let's consider the following example:

```
apiVersion: v1
kind: Pod
metadata:
  name: frontend
spec:
  containers:
  - name: db
    image: mysql
    env:
    - name: MYSQL_ROOT_PASSWORD
      value: "password"
    resources:
      requests:
        memory: "64Mi"
        cpu: "250m"
      limits:
        memory: "128Mi"
        cpu: "500m"
  - name: wp
    image: wordpress
    resources:
      requests:
        memory: "64Mi"
        cpu: "250m"
      limits:
        memory: "128Mi"
        cpu: "500m"
```

In this pod declaration, under the `containers` definition, we have two new fields that we haven't covered: `env` and `resources`. The `resources` field contains the compute resource limitations and requirements for our `containers`. By setting `limits`, you are telling the container the maximum number of resources that it can ask of that resource type. If a container exceeds the limit, it will be restarted or terminated.

The `request` field refers to how much of that resource Kubernetes will guarantee to that container. In order for the container to be able to run, the host node must have enough free resources to satisfy the request.

CPU and memory are measured in different ways. For instance, when we assign or limit CPU, we talk in CPU units. There are several ways of setting the CPU units; first, you can either specify round or fractional numbers such as 1, 2, 3, 0.1, and 1.5, which will correspond to the number of virtual cores that you want to assign to that container. Another way of assigning is to use the **milicore** expression. One milicore (1m), which is the minimum CPU quantity that you can assign, is equivalent to 0.001 CPU cores; for example, you could do the following assignment:

```
cpu: "250m"
```

That would be the same as writing the following:

```
cpu: 0.25
```

The preferred way of assigning CPU is through Millicores, as the API will convert whole numbers into Millicores either way.

For memory allocation, you can use normal memory units such as kilobytes or kibibytes; the same goes for any other memory unit, such as E, P, T, G, and M.

Going back to resource quotas, we can see how individual container resource management will play together with resource quotas on namespaces. This is because the resource quotas will tell us how many limits and requests we can set per namespace in our containers.

The second field that we haven't revised is the `env` field. With `env`, we configure the environmental variables for our containers. With variable declarations, we can pass settings, parameters, passwords, and more configurations to our containers. The simplest way to declare a variable in a pod is as follows:

```
  . . .
  env:
  -  name: VAR
     value: "Hello World"
```

Now the container will have access to the `VAR` variable content in its shell, referred to as `$VAR`. As we mentioned previously, this is the easiest way to declare a variable and provide a value to it. However, this is not the most efficient one—when you declare a value in this way, the value will only live in the pod declaration.

If we need to edit the value or pass this value to multiple pods, it becomes a hassle as you need to type the same value on every pod that requires it. This is where we will introduce two more Kubernetes API objects: `Secrets` and `ConfigMaps`.

With `ConfigMaps` and `Secrets`, we can store values for our variables in a persistent and more modular form. In essence, `ConfigMaps` and `Secrets` are the same, but secrets contain their values encoded in `base64`. Secrets are used to store sensitive information such as passwords or private keys—essentially, any type of confidential data. All the rest of the data that you don't need to be hidden can be passed through `ConfigMap`.

The way that you create these two types of objects is the same way as with any other object in Kubernetes—through `YAML`. You can create a `ConfigMap` object as follows:

```
apiVersion: v1
 kind: ConfigMap
 metadata:
  name: my-config
 data:
 super.data: much-data
 very.data: wow
```

The only difference on this definition, form all the other definitions in this chapter is that we are missing the specification field. Instead, we have data where we will be placing the key-value pairs that contain the data that we want to store.

With `Secrets`, this works a little bit differently. This is because the value for the key that we need to store has to be encoded. In order to store a value in a secret's key, we pass the value to `base64`, as follows:

```
[dsala@RedFedora]$ echo -n "our secret" | base64
WW91IEhhdmUgRGVjb2RlZCBNeSBTZWNyZXQhIENvbmdyYXR6IQ==
```

When we have the `base64` hash of our string, we are ready to create our secret.

The following code block shows a `YAML` file configured with the secret's value in `base64`:

```
apiVersion: v1
 kind: Secret
 metadata:
  name: kube-secret
 type: Opaque
 data:
  password: WW91IEhhdmUgRGVjb2RlZCBNeSBTZWNyZXQhIENvbmdyYXR6IQ==
```

To use our `ConfigMaps` and `Secrets` objects in pods, we use the `valueFrom` field in the `env` array:

```
apiVersion: v1
 kind: Pod
 metadata:
  name: secret-pod
 spec:
  containers:
 - name: secret-container
    image: busybox
    env:
     - name: SECRET_VAR
       valueFrom:
         secretKeyRef:
           name: kube-secret
           key: password
```

Here, the name under `secretKeyRef` corresponds to the `Secret` API object name, and the `key` is the `key` from the `data` field in `Secret`.

With `ConfigMaps`, it will look almost the same; however, in the `valueFrom` field, we will use `configMapKeyRef` instead of `secretKeyRef`.

The `ConfigMap` declaration is as follows:

```
    ...
    env:
       -    name: CONFMAP_VAR
            valueFrom:
              configMapKeyRef:
                name: my-config
                key: very.data
```

 Now that you understand the basics of customizing pods, you can take a look at a real-life example at `https://kubernetes.io/docs/tutorials/configuration/configure-redis-using-configmap/`.

Summary

In this chapter, we learned how to determine the compute and network requirements of a Kubernetes cluster. We also touched upon the software requirements that come along with it, such as `etcd`, and how odd-numbered clusters are preferred (due to the census algorithm) as the cluster needs to achieve more than 50% of votes for consensus.

The `etcd` cluster can either run on the kube-apiserver or have a separate set of clusters dedicated just for `etcd`. When it comes to resources, 2 CPUs and 8 GB of RAM should be enough. When deciding on the storage system for `etcd`, opt for lower latency and higher IOPS storage such as SSD. We then jumped into sizing the kube-apiserver, which can be run alongside `etcd`. Given that both components can coexist, resources should be bumped to anything between 8 and 16 GB of RAM and between 2 and 4 CPUs per node.

In order to properly size the worker nodes, we have to keep in mind that this is where the actual application workloads will be running. These nodes should be sized for application requirements, and additional resources should be considered for periods where more than the planned number of pods could be running, such as during rolling updates. Continuing with the requirements for the cluster, we touched on how a load balancer can help with the master node's communication by balancing requests among the cluster.

Storage needs for Kubernetes can be quite overwhelming as many factors can affect the overall setup, and leaning toward a storage system that benefits reads over writes is preferable. Additionally, some of the most common storage providers for Kubernetes are as follows:

- Ceph
- GlusterFS (covered in `Chapter 2`, *Defining GlusterFS Storage* to `Chapter 5`, *Analyzing Performance in a Gluster System*)
- OpenStack Cinder
- NFS

We then moved on to the networking side of things and learned how Kubernetes provides services such as DNS-based service discovery, which is in charge of creating all DNS records in the cluster and serving DNS requests for service discovery. Objects in Kubernetes can be customized to accommodate the different needs of each workload, and things such as namespaces are used as a way of segmenting your cluster into multiple virtual clusters. Resource limits can be done through resource quotas.

Finally, pods can be customized to allow an absolute maximum of resources to be allocated and to avoid a single pod from consuming all of the worker node's resources. We discussed the various storage considerations and requirements in detail, including how to customize kube objects and pods.

In the next chapter, we'll jump into deploying a Kubernetes cluster and learn how to configure it.

Questions

1. Why are odd-numbered `etcd` clusters preferred?
2. Can `etcd` run alongside kube-apiserver?
3. Why is lower latency recommended for `etcd`?
4. What are the worker nodes?
5. What should be considered when sizing worker nodes?
6. What are some of the storage providers for Kubernetes?
7. Why is a load balancer needed?
8. How can namespaces be used?

Further reading

- *Mastering Kubernetes* by Gigi Sayfan: `https://www.packtpub.com/virtualization-and-cloud/mastering-kubernetes`
- *Kubernetes for Developers* by Joseph Heck: `https://www.packtpub.com/virtualization-and-cloud/kubernetes-developers`
- *Hands-On Microservices with Kubernetes* by Gigi Sayfan: `https://www.packtpub.com/virtualization-and-cloud/hands-microservices-kubernetes`
- *Getting Started with Kubernetes – Third Edition* by Jonathan Baier, Jesse White: `https://www.packtpub.com/virtualization-and-cloud/getting-started-kubernetes-third-edition`
- *Mastering Docker – Second Edition* by Russ McKendrick, Scott Gallagher: `https://www.packtpub.com/virtualization-and-cloud/mastering-docker-second-edition`
- *Docker Bootcamp* by Russ McKendrick et al.: `https://www.packtpub.com/virtualization-and-cloud/docker-bootcamp`

9
Deploying and Configuring Kubernetes

After learning about Kubernetes internal components and how they interact with each other, it's time to learn how to set them up. Installing a Kubernetes cluster manually can be a very painful and delicate process, but by going through the required steps, we can learn and understand better its internal components. After performing a manual install, we can also explore what other alternatives and tools we have available to automate this process. The following is a summary of what we will learn in this chapter:

- Creating our compute environment
- Bootstrapping the control plane
- Bootstrapping worker nodes
- Configuring cluster networking and DNS settings
- Examples of managed Kubernetes services

With each step, we will be closer to completing a full install of Kubernetes, and ready to test it in a development environment.

Infrastructure deployment

To deploy the infrastructure that will be running our Kubernetes cluster, we will be using Microsoft Azure. You can follow along by creating a free trial or using any other public cloud provider, or your own on-premise IT infrastructure. The steps will differ depending on what you choose, though.

Installing Azure CLI

There are two ways of deploying resources in Azure when you are using Linux: you can do it either from the portal or via the Azure CLI. We will be using both, but for different scenarios.

Let's begin installing Azure CLI on our Linux workstation or on the Windows subsystem for Linux.

 Note that all commands are assumed to be issued by an account with root privileges or the root account itself (but this is not recommended).

For RHEL/Centos-based distributions, you need to perform the following steps:

1. Download and `import` the repository key, as shown in the following command:

    ```
    rpm --import https://packages.microsoft.com/keys/microsoft.asc
    ```

2. Create the repository config file, as shown in the following command:

    ```
    cat << EOF > /etc/yum.repos.d/azure-cli.repo
    [azure-cli]
    name=Azure CLI
    baseurl=https://packages.microsoft.com/yumrepos/azure-cli
    enabled=1
    gpgcheck=1
    gpgkey=https://packages.microsoft.com/keys/microsoft.asc
    EOF
    ```

3. Install `azure-cli` using the following command:

    ```
    yum install azure-cli
    ```

4. Log in to your Azure subscription using the following command:

    ```
    az login
    ```

 If you are not in a Desktop environment, you can use: az login --use-device-code, because the regular "az login" requires a web browser to perform the login.

After installing Azure CLI, we still need to set up some defaults so we won't have to type the same flag options over and over again.

Configuring Azure CLI

Every resource on Azure lives in a resource group and a geographical location. Because all our resources will be living in the same resource group and location, let's configure them as defaults. To do this, run the following command:

```
az configure --defaults location=eastus group=Kube_Deploy
```

For our example, we are using `east us` for the location, as this is the location closest to where we are based. The group name will depend on how you are going to name your resource group—in our case, `Kube_Deploy`.

With the defaults configured, let's move on to actually create the resource group that will contain our resources, using the following command:

```
az group create -n "Kube_Deploy"
```

High-level design overview

With our resource group created and our location selected, let's take a high-level look at the design that we are going to create using the following code:

```
<design picture>
```

The important things that we need to note right now are the number of VMs, the network architecture, and firewall rules, because these are the elements that we will be configuring directly in our first steps.

Let's take a look at our network requirements before we start provisioning our resources.

We have the following requirements:

- The following three sets of different, non-overlapping subnets:
    - VM subnet
    - Pod subnet
    - Service subnet

- Statically allocated IP addresses for the following resources:
    - Master nodes
    - Worker nodes
    - Management VM
    - Public IP for the load-balancer
    - DNS server

For our VM subnet, we are going to use the following address space:

```
192.168.0.0/24
```

The service CIDR will be the following:

```
10.20.0.0/24
```

And finally, our POD CIDR will be a little bit bigger so that it can allocate more pods, as shown in the following code:

```
10.30.0.0/16
```

Now let's start provisioning the network resources that we need to make this architecture possible.

Provisioning network resources

First, we will create the virtual network that will contain our VM subnet. To do this, run the following command:

```
az network vnet create -n kube-node-vnet \
  --address-prefix 192.168.0.0/16 \
  --subnet-name node-subnet \
  --subnet-prefix 192.168.0.0/24
```

The two key points in this command are the `address-prefix` flag and the `subnet-prefix` flag.

With the `address-prefix` flag, we will be specifying the address space that will define which subnets we can put on the VNET. For example, our VNET prefix is `192.16.0.0/16`. This means that we cannot put any address outside this CIDR; for example, `10.0.0.0/24` won't work.

The subnet prefix will be the address space that will be provided to the VMs connected to our subnet. Now that we have created our VNET and the subnet, we require a static public IP address. In Azure and in any public cloud provider, public IPs are resources that are separate from the VM.

Let's create our public IPs by running the following:

```
az network public-ip create -n kube-api-pub-ip \
    --allocation-method Static \
    --sku Standard
```

Once created, we can take note of the IP by running the following query:

```
az network public-ip show -n kube-api-pub-ip --query "ipAddress"
```

With our VNET, subnet, and public IP all allocated, we just need one final resource, a firewall, to provide security for our VMS. In Azure, firewalls are called **network security groups** (**NSGs**). The process of creating an NSG is fairly simple, as shown in the following command:

```
az network nsg create -n kube-nsg
```

After creating the NSG, we assign the NSG to our subnet using the following command:

```
az network vnet subnet update -n node-subnet \
    --vnet-name kube-node-vnet \
    --network-security-group kube-nsg
```

Provisioning compute resources

With our network all set up, we are ready to start creating some VMs. But before we create any VM, we need to create the SSH keys that we will use to access our VMs.

The first pair of keys that we will create is for our management VM. This VM will be the only one that will have SSH access from the outside world. We do not want to expose port 22 of any of our cluster nodes for security reasons. Any time when we want to access any of our nodes, we will be doing it from this VM.

To create the SSH keys, run ssh-keygen on your Linux workstation:

```
ssh-keygen
```

Now let's create the management VM using the following command:

```
az vm create -n management-vm \
    --admin-username <USERNAME> \
    --size Standard_B1s \
    --image CentOS \
    --vnet-name kube-node-vnet \
    --subnet node-subnet \
    --private-ip-address 192.168.0.99 \
    --nsg kube-nsg \
    --ssh-key-value ~/.ssh/id_rsa.pub
```

Remember to replace the <USERNAME> field with the desired username.

The next step is where we need to configure our first NSG rule. This rule will allow traffic from our own network to our management VM on port 22 so that we can SSH into it. Let's set this up using the following command:

```
az network nsg rule create --nsg-name kube-nsg \
    -n mgmt_ssh_allow \
    --direction Inbound \
    --priority 100 \
    --access Allow \
    --description "Allow SSH From Home" \
    --destination-address-prefixes '192.168.0.99' \
    --destination-port-ranges 22 \
    --protocol Tcp \
    --source-address-prefixes '<YOUR IP>' \
    --source-port-ranges '*' \
    --direction Inbound
```

 The `source-address-prefixes` is your ISP provided public IP address, as this IPs can be dynamic, in the even that it changes, you can edit the IP on the Network Security Group rules in your Azure Portal.

Now let's connect to our VM to create SSH keys that will allow us to connect to our cluster VMs. To retrieve the public IP address of our management vm, run the following query:

```
az vm show -d -n management-vm --query publicIps
```

Now let's SSH into our VM using our previously created private key, as follows:

```
ssh <username>@<public ip> -i <path to private key>
```

You will only need to specify the private key if you are logged in with a different user than the one with which you created the key pair.

Now that we are in the management VM, run `ssh-keygen` again and finally exit the VM.

To provide high availability in the case of a disaster in the Azure data centers, our master nodes will be on an availability set. Let's create the availability set.

If you don't recall what an availability set is, you can go back to our Gluster chapters and revisit its functionalities.

To create the availability set, run the following:

```
az vm availability-set create -n control-plane \
  --platform-fault-domain-count 3 \
  --platform-update-domain-count 3
```

Now we can go ahead and create our first control plane nodes. Let's save our management's VM public SSH key into a variable first to pass the key to the master nodes, as shown in the following command:

```
MGMT_KEY=$(ssh <username>@<public ip> cat ~/.ssh/id_rsa.pub)
```

To create the three controller nodes, run the following `for` loop:

```
for i in 1 2 3; do
az vm create -n kube-controller-${i} \
  --admin-username <USERNAME> \
  --availability-set control-plane \
  --size Standard_B2s \
  --image CentOS \
  --vnet-name kube-node-vnet \
  --subnet node-subnet \
  --private-ip-address 192.168.0.1${i} \
  --public-ip-address "" \
  --nsg kube-nsg \
  --ssh-key-value ${MGMT_KEY};
done
```

The sizes that we are using on these VMs are small because this is only a test environment, and we will not really require a lot of compute resources. In a real environment, we would size the VMs based on the considerations that we explored in the Chapter 8, *Architecting a Kubernetes Cluster*.

Last but not least, we create our worker nodes using the following command:

```
for i in 1 2; do
az vm create -n kube-node-${i} \
  --admin-username <USERNAME>\
  --size Standard_B2s \
  --image CentOS \
  --vnet-name kube-node-vnet \
  --subnet node-subnet \
  --private-ip-address 192.168.0.2${i} \
  --public-ip-address "" \
  --nsg kube-nsg \
  --ssh-key-value ${MGMT_KEY}
done
```

Preparing the management VM

With our controller and worker nodes created, we can now log in to our management VM and start installing and configuring the tools that we will need to bootstrap our Kubernetes cluster.

From here on out, we will mostly be working on the management VM. Let's SSH to the VM and start installing our toolset.

First, we will need to download the tools to create the certificates that our cluster's services will be using to talk with one another.

We will install dependencies first using the following command:

```
johndoe@management-vm$ sudo yum install git gcc

johndoe@management-vm$ sudo wget -O golang.tgz
https://dl.google.com/go/go1.11.1.linux-amd64.tar.gz

johndoe@management-vm$ sudo tar -C /usr/local -xzvf golang.tgz
```

With **Go lang** installed, you need to update your PATH variable and create a new one named GOPATH. Your TLS certificate-generating tool, CFFSL, will be installed in this path. To do this, you can do the following:

```
johndoe@management-vm$ sudo cat << EOF > /etc/profile.d/paths.sh
export PATH=$PATH:/usr/local/go/bin:/usr/local/bin
export GOPATH=/usr/local/
EOF
```

Then run the following to load the variables in your current shell:

```
johndoe@management-vm$ sudo source /etc/profile.d/paths.sh
```

With the variables set, now we are ready to go and get our `cffsl` toolkit using the following command:

```
johndoe@management-vm$ go get -u github.com/cloudflare/cfssl/cmd/cfssl
```

```
johndoe@management-vm$ go get -u github.com/cloudflare/cfssl/cmd/cfssljson
```

Both binaries will be saved under our GOPATH variable.

Generating certificates

With the CFSSL binaries installed and loaded to our PATH, we can start generating our certificate files. We will be generating a lot of files in this part of the install, so it will be a good idea to create a directory structure to store them appropriately.

Certificate authority

The first files that we need to generate are the files for our certificate authority, which will be signing the rest of our component's certificates.

We will be storing all of our certificates under the ~/certs/ directory, but first we need to create the directory. Let's set this up using the following command:

```
johndoe@management-vm$ mkdir ~/certs
```

Now that we have the directory, let's start by using the following command to generate the CA configuration file, which will have information such as the expiration date of the certificates issued by our CA and what the CA is going to be used for:

```
johndoe@management-vm$ cd ~/certs

johndoe@management-vm$ cat << EOF > ca-config.json
{
  "signing": {
    "default": {
      "expiry": "8760h"
    },
    "profiles": {
      "kubernetes": {
        "usages": [
            "signing",
```

```
                "key encipherment",
                "server auth",
                "client auth"
        ],
        "expiry": "8760h"
    }
    }
    }
}
EOF
```

With our CA config, we can now start issuing certificate signing requests.

The first CSR that we are going to generate is the one for our CA. Let's set this up using the following command:

```
johndoe@management-vm$ cat << EOF > ca-csr.json
{
  "CN": "Kubernetes",
  "key": {
    "algo": "rsa",
    "size": 2048
  },
  "names": [
    {
      "C": "US",
      "L": "New York",
      "O": "Kubernetes",
      "OU": "CA",
      "ST": "NY"
    }
  ]
}
EOF
```

Now that we have both our JSON files, we can actually use cffsl and generate our certificates using the following command:

```
johndoe@management-vm$ cfssl gencert -initca ca-csr.json | cfssljson -bare
ca
```

As shown in the following command, three files will be generated, ca.csr, ca.pem, and ca-key.pem. The first one, ca.csr, is the certificate signing request. The other two are our public certificate and the private key respectively:

```
johndoe@management-vm$ ls
ca-config.json   ca.csr ca-csr.json   ca-key.pem ca.pem
```

This will be the case for any certificates that we generate from here on in.

Client certificates

Now that our CA is configured and its certificate files generated, we can start issuing certificates for our admin user and for the kubelet on each worker node.

The process and the files that we are going to create are very similar to the CA ones, but with slight differences in the commands that we use to generate them.

Let's create a directory for our `admin certs` using the following command:

```
johndoe@management-vm$ mkdir ~/certs/admin/

johndoe@management-vm$ cd ~/certs/admin/
```

First, create the admin user certificate. This certificate is for our administrators to manage our cluster via `kubectl`.

Again, we will generate the `json` for the `csr` using the following command:

```
johndoe@management-vm$ cat << EOF > admin-csr.json
{
  "CN": "admin",
  "key": {
    "algo": "rsa",
    "size": 2048
  },
  "names": [
    {
      "C": "US",
      "L": "New York",
      "O": "system:masters",
      "OU": "Kubernetes",
      "ST": "NY"
    }
  ]
}
EOF
```

With our JSON ready, let's now sign and create the admin certificates using the following command:

```
johndoe@management-vm$ cfssl gencert \
  -ca=../ca.pem \
  -ca-key=../ca-key.pem \
  -config=../ca-config.json \
```

```
-profile=kubernetes \
admin-csr.json | cfssljson -bare admin
```

The process for creating the kubelet certificates is a little bit different compared to the admin and CA certs. The kubelet certificate requires us to have the hostname field filled up in the certificate, as this is how it will be identified.

Create the directory using the following command:

```
johndoe@management-vm$ mkdir ~/certs/kubelet/

johndoe@management-vm$ cd ~/certs/kubelet/
```

Then use the following command to create the json csr, in which not much has changed:

```
johndoe@management-vm$ cat << EOF > kube-node-1-csr.json
{
  "CN": "system:node:kube-node-1",
  "key": {
    "algo": "rsa",
    "size": 2048
  },
  "names": [
    {
      "C": "US",
      "L": "New York",
      "O": "system:nodes",
      "OU": "Kubernetes",
      "ST": "NY"
    }
  ]
}
EOF
```

However, the process is a little bit different when it comes to generating the certs, as you can see from the following command:

```
johndoe@management-vm$ cfssl gencert \
  -ca=../ca.pem \
  -ca-key=../ca-key.pem \
  -config=../ca-config.json \
  -hostname=192.168.0.21,kube-node-1 \
  -profile=kubernetes \
  kube-node-1-csr.json | cfssljson -bare kube-node-1
```

As you can see, the hostname field will contain any IP or FQDN that the node will have. Now generate a cert for each worker node, filling in the information corresponding to the node that you are generating the cert for.

Control plane certificates

Let's start creating the certificate for our kube master components.

As with the previous steps, create a directory that will contain the master node components' certificates and generate the certificate files for each of them in the following way:

```
johndoe@management-vm$ mkdir ~/certs/control-plane/

johndoe@management-vm$ cd ~/certs/control-plane/
```

For `kube-controller-manager`, use the following command:

```
johndoe@management-vm$ cat << EOF > kube-controller-manager-csr.json
{
  "CN": "system:kube-controller-manager",
  "key": {
    "algo": "rsa",
    "size": 2048
  },
  "names": [
    {
      "C": "US",
      "L": "New York",
      "O": "system:kube-controller-manager",
      "OU": "Kubernetes",
      "ST": "NY"
    }
  ]
}
EOF

johndoe@management-vm$ cfssl gencert \
  -ca=../ca.pem \
  -ca-key=../ca-key.pem \
  -config=../ca-config.json \
  -profile=kubernetes \
  kube-controller-manager-csr.json | cfssljson -bare kube-controller-manager
```

For the `kube-proxy`, use the following command:

```
johndoe@management-vm$ cat << EOF > kube-proxy-csr.json
{
  "CN": "system:kube-proxy",
  "key": {
    "algo": "rsa",
    "size": 2048
  },
  "names": [
    {
      "C": "US",
      "L": "New York",
      "O": "system:node-proxier",
      "OU": "Kubernetes",
      "ST": "NY"
    }
  ]
}
EOF

johndoe@management-vm$ cfssl gencert \
  -ca=../ca.pem \
  -ca-key=../ca-key.pem \
  -config=../ca-config.json \
  -profile=kubernetes \
  kube-proxy-csr.json | cfssljson -bare kube-proxy
```

For the `kube-scheduler`, use the following command:

```
johndoe@management-vm$ cat << EOF > kube-scheduler-csr.json
{
  "CN": "system:kube-scheduler",
  "key": {
    "algo": "rsa",
    "size": 2048
  },
  "names": [
    {
      "C": "US",
      "L": "New York",
      "O": "system:kube-scheduler",
      "OU": "Kubernetes",
      "ST": "NY"
    }
  ]
}
EOF
```

```
johndoe@management-vm$ cfssl gencert \
  -ca=../ca.pem \
  -ca-key=../ca-key.pem \
  -config=../ca-config.json \
  -profile=kubernetes \
  kube-scheduler-csr.json | cfssljson -bare kube-scheduler
```

Now we need to create the API server. You will notice that it is similar to the process we used with the `kubelets`, as this certificate requires the hostname parameter. But with the `kube-api` cert, we will not only provide the hostname and IP address of the individual nodes, we will also provide instead all of the possible hostnames and IPs that our API server will be using: the load-balancer public IP, the IP of each master node, and a special FQDN, `kubernetes.default`. All of them will be in a single cert.

Let's create a separate directory first using the following command:

```
johndoe@management-vm$ mkdir ~/certs/api/
```

```
johndoe@management-vm$ cd ~/certs/api/
```

Now, let's create a variable for the hostname using the following command:

```
johndoe@management-vm$API_HOSTNAME=10.20.0.1,192.168.0.11,kube-
controller-1,192.168.0.12,kube-
controller-2,<PUBLIC_IP>,127.0.0.1,localhost,kubernetes.default
```

 Note that you should replace `<PUBLIC_IP>` with your public IP address.

Now, let's create the certificate using the following command:

```
johndoe@management-vm$ cat << EOF > kubernetes-csr.json
{
  "CN": "kubernetes",
  "key": {
    "algo": "rsa",
    "size": 2048
  },
  "names": [
    {
      "C": "US",
      "L": "New York",
      "O": "Kubernetes",
      "OU": "Kubernetes",
      "ST": "NY"
```

```
        }
    ]
}
EOF

johndoe@management-vm$ cfssl gencert \
  -ca=../ca.pem \
  -ca-key=../ca-key.pem \
  -config=../ca-config.json \
  -hostname=${API_HOSTNAME} \
  -profile=kubernetes \
  kubernetes-csr.json | cfssljson -bare kubernetes
```

At this point, only one certificate is missing—the service account certificate. This certificate is not for any normal user or Kubernetes component specifically. Service account certificates are used by the API server to sign tokens that are used for service accounts.

We will be storing these key pairs in the same directory as the API certs, so we will just create the json and run the cfssl gencert command, as shown in the following command:

```
johndoe@management-vm$ cat << EOF > service-account-csr.json
{
  "CN": "service-accounts",
  "key": {
    "algo": "rsa",
    "size": 2048
  },
  "names": [
    {
      "C": "US",
      "L": "New York",
      "O": "Kubernetes",
      "OU": "Kubernetes",
      "ST": "NY"
    }
  ]
}
EOF

johndoe@management-vm$ cfssl gencert \
  -ca=../ca.pem \
  -ca-key=../ca-key.pem \
  -config=../ca-config.json \
  -profile=kubernetes \
  service-account-csr.json | cfssljson -bare service-account
```

Sending our certificates home

With all our certificates generated, it's time to move them to their corresponding nodes. Microsoft Azure can resolve internally via the VM name, so we can move the certificates easily.

To move the certificates to the `kubelets`, use the following command:

```
johndoe@management-vm$ cd ~/certs/kubelets

johndoe@management-vm$ scp ../ca.pem \
kube-node-1.pem \
kube-node-1-key.pem \
johndoe@kube-node-1:~/
```

Repeat for the rest of the nodes.

To move the certificates to the control plane, use the following command:

```
johndoe@management-vm$ cd ~/certs/api

johndoe@management-vm$ scp ../ca.pem \
../ca-key.pem \
kubernetes.pem \
kubernetes-key.pem \
service-account.pem \
service-account-key.pem \
johndoe@kube-controller-1:~/
```

Repeat for the last controllers.

Kubeconfigs

For you to be able to talk to Kubernetes, you need to know where your API is. You also need to tell the API who you are and what your credentials are. All of this information is provided with `kubeconfigs`. These configuration files contain all the information necessary for you to reach and authenticate against the cluster. Not only will users be using `kubeconfig` files to reach the cluster, they will also be using it to reach other services. That is why we will be generating multiple `kubeconfig` files for every component and user.

Installing kubectl

To be able to create the `kubeconfig` files, we require `kubectl`. You will be installing `kubectl` in the management VM first to generate the config files, but later we will also use it to manage our cluster.

First, add the repository from where we will be getting `kubectl`, as shown in the following command:

```
johndoe@management-vm$ sudo cat << EOF > /etc/yum.repos.d/kubernetes.repo
[kubernetes]
name=Kubernetes
baseurl=https://packages.cloud.google.com/yum/repos/kubernetes-el7-x86_64
enabled=1
gpgcheck=1
repo_gpgcheck=1
gpgkey=https://packages.cloud.google.com/yum/doc/yum-key.gpg
https://packages.cloud.google.com/yum/doc/rpm-package-key.gpg
EOF
```

Finally, we install it using `yum`, as shown in the following command:

```
johndoe@management-vm$sudo yum install kubectl
```

Control plane kubeconfigs

The first kubeconfigs that we will be generating are for our control plane components.

To maintain order, we will keep organizing our files into directories. All our `kubeconfigs` will go in the same directory, though, as shown in the following command:

```
johndoe@management-vm$ mkdir ~/kubeconfigs
```

```
johndoe@management-vm$ cd ~/kubeconfigs
```

With our directory created, let's begin generating `kubeconfigs`!

Kube-controller-manager

`kube-controller-manager kubeconfig`:

```
johndoe@management-vm$ kubectl config set-cluster kubernetes \
    --certificate-authority=../certs/ca.pem \
    --embed-certs=true \
    --server=https://127.0.0.1:6443 \
```

```
    --kubeconfig=kube-controller-manager.kubeconfig

johndoe@management-vm$ kubectl config set-credentials \
system:kube-controller-manager \
    --client-certificate=../certs/control-plane/kube-controller-manager.pem
\
    --client-key=../certs/control-plane/kube-controller-manager-key.pem \
    --embed-certs=true \
    --kubeconfig=kube-controller-manager.kubeconfig

johndoe@management-vm$ kubectl config set-context default \
    --cluster=kubernetes \
    --user=system:kube-controller-manager \
    --kubeconfig=kube-controller-manager.kubeconfig

johndoe@management-vm$ kubectl config use-context default --
kubeconfig=kube-controller-manager.kubeconfig
```

Kube-scheduler

Kube-scheduler kubeconfig:

```
johndoe@management-vm$ kubectl config set-cluster kubernetes \
    --certificate-authority=../certs/ca.pem \
    --embed-certs=true \
    --server=https://127.0.0.1:6443 \
    --kubeconfig=kube-scheduler.kubeconfig

johndoe@management-vm$ kubectl config set-credentials system:kube-scheduler
\
    --client-certificate=../certs/control-plane/kube-scheduler.pem \
    --client-key=../certs/control-plane/kube-scheduler-key.pem \
    --embed-certs=true \
    --kubeconfig=kube-scheduler.kubeconfig

johndoe@management-vm$ kubectl config set-context default \
    --cluster=kubernetes \
    --user=system:kube-scheduler \
    --kubeconfig=kube-scheduler.kubeconfig

johndoe@management-vm$ kubectl config use-context default --
kubeconfig=kube-scheduler.kubeconfig
```

Kubelet configs

For our `kubelets`, we will require one `kubeconfig` for each node. To make things easier, we will just make a for loop to create a config for each node, as shown in the following command. Note that you need to replace `<KUBE_API_PUBLIC_IP>` with your own public IP address:

```
johndoe@management-vm$ for i in 1 2; do
kubectl config set-cluster kubernetes \
--certificate-authority=../certs/ca.pem \
--embed-certs=true \
--server=https://<KUBE_API_PUBLIC_IP>:6443 \
--kubeconfig=kube-node-${i}.kubeconfig

kubectl config set-credentials system:node:kube-node-${i} \
--client-certificate=../certs/kubelets/kube-node-${i}.pem \
--client-key=../certs/kubelets/kube-node-${i}-key.pem \
--embed-certs=true \
--kubeconfig=kube-node-${i}.kubeconfig

kubectl config set-context default \
--cluster=kubernetes \
--user=system:node:kube-node-${i} \
--kubeconfig=kube-node-${i}.kubeconfig

kubectl config use-context default --kubeconfig=kube-node-${i}.kubeconfig
done
```

Finally, the last `kubeconfig` that our worker nodes will need is the `kube-proxy` `kubeconfig`. We will only be generating one as it does not contain any specific node configurations, and we can just copy the same config to all our nodes.

Kube-proxy

`kube-proxy kubeconfig`:

```
johndoe@management-vm$ kubectl config set-cluster kubernetes \
    --certificate-authority=../certs/ca.pem \
    --embed-certs=true \
    --server=https://<PUBLIC_IP>:6443 \
    --kubeconfig=kube-proxy.kubeconfig

johndoe@management-vm$ kubectl config set-credentials system:kube-proxy \
    --client-certificate=../certs/controllers/kube-proxy.pem \
    --client-key=../certs/controllers/kube-proxy-key.pem \
    --embed-certs=true \
    --kubeconfig=kube-proxy.kubeconfig
```

```
johndoe@management-vm$ kubectl config set-context default \
    --cluster=kubernetes \
    --user=system:kube-proxy \
    --kubeconfig=kube-proxy.kubeconfig

johndoe@management-vm$ kubectl config use-context default \ --
kubeconfig=kube-proxy.kubeconfig
```

Now that we have the control plane kubeconfigs and worker nodes, we will now create the `kubeconfig` for the administrator user, using the following command. This `kubeconfig` file is the one that we will be using to connect to the cluster and manage its API objects:

```
johndoe@management-vm$ kubectl config set-cluster kubernetes \
    --certificate-authority=../certs/ca.pem \
    --embed-certs=true \
    --server=https://127.0.0.1:6443 \
    --kubeconfig=admin.kubeconfig

johndoe@management-vm$ kubectl config set-credentials admin \
    --client-certificate=../certs/admin/admin.pem \
    --client-key=../certs/admin/admin-key.pem \
    --embed-certs=true \
    --kubeconfig=admin.kubeconfig

johndoe@management-vm$ kubectl config set-context default \
    --cluster=kubernetes \
    --user=admin \
    --kubeconfig=admin.kubeconfig

johndoe@management-vm$ kubectl config use-context default \ --
kubeconfig=admin.kubeconfig
```

Moving configs around

Our kubeconfigs now need to be transferred to each of their corresponding VMs. To do this, we will follow the same procedure that we used to move the certificates.

First, let's move kubeconfigs that go in the worker nodes using the following command:

```
johndoe@management-vm$ scp kube-node-1.kubeconfig kube-proxy.kubeconfig
johndoe@kube-node-1:~/
```

Repeat for every node.

With the kubeconfigs in place on the nodes, we can now move the `kube-api` server configs using the following command:

```
johndoe@management-vm$ scp admin.kubeconfig kube-controller-
manager.kubeconfig \
kube-scheduler.kubeconfig johndoe@kube-controller-1:~/
```

Repeat for every controller.

Installing the control plane

Now we will install the binaries required for our control plane.

ETCD

In this design, we have decided to run `etcd` alongside our `kube-apiserver`. We will start downloading the binaries and configuring the `systemd` units for our database.

Installing etcd

It's time to start installing the `etcd` cluster in our controller nodes. To install `etcd`, we will SSH into each of the controllers from our management VM and run the following procedures.

We will begin by downloading and extracting the binaries using the following command:

```
johndoe@kube-controller-1$ wget -O etcd.tgz \
https://github.com/etcd-io/etcd/releases/download/v3.3.10/etcd-v3.3.10-linu
x-amd64.tar.gz

johndoe@kube-controller-1$ tar xzvf etcd.tgz

johndoe@kube-controller-1$ sudo mv etcd-v3.3.10-linux-amd64/etcd*
/usr/local/bin/

johndoe@kube-controller-1$ sudo mkdir -p /etc/etcd /var/lib/etcd
```

After we have extracted the binaries, we need to copy the kubernetes API and CA certificates to our `etcd` directory using the following command:

```
johndoe@kube-controller-1$ cp /home/johndoe/ca.pem \
/home/johndoe/kubernetes-key.pem \
/home/johndoe/kubernetes.pem /etc/etcd
```

Before creating the `systemd` unit file, let's set up some variables to make things a little easier.

These two first variables will be host-unique, as shown in the following commands:

```
johndoe@kube-controller-1$ ETCD_NAME=$(hostname)

johndoe@kube-controller-1$ I_IP=192.168.0.11
```

The next and last variable will be the same across all the nodes; it will contain the hostname and IP of each of our `ectd` cluster members, as shown in the following command:

```
I_CLUSTER=kube-
controller-1=https://192.168.0.11:2380,kube-controller-2=https://192.168.0.
12:2380,kube-controller-3=https://192.168.0.13:2380
```

Now that we have the variables, let's create the `systemd` unit file, as shown in the following command:

```
johndoe@kube-controller-1$sudo cat << EOF | sudo tee
/etc/systemd/system/etcd.service
[Unit]
Description=etcd
Documentation=https://github.com/coreos

[Service]
ExecStart=/usr/local/bin/etcd \\
  --name ${ETCD_NAME} \\
  --cert-file=/etc/etcd/kubernetes.pem \\
  --key-file=/etc/etcd/kubernetes-key.pem \\
  --peer-cert-file=/etc/etcd/kubernetes.pem \\
  --peer-key-file=/etc/etcd/kubernetes-key.pem \\
  --trusted-ca-file=/etc/etcd/ca.pem \\
  --peer-trusted-ca-file=/etc/etcd/ca.pem \\
  --peer-client-cert-auth \\
  --client-cert-auth \\
  --initial-advertise-peer-urls https://${I_IP}:2380 \\
  --listen-peer-urls https://${I_IP}:2380 \\
  --listen-client-urls https://${I_IP}:2379,https://127.0.0.1:2379 \\
  --advertise-client-urls https://${I_IP}:2379 \\
  --initial-cluster-token etcd-cluster-0 \\
  --initial-cluster ${I_CLUSTER} \\
  --initial-cluster-state new \\
  --data-dir=/var/lib/etcd
Restart=on-failure
RestartSec=5

[Install]
```

```
WantedBy=multi-user.target
EOF
```

Now we reload, enable, and start the daemon using the following command:

```
johndoe@kube-controller-1$ systemctl daemon-reload && \
systemctl enable etcd && \
systemctl start etcd && \
systemctl status etcd
```

Once you have repeated this process for each of the nodes, you can check the status of the cluster by running the following:

```
johndoe@kube-controller-3$ ETCDCTL_API=3 etcdctl member list \
--endpoints=https://127.0.0.1:2379 \
--cacert=/etc/etcd/ca.pem \
--cert=/etc/etcd/kubernetes.pem \
--key=/etc/etcd/kubernetes-key.pem
```

Encrypting etcd data

The API server can encrypt data stored in etcd. To do this, we will be using a flag called `--experimental-encryption-provider-config` when we create our `kube-apiserver` `systemd` unit file. But before we pass the flag, we need to create a YAML that will contain our encryption key.

We will only create one YAML definition and copy it to every controller node. You should do this from the management VM so that you can easily transfer the file to all the controllers. Let's set this up using the following command:

```
johndoe@management-vm$ CRYPT_KEY=$(head -c 32 /dev/urandom | base64)
```

Input the YAML definition as follows:

```
johndoe@management-vm$ cat << EOF > crypt-config.yml
kind: EncryptionConfig
apiVersion: v1
resources:
  - resources:
      - secrets
    providers:
      - aescbc:
          keys:
            - name: key1
              secret: ${CRYPT_KEY}
      - identity: {}
EOF
```

Finally, move the key to every node as follows:

```
johndoe@management-vm$ for i in 1 2 3; do
scp crypt-config.yml johndoe@kube-controller-${i}:~/
done
```

Installing the Kubernetes controller binaries

Now that `etcd` is in place, we can start installing `kube-apiserver`, `kube-controller-manager`, and `kube-scheduler`.

Kube-apiserver

Let's begin by SSHing into our first controller node and downloading the required binary using the following command:

```
johndoe@management-vm$ ssh johndoe@kube-controller-1

johndoe@kube-controller-1$ wget
"https://storage.googleapis.com/kubernetes-release/release/v1.12.0/bin/linux/amd64/kube-apiserver" \
"https://storage.googleapis.com/kubernetes-release/release/v1.12.0/bin/linux/amd64/kubectl"
```

Now move the binaries to `/usr/local/bin/` using the following command:

```
johndoe@kube-controller-1$ sudo mkdir -p /etc/kubernetes/config

johndoe@kube-controller-1$ sudo chmod +x kube*

johndoe@kube-controller-1$ sudo mv kube-apiserver kubectl /usr/local/bin/
```

Next, we will be creating and moving all the directories and certificates that are needed for our API server to work using the following command:

```
johndoe@kube-controller-1$ sudo mkdir -p /var/lib/kubernetes/

johndoe@kube-controller-1$ sudo cp /home/johndoe/ca.pem \
/home/johndoe/ca-key.pem \
/home/johndoe/kubernetes-key.pem \
/home/johndoe/kubernetes.pem \
/home/johndoe/service-account-key.pem \
/home/johndoe/service-account.pem \
/home/johndoe/crypt-config.yml \
/var/lib/kubernetes/
```

Before creating the `systemd` unit file, let's declare some variables using the following command:

```
johndoe@kube-controller-1$ I_IP=192.168.0.11

johndoe@kube-controller-1$ CON1_IP=192.168.0.11

johndoe@kube-controller-1$ CON2_IP=192.168.0.12

johndoe@kube-controller-1$ CON2_IP=192.168.0.13
```

Only the `I_IP` variable will be unique on each node, and it will depend on the IP of the node on which you are doing the procedure. The other three will be the same on all nodes.

Now that the variables are set up, we can start creating the unit file, as shown in the following command:

```
johndoe@kube-controller-1$ sudo cat << EOF | sudo tee
/etc/systemd/system/kube-apiserver.service
[Unit]
Description=Kubernetes API Server
Documentation=https://github.com/kubernetes/kubernetes

[Service]
ExecStart=/usr/local/bin/kube-apiserver \\
  --advertise-address=${I_IP} \\
  --allow-privileged=true \\
  --apiserver-count=3 \\
  --audit-log-maxage=30 \\
  --audit-log-maxbackup=3 \\
  --audit-log-maxsize=100 \\
  --audit-log-path=/var/log/audit.log \\
  --authorization-mode=Node,RBAC \\
  --bind-address=0.0.0.0 \\
  --client-ca-file=/var/lib/kubernetes/ca.pem \\
  --enable-admission-
plugins=Initializers,NamespaceLifecycle,NodeRestriction,LimitRanger,Service
Account,DefaultStorageClass,ResourceQuota \\
  --enable-swagger-ui=true \\
  --etcd-cafile=/var/lib/kubernetes/ca.pem \\
  --etcd-certfile=/var/lib/kubernetes/kubernetes.pem \\
  --etcd-keyfile=/var/lib/kubernetes/kubernetes-key.pem \\
  --etcd-servers=https://$CON1_IP:2379,https://$CON2_IP:2379 \\
  --event-ttl=1h \\
  --experimental-encryption-provider-config=/var/lib/kubernetes/crypt-
config.yml \\
  --kubelet-certificate-authority=/var/lib/kubernetes/ca.pem \\
  --kubelet-client-certificate=/var/lib/kubernetes/kubernetes.pem \\
```

```
--kubelet-client-key=/var/lib/kubernetes/kubernetes-key.pem \\
--kubelet-https=true \\
--runtime-config=api/all \\
--service-account-key-file=/var/lib/kubernetes/service-account.pem \\
--service-cluster-ip-range=10.20.0.0/24 \\
--service-node-port-range=30000-32767 \\
--tls-cert-file=/var/lib/kubernetes/kubernetes.pem \\
--tls-private-key-file=/var/lib/kubernetes/kubernetes-key.pem \\
--v=2 \\
--kubelet-preferred-address-
types=InternalIP,InternalDNS,Hostname,ExternalIP,ExternalDNS
Restart=on-failure
RestartSec=5

[Install]
WantedBy=multi-user.target
EOF
```

Kube-controller-manager

To install the `kube-controller-manager`, the steps will be very similar, except that at this point we will start using the kubeconfigs.

First, download `kube-controller-manager` using the following command:

```
johndoe@kube-controller-1$ wget
"https://storage.googleapis.com/kubernetes-release/release/v1.12.0/bin/linu
x/amd64/kube-controller-manager"

johndoe@kube-controller-1$sudo chmod +x kube-controller-manager

johndoe@kube-controller-1$sudo mv kube-controller-manager /usr/local/bin/
```

Move the `kubeconfig` and create the unit file for the `kube-controller-manager` using the following command:

```
johndoe@kube-controller-1$ sudo cp \
/home/johndoe/kube-controller-manager.kubeconfig /var/lib/kubernetes/

johndoe@kube-controller-1$ cat << EOF | sudo tee \
/etc/systemd/system/kube-controller-manager.service
[Unit]
Description=Kubernetes Controller Manager
Documentation=https://github.com/kubernetes/kubernetes

[Service]
ExecStart=/usr/local/bin/kube-controller-manager \\
```

```
    --address=0.0.0.0 \\
    --cluster-cidr=10.30.0.0/16 \\
    --cluster-name=kubernetes \\
    --cluster-signing-cert-file=/var/lib/kubernetes/ca.pem \\
    --cluster-signing-key-file=/var/lib/kubernetes/ca-key.pem \\
    --kubeconfig=/var/lib/kubernetes/kube-controller-manager.kubeconfig \\
    --leader-elect=true \\
    --root-ca-file=/var/lib/kubernetes/ca.pem \\
    --service-account-private-key-file=/var/lib/kubernetes/service-account-
key.pem \\
    --service-cluster-ip-range=10.20.0.0/24 \\
    --use-service-account-credentials=true \\
    --v=2
Restart=on-failure
RestartSec=5

[Install]
WantedBy=multi-user.target
EOF
```

Kube-scheduler

The final component to install in the control plane is kube-scheduler. With the scheduler, besides creating the systemd unit file we will also be creating a YAML file that contains the basic configuration of the scheduler.

First, let's download the binaries. Use the following commands to download kube-scheduler and move it to /usr/local/bin/:

```
johndoe@kube-controller-1$ wget \
"https://storage.googleapis.com/kubernetes-release/release/v1.12.0/bin/linu
x/amd64/kube-scheduler"

johndoe@kube-controller-1$ chmod +x kube-scheduler

johndoe@kube-controller-1$ sudo mv kube-scheduler /usr/local/bin/
```

We move the kubeconfig file to the kubernetes folder using the following command:

```
johndoe@kube-controller-1$sudo cp /home/johndoe/kube-scheduler.kubeconfig
/var/lib/kubernetes/
```

`kube-scheduler.yml` is given as follows:

```
johndoe@kube-controller-1$sudo cat << EOF | sudo tee
/etc/kubernetes/config/kube-scheduler.yml
apiVersion: componentconfig/v1alpha1
kind: KubeSchedulerConfiguration
clientConnection:
  kubeconfig: "/var/lib/kubernetes/kube-scheduler.kubeconfig"
leaderElection:
  leaderElect: true
EOF
```

`kube-scheduler.service` is given as follows:

```
johndoe@kube-controller-1$ sudo cat << EOF | sudo tee
/etc/systemd/system/kube-scheduler.service
[Unit]
Description=Kubernetes Scheduler
Documentation=https://github.com/kubernetes/kubernetes

[Service]
ExecStart=/usr/local/bin/kube-scheduler \\
  --config=/etc/kubernetes/config/kube-scheduler.yml \\

  --v=2
Restart=on-failure
RestartSec=5

[Install]
WantedBy=multi-user.target
EOF
```

Repeat all the steps in the *Installing the control plane* section on each controller node before moving on to the next steps.

Starting the control plane

After finishing the installation of each component on every controller node, we are ready to start and test the services.

To do this, we will first enable and start all `systemd` units using the following command:

```
johndoe@kube-controller-1$ sudo systemctl daemon-reload

johndoe@kube-controller-1$ sudo systemctl enable kube-apiserver kube-
controller-manager kube-scheduler

johndoe@kube-controller-1$ sudo systemctl start kube-apiserver kube-
controller-manager kube-scheduler

johndoe@kube-controller-1$ sudo systemctl status kube-apiserver kube-
controller-manager kube-scheduler
```

Finally, to be able to use `kubectl` ourselves, we need to set the context of the cluster that we want to connect to and set up the `kubeconfig` admin as our default one.
The `kubeconfig` admin that we have is currently set to point to `localhost` as the `kube-apiserver` endpoint. This will be OK for now, because we only want to test our components.

Enter the following command in your `kube-controller-1`:

```
johndoe@kube-controller-1$ mkdir /home/johndoe/.kube/

johndoe@kube-controller-1$ cat /home/johndoe/admin.kubeconfig >
/home/johndoe/.kube/config

johndoe@kube-controller-1$ kubectl get cs
```

The output should look as follows:

```
NAME                   STATUS    MESSAGE                ERROR
controller-manager     Healthy   ok
scheduler              Healthy   ok
etcd-0                 Healthy   {"health": "true"}
etcd-1                 Healthy   {"health": "true"}
etcd-2                 Healthy   {"health": "true"}
```

Setting RBAC permissions for kubelets.

Our API server will require permissions to talk to the `kubelets` API. To accomplish this, we create cluster roles that we will bind to the Kubernetes user. We will do this on just one of the controller nodes because we will use `kubectl`, and the changes will be applied to the entire cluster.

Cluster role

Create a cluster role that contains the permissions using the following command:

```
johndoe@kube-controller-1$ cat << EOF | kubectl apply -f -
apiVersion: rbac.authorization.k8s.io/v1beta1
kind: ClusterRole
metadata:
  annotations:
    rbac.authorization.kubernetes.io/autoupdate: "true"
  labels:
    kubernetes.io/bootstrapping: rbac-defaults
  name: system:kube-apiserver-to-kubelet
rules:
  - apiGroups:
      - ""
    resources:
      - nodes/proxy
      - nodes/stats
      - nodes/log
      - nodes/spec
      - nodes/metrics
    verbs:
      - "*"
EOF
```

Cluster role binding

Now bind the role to the Kubernetes user using the following command:

```
johndoe@kube-controller-1$ cat << EOF | kubectl apply -f -
apiVersion: rbac.authorization.k8s.io/v1beta1
kind: ClusterRoleBinding
metadata:
  name: system:kube-apiserver
  namespace: ""
roleRef:
  apiGroup: rbac.authorization.k8s.io
  kind: ClusterRole
  name: system:kube-apiserver-to-kubelet
subjects:
  - apiGroup: rbac.authorization.k8s.io
    kind: User
    name: kubernetes
EOF
```

Load-balancer setup

We need to load-balance the request to all our kube-controller-nodes. Because we are running on the cloud, we can create a load-balancer object that will load-balance requests across all our nodes. Not only that, but we can configure health probes that will monitor the status of our controller nodes to see if they are available to receive requests.

Creating the load-balancer

The load-balancer is what we have been saving the public IP for. The LB is going to be our point of access to our cluster from the outside. We will need to create rules to health-check port 80 and to redirect kubectl requests to 6443.

Let's go through the following steps to achieve this.

Azure load-balancer

We will have to go back to our workstation with the Azure CLI installed to go through the next set of steps.

To create the load-balancer in your workstation and assign it the public IP, run the following:

```
az network lb create -n kube-lb \
--sku Standard \
--public-ip-address kube-api-pub-ip
```

Now that we have created our load-balancer, we still need to configure three more things:

- The backend pool
- Health probes
- Load balancing rules

The backend pool

So far ,we have been doing everything related to Azure via the Azure CLI. Let's go through the following steps via the Azure portal so you can familiarize yourself with the portal as well:

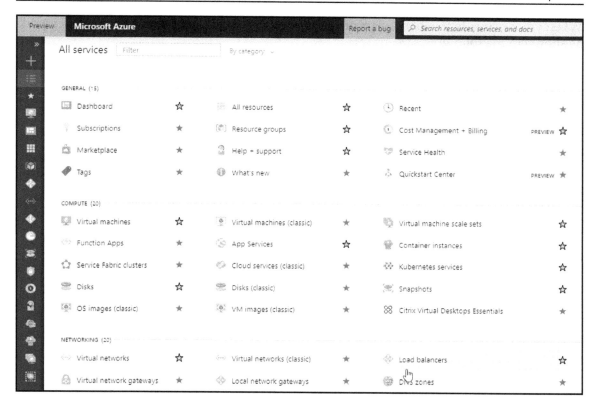

To create the backend pool, navigate to your **kube-lb** object as shown in the following screenshots:

When you are inside the load-balancer object, navigate to **Backend Pools** and click on **Add**, as shown in the following screenshot:

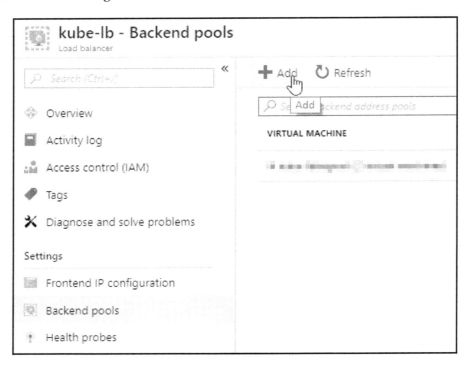

When you click on **Add**, a menu will appear. Name your backend pool `kube-lb-backend` and make sure you select all the kube-controller-nodes and their respective IPs, as shown in the following screenshot:

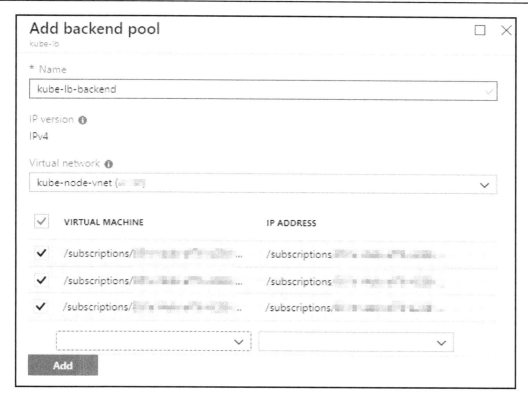

Example

Click on **Add** to finish. We have successfully set up backend VMs.

Health probes

Before we can create load balancing rules, we need to create the health probes that will tell our LB which nodes are available to receive traffic. Because, at the time of writing this chapter, load-balancers in Azure do not support HTTPS health probes, we will need to expose the /healthz endpoint through HTTP. To do this, we will install Nginx in our controller nodes, and pass proxy requests coming to port 80 to port 6443.

SSH back to your controller nodes and perform the following procedures in each one of them:

```
johndoe@kube-controller-1$ sudo yum install epel-release && yum install
nginx
```

Once Nginx is installed, replace the `server` entry in `/etc/nginx/nginx.conf` with the following:

```
server {
  listen 80;
  server_name kubernetes.default.svc.cluster.local;

  location /healthz {
     proxy_pass https://127.0.0.1:6443/healthz;
     proxy_ssl_trusted_certificate /var/lib/kubernetes/ca.pem;
  }
}
```

Because we are running a RHEL-based distribution, SELINUX is enabled by default; therefore, it will be preventing Nginx from accessing the TCP socket on port 6443. To permit this behavior, we need to run the following commands.

First, we install the required packages to manage SELINUX, as shown in the following command:

```
johndoe@kube-controller-1$ sudo yum install policycoreutils-python
```

Once the packages are installed, we run the following to allow connections to port 6443:

```
johndoe@kube-controller-1$ sudo semanage port -a -t http_port_t -p tcp 6443
```

Lastly, we use the following command to start `nginx`:

```
johndoe@kube-controller-1$ sudo systemctl daemon-reload && \
systemctl enable nginx --now
```

If you want to test this, you can always run a `curl` on `localhost`, like this:

```
johndoe@kube-controller-1$ curl -v http://localhost/healthz
```

The following output will be generated if everything was correctly configured:

```
* About to connect() to localhost port 80 (#0)
*   Trying 127.0.0.1...
* Connected to localhost (127.0.0.1) port 80 (#0)
> GET /healthz HTTP/1.1
> User-Agent: curl/7.29.0
> Host: localhost
> Accept: /
< HTTP/1.1 200 OK
< Server: nginx/1.12.2
< Date: Sun, 28 Oct 2018 05:44:35 GMT
< Content-Type: text/plain; charset=utf-8
```

```
< Content-Length: 2
< Connection: keep-alive
<
* Connection #0 to host localhost left intact
Ok
```

Remember to repeat all these procedures for each of the controller nodes.

Now that the health endpoints are exposed, we are ready to create health probe rules in the load-balancer.

Back in the `kube-lb` menu, under **Settings**—the same place where we configure backend pools—select health probes and click on **Add**.

Once the menu appears, fill in the fields as shown in the following screenshot:

Load-balancing rules

We have everything ready to create load-balancing rules and get our load-balancer ready for use.

The process is the same one that we used with backend pools and health probes. Go to the **Settings** menu under **kube-lb** and select **Load Balancing Rules**. Click on **Add** and fill in the dialog that appears, as shown in the following screenshot:

Once what is ready, we just need to open our network security group to allow connections on port 6443.

On your Azure CLI workstation, run the following command to create the rule:

```
az network nsg rule create --nsg-name kube-nsg \
    -n pub_https_allow \
    --direction Inbound \
    --priority 110 \
    --access Allow \
    --description "Allow HTTPS" \
    --destination-address-prefixes '*' \
    --destination-port-ranges 6443 \
    --protocol Tcp \
    --source-address-prefixes '*' \
    --source-port-ranges '*' \
    --direction Inbound
```

Give it a few minutes to take effect, and then navigate in your browser to `https://<LB_IP>:6443/version`.

You should see something like the following:

```
{
  "major": "1",
  "minor": "12",
  "gitVersion": "v1.12.0",
  "gitCommit": "0ed33881dc4355495f623c6f22e7dd0b7632b7c0",
  "gitTreeState": "clean",
  "buildDate": "2018-09-27T16:55:41Z",
  "goVersion": "go1.10.4",
  "compiler": "gc",
  "platform": "linux/amd64"
}
```

This will indicate that you can access the API server through the LB.

Worker node setup

It's time to configure and install our worker nodes. In these, we will be installing `kubelet`, the kube proxy, the container runtime, and the container network interface plugins.

SSH into the first worker node from your management VM, as shown in the following command:

```
johndoe@management-vm$ ssh johndoe@kube-node-1
```

Downloading and preparing binaries

Before configuring any service, we need to download any dependencies and set up the required repositories. After this, we can start downloading the binaries and moving them to their respective locations.

Adding the Kubernetes repository

The repository that we need to configure is the Kubernetes repository. With this, we will be able to download `kubectl`. Let's set this up using the following command:

```
johndoe@kube-node-1$ sudo cat << EOF > /etc/yum.repos.d/kubernetes.repo
[kubernetes]
name=Kubernetes
baseurl=https://packages.cloud.google.com/yum/repos/kubernetes-el7-x86_64
enabled=1
gpgcheck=1
repo_gpgcheck=1
gpgkey=https://packages.cloud.google.com/yum/doc/yum-key.gpg
https://packages.cloud.google.com/yum/doc/rpm-package-key.gpg
EOF
```

Installing dependencies and kubectl

With the `repo` configured, we can start downloading `kubectl` and any required dependencies for the binaries that we will download. Let's set this up using the following command:

```
johndoe@kube-node-1$ sudo yum install -y kubectl socat conntrack ipset
libseccomp
```

Downloading and storing worker binaries

Now that we have the dependencies ready, we can download our required worker binaries using the following command:

```
johndoe@kube-node-1$ wget \
https://github.com/kubernetes-sigs/cri-tools/releases/download/v1.12.0/cric
tl-v1.12.0-linux-amd64.tar.gz \
https://storage.googleapis.com/kubernetes-release/release/v1.12.0/bin/linux
/amd64/kubelet \
https://github.com/containernetworking/plugins/releases/download/v0.6.0/cni
-plugins-amd64-v0.6.0.tgz \
https://github.com/opencontainers/runc/releases/download/v1.0.0-rc5/runc.am
d64 \
https://storage.googleapis.com/kubernetes-release/release/v1.12.0/bin/linux
/amd64/kube-proxy \
https://github.com/containerd/containerd/releases/download/v1.1.2/container
d-1.1.2.linux-amd64.tar.gz
```

Now let's create the folder structure for the recently downloaded binaries using the following command:

```
johndoe@kube-node-1$ sudo mkdir -p \
/etc/cni/net.d \
/opt/cni/bin \
/var/lib/kube-proxy \
/var/lib/kubelet \
/var/lib/kubernetes \
/var/run/kubernetes
```

We change the name to runc for ease of use and to conform to the convention, as shown in the following command:

```
johndoe@kube-node-1$ mv runc.amd64 runc
```

We give executable permissions to the rest of our binaries using the following command:

```
johndoe@kube-node-1$ chmod +x kube-proxy kubelet runc
```

After giving them executable rights, we can move them to /usr/local/bin/ using the following command:

```
johndoe@kube-node-1$ sudo mv kube-proxy kubelet runc /usr/local/bin/
```

Some of the downloaded files are TAR archives, which we need to `untar` and store in their respective locations using the following command:

```
johndoe@kube-node-1$ tar xvzf crictl-v1.12.0-linux-amd64.tar.gz

johndoe@kube-node-1$ sudo mv crictl /usr/local/bin/

johndoe@kube-node-1$ sudo tar xvzf cni-plugins-amd64-v0.6.0.tgz -C
/opt/cni/bin/

johndoe@kube-node-1$ tar xvzf containerd-1.1.2.linux-amd64.tar.gz

johndoe@kube-node-1$ sudo mv ./bin/* /bin/
```

Containerd setup

We are ready now to start configuring each service. The first one is `containerd`.

Let's create the configuration directory using the following command:

```
johndoe@kube-node-1$ sudo mkdir -p /etc/containerd/
```

Now we create the `toml` config file, which will tell `containerd` what container runtime to use. Let's set this up using the following command:

```
johndoe@kube-node-1$ sudo cat << EOF | sudo tee /etc/containerd/config.toml
[plugins]
[plugins.cri.containerd]
snapshotter = "overlayfs"
[plugins.cri.containerd.default_runtime]
runtime_type = "io.containerd.runtime.v1.linux"
runtime_engine = "/usr/local/bin/runc"
runtime_root = ""
EOF
```

Finally, let's set up the `systemd` unit file using the following command:

```
johndoe@kube-node-1$ sudo cat << EOF | sudo tee
/etc/systemd/system/containerd.service
[Unit]
Description=containerd container runtime
Documentation=https://containerd.io
After=network.target

[Service]
ExecStartPre=/sbin/modprobe overlay
ExecStart=/bin/containerd
```

```
Restart=always
RestartSec=5
Delegate=yes
KillMode=process
OOMScoreAdjust=-999
LimitNOFILE=1048576
LimitNPROC=infinity
LimitCORE=infinity

[Install]
WantedBy=multi-user.target
EOF
```

The kubelet

Our main service in the worker nodes is the `kubelet`. Let's create its configuration files.

First, we need to move the `kubelet` certificates to their locations using the following command:

```
johndoe@kube-node-1$ sudo mv /home/johndoe/${HOSTNAME}-key.pem
/home/johndoe/${HOSTNAME}.pem /var/lib/kubelet/

johndoe@kube-node-1$ sudo mv /home/johndoe/${HOSTNAME}.kubeconfig
/var/lib/kubelet/kubeconfig

johndoe@kube-node-1$ sudo mv /home/johndoe/ca.pem /var/lib/kubernetes/
```

Now we create the YAML config file that will contain things such as the DNS server IP address, the cluster domain, and the location of the certificate files. Let's set this up using the following command:

```
johndoe@kube-node-1$ sudo cat << EOF | sudo tee /var/lib/kubelet/kubelet-config.yaml
kind: KubeletConfiguration
apiVersion: kubelet.config.k8s.io/v1beta1
authentication:
  anonymous:
    enabled: false
  webhook:
    enabled: true
  x509:
    clientCAFile: "/var/lib/kubernetes/ca.pem"
authorization:
  mode: Webhook
clusterDomain: "cluster.local"
```

```
clusterDNS:
  - "10.20.0.10"
runtimeRequestTimeout: "15m"
tlsCertFile: "/var/lib/kubelet/${HOSTNAME}.pem"
tlsPrivateKeyFile: "/var/lib/kubelet/${HOSTNAME}-key.pem"
EOF
```

Finally, we create the service unit file using the following command:

```
johndoe@kube-node-1$ sudo cat << EOF | sudo tee
/etc/systemd/system/kubelet.service
[Unit]
Description=Kubernetes Kubelet
Documentation=https://github.com/kubernetes/kubernetes
After=containerd.service
Requires=containerd.service

[Service]
ExecStart=/usr/local/bin/kubelet \\
  --config=/var/lib/kubelet/kubelet-config.yaml \\
  --container-runtime=remote \\
  --container-runtime-endpoint=unix:///var/run/containerd/containerd.sock
\\
  --image-pull-progress-deadline=2m \\
  --kubeconfig=/var/lib/kubelet/kubeconfig \\
  --network-plugin=cni \\
  --register-node=true \\
  --v=2 \\
  --hostname-override=${HOSTNAME} \\
  --allow-privileged=true
Restart=on-failure
RestartSec=5

[Install]
WantedBy=multi-user.target
EOF
```

kube-proxy

The next service to create is kube-proxy.

We move the previously created kubeconfigs using the following command:

```
johndoe@kube-node-1$ sudo mv /home/johndoe/kube-proxy.kubeconfig
/var/lib/kube-proxy/kubeconfig
```

As with `kubelet`, `kube-proxy` also requires a config `YAML` that has the cluster CIDR and the mode in which `kube-proxy` will operate. Let's set this up using the following command:

```
johndoe@kube-node-1$ sudo cat << EOF | sudo tee /var/lib/kube-proxy/kube-
proxy-config.yaml
kind: KubeProxyConfiguration
apiVersion: kubeproxy.config.k8s.io/v1alpha1
clientConnection:
  kubeconfig: "/var/lib/kube-proxy/kubeconfig"
mode: "iptables"
clusterCIDR: "10.30.0.0/16"
EOF
```

Finally, we create a unit file for `kube-proxy` using the following command:

```
johndoe@kube-node-1$ sudo cat << EOF | sudo tee /etc/systemd/system/kube-
proxy.service
[Unit]
Description=Kubernetes Kube Proxy
Documentation=https://github.com/kubernetes/kubernetes

[Service]
ExecStart=/usr/local/bin/kube-proxy \\
  --config=/var/lib/kube-proxy/kube-proxy-config.yaml
Restart=on-failure
RestartSec=5

[Install]
WantedBy=multi-user.target
EOF
```

Starting services

Once you have completed these procedures on ALL kube-nodes, you can start the services on each node with the following command:

```
johndoe@kube-node-1$ sudo systemctl daemon-reload && \
systemctl enable containerd kubelet kube-proxy && \
systemctl start containerd kubelet kube-proxy && \
systemctl status containerd kubelet kube-proxy
```

Kubernetes networking

We still have a couple more things to do in our cluster: we need to install a network provider and configure the DNS.

Getting the nodes ready

Our nodes will have to be able to forward packets in order for our pods to be able to talk to the outside world. Azure VMs do not have IP forwarding enabled out-of-the-box, so we will have to enable it manually.

To do this, go to your Azure CLI workstation and run the following:

```
for i in 1 2; do
az network nic update \
-n $(az vm show --name kube-node-${i} --query
[networkProfile.networkInterfaces[*].id] --output tsv | sed 's:.*/::') \
--ip-forwarding true
done
```

This will enable IP forwarding capabilities on the VM's NIC.

Now we have to enable the IP-forwarding kernel parameter on the worker nodes.

SSH into each worker node from the management VM and enable IPv4 forwarding using the following command:

```
johndoe@kube-node-1$ sudo sysctl net.ipv4.conf.all.forwarding=1
```

```
johndoe@kube-node-1$ sudo echo "net.ipv4.conf.all.forwarding=1" | tee -a
/etc/sysctl.conf
```

Configuring remote access

Now, in order to run `kubectl` commands from your management VM, we need to create a `kubeconfig` that uses the admin certificate and the public IP address of our cluster. Let's set this up using the following command:

```
johndoe@management-vm$ kubectl config set-cluster kube \
  --certificate-authority=/home/johndoe/certs/ca.pem \
  --embed-certs=true \
  --server=https://104.45.174.96:6443

johndoe@management-vm$ kubectl config set-credentials admin \
```

```
--client-certificate=/home/johndoe/certs/admin/admin.pem \
--client-key=~/certs/admin/admin-key.pem

johndoe@management-vm$ kubectl config set-context kube \
  --cluster=kube \
  --user=admin

johndoe@management-vm$ kubectl config use-context kube
```

Installing Weave Net

With remote access on our management VM configured, we can now run `kubectl` commands without having to log in to our controller nodes.

To install Weave Net, run the following `kubectl` command from the management VM:

```
johndoe@management-vm$ kubectl apply -f
"https://cloud.weave.works/k8s/net?k8s-version=$(kubectl version | base64 |
tr -d '\n')&env.IPALLOC_RANGE=10.30.0.0/16"
```

With Weave Net installed, now our pods will have IP allocations.

DNS server

Now we will provision our DNS server, which will be provided by Core DNS, an open source DNS server based on plugins. Let's set this up using the following command:

```
johndoe@management-vm$ kubectl create -f
https://raw.githubusercontent.com/dsalamancaMS/CoreDNSforKube/master/coredn
s.yaml
```

Check the DNS pods with the following command:

```
johndoe@management-vm$  kubectl get pods -n kube-system
```

With the DNS server pods created, we have successfully finished the installation of our Kubernetes cluster. If you want, you can create the following deployment to test the cluster one more time:

```
apiVersion: apps/v1
kind: Deployment
metadata:
  name: nginx-deployment
  labels:
    app: nginx
```

```
spec:
  replicas: 3
  selector:
    matchLabels:
      app: nginx
  template:
    metadata:
      labels:
        app: nginx
    spec:
      containers:
      - name: nginx
        image: nginx:1.7.9
        ports:
        - containerPort: 80
```

Now that we have seen the steps needed to create a cluster from scratch, I want to talk a little bit about managed Kubernetes solutions.

Managing Kubernetes on the cloud

Installing and making a Kubernetes cluster usable and ready for production, as you saw in this chapter, is a very long and complex process. If any step goes wrong, your entire deployment might be useless. Because of this, many cloud providers are offering managed Kubernetes solutions—Kubernetes as a service, in a way. In this type of managed solution, the cloud provider or service provider will manage the master nodes of the cluster, which include all the Kubernetes controllers, the API server, and even the etcd database. This is a major advantage because using a managed service will mean that you don't have to worry about the maintenance of the master nodes, and so you won't have to worry about the following:

- Renewing SSL certificates
- Updating/upgrading the etcd database
- Updating/upgrading each of the master node binaries
- Registering extra nodes to the cluster
- Lack of support if something goes wrong
- Transparent integration with the cloud infrastructure
- Operating system patching and maintenance

By forgetting these, we can focus on what's important, such as provisioning pods and creating workloads on our cluster. With managed services, the learning curve decreases dramatically because our staff can focus mainly on the functionality of Kubernetes instead of how it works in order for them to maintain it.

At the time of writing, some managed Kubernetes services worth mentioning are from the following three biggest cloud providers:

- **Azure Kubernetes Services (AKS)**
- **Amazon Web Services Elastic Container Service for Kubernetes (EKS)**
- **Google Kubernetes Engine (GKE)**

Besides managed Kubernetes services, there are also several open-source projects and non-open-source projects that are Kubernetes-based. These projects are not entirely managed, but instead use Kubernetes in the backend to achieve their goals. The following are some more well-known projects:

- Okd (Red Hat's upstream community project for Red Hat OpenShift)
- Red Hat OpenShift
- SUSE **Container as a Service (Caas)** platform
- Mesosphere Kubernetes Engine

Summary

In this chapter, we learned the basic steps of provisioning a Kubernetes cluster. We also learned about the Azure command-line interface and how to provision resources in Azure. We also tried different tools across the whole deployment, such as CFSSL and Nginx.

We learned about and provisioned `kubectl` configuration files that enabled us to access our cluster and deployed a dummy deployment to test our cluster. Finally, we looked at the benefits of running a managed cluster and the different types of managed service that we can find in the major public cloud providers.

The next chapter will explain what each component does. The reader will learn about the different components and their purposes.

Questions

1. How do you install Kubernetes?
2. What is a `kubeconfig`?
3. How do we create SSL certificates?
4. What is AKS?
5. How do we use the Azure CLI?
6. How do we provision a resource group in Azure?
7. How do we install `etcd`?

Further reading

- *Mastering Kubernetes* by Packt Publishing: `https://prod.packtpub.com/in/application-development/mastering-kubernetes-second-edition`
- *Kubernetes for Developers* by Packt Publishing: `https://prod.packtpub.com/in/virtualization-and-cloud/kubernetes-developers`
- *Hands-On Microservices with Kubernetes* by Packt Publishing: `https://prod.packtpub.com/in/virtualization-and-cloud/hands-microservices-kubernetes`

Bibliography/sources:

- **Generating self-signed certificates:** `https://coreos.com/os/docs/latest/generate-self-signed-certificates.html`
- **CloudFlare's PKI/TLS toolkit:** `https://github.com/cloudflare/cfssl`
- **The Go Programming Language:** `https://golang.org/doc/install`

3
Section 3: Elastic Stack

This section focuses on how to implement an **ELK stack** that comprises Elasticsearch, Logstash, and Kibana for environment log awareness.

This section contains the following chapters:

- Chapter 10, *Monitoring with the ELK stack*
- Chapter 11, *Designing an ELK Stack*
- Chapter 12, *Using Elasticsearch, Logstash, and Kibana to Manage Logs*

Monitoring with the ELK Stack 10

Monitoring is an essential part of any environment, whether it is production, QA, or development; the **Elastic Stack (ELK Stack)** helps simplify this task by allowing logs, metrics, and events from different sources to be aggregated in a single indexable location: Elasticsearch.

The ELK Stack is a collection of three different pieces of software:

- Elasticsearch
- Logstash
- Kibana

In this chapter, we will explain the role of each component.

In this chapter, we will cover the following topics:Defining the main functionality of Elasticsearch

- Exploring the concept of centralized logs
- How Kibana helps bring together the other components

Technical requirements

Here's the list of technical requirements for this chapter:

- Elasticsearch product page: `https://www.elastic.co/products/elasticsearch`
- Overview of Logstash: `https://www.elastic.co/products/logstash`
- Available input plugins for Logstash: `https://www.elastic.co/guide/en/logstash/current/input-plugins.html`
- Grok pattern matching: `https://www.elastic.co/guide/en/logstash/current/plugins-filters-grok.html`
- Kibana user guide: `https://www.elastic.co/guide/en/kibana/current/index.html`

Understanding the need for monitoring

Imagine that you're asked to provide historical data to the CIO, as an ongoing project requires information on how much CPU the entire ecosystem is using on average, but the business never invested the time to implement a good monitoring system. Therefore, your only option is to log into each system and run local commands, record results into a spreadsheet, do some math to obtain the average results, and, after all this, you realize that the data is no longer valid and you have to go through all of this again. This is precisely why we have monitoring systems such as Elasticsearch. The same process could've taken you a couple of minutes. Not just that, you would be getting accurate data and real-time reports. Let's find out more about what monitoring is, and why you, as an architect, should consider it to be the best thing ever to exist.

Monitoring refers to the process of taking raw data from any given environment, aggregating it, storing it, and analyzing it in a way that is understandable.

All environments should have some form of monitoring in place, from a simple log file for keeping track of failed logins, to a more robust system that is in charge of analyzing data from thousands of hosts. Monitoring data allows system administrators to detect problems before they occur, and allows architects to make decisions for future or ongoing projects based on data.

You may recall from the `Chapter 1`, *Introduction to Design Methodology*, that we spoke about how asking the right questions can help design a better solution, and, at the same time, give the right answers; for example, it could help make sizing decisions based on historical usage data. Providing usage data to architects helps size the solution correctly. They not only leverage future usage statistics, but also past instances, where usage spikes have been recorded during peak times, such as during weekends.

Let's try to condense why we need monitoring into four main areas:

- Make decisions through historical data
- Proactively detect problems
- Understand environment performance
- Plan for budget

Decisions made through historical data

Monitoring gives the ability to go back in time and analyze usage trends to help identify areas of opportunity. For example, in the scenario presented in the `Chapter 1`, *Introduction to Design Methodology*, where the customer needed a web server solution able to sustain 10,000 hits per second. You, as an architect, requested access to usage data from their existing solution, and, after looking at their usage trends, you determined that usage increased tenfold during the first week of each month.

While users might not complain about problems during these days, you should take into account that this high usage tends to leverage resources during this times. The data taken from the monitoring system might lead to a decision where either more resources need to be destined to the server (for example, more CPU and RAM) than previously calculated, or more servers need to be added to the cluster (if possible).

Without this data, no one would ever know that more resources are needed due to spiking. The ability to discern normal usage from spikes helps make the right choices when designing and sizing a solution.

From the same scenario, we could conclude from the historical data usage that the current solution had been sustaining 10,000 hits per second for the last several months. This might mean that the customers were able to achieve the desired performance all along, but in reality what they needed was a solution that could handle the usage spikes, as mentioned earlier.

Proactively detect problems

Imagine that you're almost ready to go home for the day when suddenly someone reports that a database server is unable to receive connections. You log into the server and notice that the problem is a lot worse than initially reported. The disks where the data from the database resides are now all reported as failed. You look closer at the logs on the system and notice that disk errors had been reported for the last four months; however, as a robust monitoring system was not in place, no one ever knew that the errors were there. Now, the data is lost, and you have to retrieve an old backup that takes several hours to go back to production.

Unfortunately, this situation is not uncommon, and most of the time, IT works reactively, meaning that if something breaks, someone reports the broken something, and someone then goes and fix the broken something. This could've been avoided altogether if a monitoring system had been implemented and configured to report errors. The disks could have been replaced before they catastrophically failed.

Being able to proactively detect problems before they occur is, in our opinion, one of the most critical aspects of a monitoring system. Predicting where a problem might occur before it happens helps decrease downtime by allowing actions to be taken. For example, in the previous scenario, replacing the drives could have prevented data loss. Predicting changes also helps to decrease operational costs by preventing business losses due to downtime or failures, and by increasing production (or uptime).

Understand environment performance

In Chapter 5, *Analyzing Performance in a Gluster System*, we went through performance testing of a GlusterFS implementation. With monitoring systems, the process of obtaining a baseline for performance can be streamlined by aggregating historical data and averaging statistics.

By looking at historical data, we can see the average performance of any given system through a certain amount of time, allowing an architect to define what is normal and what is not. By obtaining a baseline, we can understand on a deeper level how the environment behaves throughout the day, week, or even month. For example, we can identify that storage servers have a constant throughput of about 200 MB/s through the day, and when users log in during the first hours of the day, throughput spikes to 300 MB/s. A spike of 100 MB/s might seem like a problem at first, but, looking at the data, this appears to be a trend, and is standard behavior.

With this information, we know that the baseline is around 200 MB/s with spikes of 300 MB/s. When the solution is benchmarked, it is expected to perform to this spec. If we obtain results below this number, we know that there is a problem, and an investigation is required to determine the cause of the poor performance. This might be either a redesign of the solution, or an actual problem with the configuration. On the other hand, a high number indicates that the solution can perform to spec even under load spikes.

Without this data, we wouldn't know what erratic behavior looks like, be able to confirm whether or not this is an actual problem, or see what is normal for the environment. Knowing the performance and usage of a solution can help spot problems where there might not seem to be one. For example, consider a situation with the previous numbers, where users interact normally with the storage server and have average response times; however, from the monitoring data, we observe that even with the regular user load we get a throughput of only 50 MB/s. From the user's perspective, everything seems fine, but when asked, they do report that even when response times are good, transfers are taking longer than usual, and upon further investigation a problem is found, with one of the nodes requiring maintenance.

In the preceding example, by merely looking at the performance data, an instance where the solution was under-performing was identified, and actions were taken that avoided downtime and loss to the business. This is the power of understanding the environment through the use of data.

Plan for budget

Data usage trends allow for more granular control of budget planning, as knowing how much storage space is required can help avoid situations where not enough space has been provisioned.

In the Chapter 1, *Introduction to Design Methodology*, we spoke about the procurement process of businesses, and how trying to stick to the timelines is essential as this varies from company to company. Understanding space requirements and usage is crucial for this process, since it can help predict, for example, when the solution will run out of space and can help make decisions around acquiring new storage space.

Knowing if the business consumes X amount of storage per day (also known as the daily change rate) through the use of a monitoring system allows system administrators and architects to predict how long the business can run with the space that is currently available. This will also allow them to predict when the solution will run out of space so that they can act before it runs out of storage—which is a situation that every IT department should avoid.

Understanding resource utilization is crucial to any business, as it prevents unnecessary equipment acquisition. Using data to decide whether more resources should be added to the existing environment or not reduces costs by choosing the right amount of equipment to be added in the case of upgrades. It's not the same when the application is under-performing due to a lack of resources (or outdated hardware) rather than having data that confirms that the current environment is working as expected and still has some room for growth.

Today, the need for monitoring is more crucial than ever. With the almost exponential growth of data within IT environments, being able to predict behaviors and act proactively can be achieved through data-driven decisions, which is only possible through monitoring systems, such as the ELK Stack.

Centralized logs

Before jumping deeper into what makes the ELK Stack, let's explore the concept of centralized logs.

Imagine the following scenario; there seems to be a security breach in the environment, and some strange looking files have been spotted in some servers. Looking at the /var/log/secure file, you find root logins from several addresses, and you want to know which systems have been affected. There's just one problem—the environment has 5,000+ Linux servers, and you have to log into each of the systems and look at the logs. It might take about a minute to grep each host; that's 83+ hours straight looking at system logs.

This problem of having to go to each node can be solved by aggregating and having the logs in a centralized location. While the rest of the industry seems to be going the route of de-centralizing services, having all of the environment's log in a single location can help simplify tasks, such as investigating events that might have affected multiple systems. Having a single location to look for decreases the amount of time required to troubleshoot, and at the same time allows administrators to look for problems within the environment more effectively.

A centralized logging architecture looks like this:

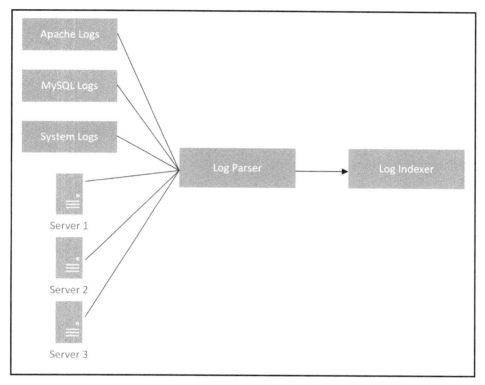

Logs from multiple applications are sent to a log parser (such as Logstash) and later moved to an indexer (such as Elasticsearch). Each host has an agent that is in charge of shipping the logs to the parser.

The parser's job is to transform the data for easy indexing, later shipping the data to the indexer.

In the next segment, we will look at the components that make up the ELK Stack.

Elasticsearch overview

Now, we will dive deep into the components of the ELK Stack, and we will start with the most important component: Elasticsearch.

Elasticsearch is based on an Apache project named Lucene. Its role is to index data and store it for later retrieval. Elasticsearch receives data from different sources and stores it in a centralized location, or multiple nodes if they are set up as a cluster. For this setup, we'll be using Logstash as a data source; however, Elasticsearch can receive data directly from Beats, which we will discuss later on. At its core, Elasticsearch is an analytics and search engine capable of retrieving data very quickly; since data is indexed once it is stored, Elasticsearch stores the data as a JSON document.

A couple of things that define Elasticsearch are as follows:

- Fast
- Scalable
- Highly available

Fast

Searches are almost real-time; what this means is, when you input a search term, Elasticsearch returns results almost immediately. This is thanks to the indexes and data being stored as JSON.

Scalable

Scaling an Elasticsearch cluster can be done quickly by simply adding more nodes to the cluster.

Highly available

When configured as a cluster, Elasticsearch allocates shards between multiple nodes, creating replicas of the shards in case one or more nodes fail.

A shard is a fragment of the JSON document. Elasticsearch creates replicas of the shards and allocates them on the cluster nodes. This allows the cluster to sustain a catastrophic failure, as data is still present as a replica.

Logstash

Most of the time, data, such as log files, is designed so that humans can easily understand what the events mean. This type of data is unstructured, as machines can't easily index the events since they don't follow the same structure or format. Take system logs and Apache, for example. While each log provides different types of events, none follow the same format or structure, and, for an indexing system, this becomes a problem. That's where Logstash comes in.

Logstash data processing parser is capable of receiving data from several sources simultaneously, and then transforming the data by parsing it into a structured form, and later shipping it to Elasticsearch as indexed, easily-searchable data.

One of the main features of Logstash is the vast amount of plugins available for filters such as Grok, allowing greater flexibility on what type of data can be parsed and indexed.

Grok

Grok is a plugin available in Logstash; it takes unstructured data from sources such as system logs, MySQL, Apache, and other webserver logs and transforms them into structured and queryable data for easy ingestion into Elasticsearch.

Grok combines text patterns into something that matches the logs, for example, numbers or IP address. The pattern for this is as follows:

```
%{SYNTAX:SEMANTIC}
```

Here, SYNTAX is the name of the pattern that matches the text and SEMANTIC is the identifier given to the segment of text.

An example of an event for HTTP would be as follows:

```
55.3.244.1 GET /index.html 15824 0.043
```

One pattern match for this could be the following:

```
%{IP:client} %{WORD:method} %{URIPATHPARAM:request} %{NUMBER:bytes}
%{NUMBER:duration}
```

So, by putting it all together in an actual filter configuration, it looks like this:

```
input {
  file {
    path => "/var/log/http.log"
  }
}
filter {
  grok {
    match => { "message" => "%{IP:client} %{WORD:method}
%{URIPATHPARAM:request} %{NUMBER:bytes} %{NUMBER:duration}" }
  }
}
```

Custom patterns

When running a custom application, Logstash won't have the correct pattern to match the syntaxes and semantics. Logstash allows the creation of custom patterns that can match custom data. The same logic from the previous example can be used to match data.

Kibana brings everything together

While Elasticsearch is the heavy lifting part of the ELK Stack, and Logstash is the parsing and processing bit, Kibana is what aggregates everything else together.

The ability to visualize the data allows users to give meaning to their data. By just looking at the raw data, it is difficult to make any sense of it. Kibana visualizes the data that is stored within Elasticsearch through graphs, maps, and other methods of shaping data.

The following is a quick glance at Kibana's interface taken from the live demo:

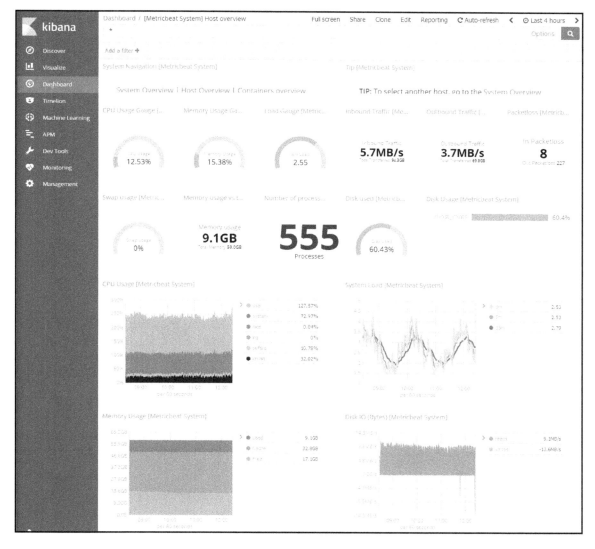

Kibana Dashboard

We can see how easy is to interpret data with multiple modules showing different metrics.

Kibana enables easy understanding of large datasets. Being a browser-based application, it can be accessed from anywhere. This also allows dashboards and reports to be easily shared with others. It can be installed alongside Elasticsearch; however, for larger deployments, it is a good practice to allocate a host to Kibana. Also, Kibana runs on Node.js, so it can be installed on pretty much every system that can run Node.js, from all of the flavors of Linux to Windows and MacOS.

Summary

In this chapter, we explored the need for monitoring, and learned the process of acquiring data from an environment, aggregating it, and storing it so that it can be retrieved later for further analysis. Being able to shape data and understand how the environment behaves by just glancing at the data helps to enhance operational efficiency.

Monitoring allows us to proactively detect problems before they happen or become a bigger problem. This is done by looking at trends, and is by far one of the most crucial reasons to implement and design a monitoring solution. We also spoke about being able to act proactively, and how that can help decrease downtime and wasting money on problems; something that can be achieved by giving shape to data.

Performance is also an area that benefits from data analysis. You may recall from previous chapters that being able to baseline and measure performance enables granular control while designing a solution. Having historical data to refer back to can help make decisions that would affect a design performance-wise, while at the same time allowing us to plan for the budget based on real data taken from a running environment.

We went through the main reasons why having a centralized logging system can help simplify administration tasks; instead of connecting to each system in the environment, looking at all of the logs from a single location saves time and allows quicker, more efficient investigations.

We also went through an overview of each of the components that comprise the ELK Stack. Elasticsearch is the main component, where the storing and analysis of data happens. We noted that it is very fast, as data is stored as JSON documents; that the solution is scalable, as nodes can be easily added; and that it is highly available, as data is spread across the nodes.

Logstash provides data transformation and filtering through plugins such as GROK, where it matches a SYNTAX with a SEMANTIC, for example, an IP with a client.

Finally, we looked at how Kibana connects all of the other components by allowing the data to be visualized and analyzed through comprehensive graphics.

In the next chapter, we will jump into the requirements for each of the components.

Questions

1. What is monitoring?
2. How can monitoring help make business decisions?
3. How can problems be proactively detected?
4. How can monitoring allow for performance baselining?
5. How can monitoring help identify erratic behaviors?
6. What is the main need for centralized logs?
7. What is Elasticsearch?
8. In what format does Elasticsearch store data?
9. What is Logstash?
10. What is Kibana?

Further reading

- *Hands-on Big Data Modeling* by *James Lee, Tao Wei:* https://www.packtpub.com/big-data-and-business-intelligence/hands-big-data-modeling
- *Practical Data Analysis – Second Edition* by *Hector Cuesta, Dr. Sampath Kumar:* https://www.packtpub.com/big-data-and-business-intelligence/practical-data-analysis-second-edition

11
Designing an ELK Stack

Designing an **Elastic Stack** that performs to the required specifications needs special attention. Each of the components, **Elasticsearch, Logstash, and Kibana** (**ELK**), have specific requirements. Correct sizing is crucial for best performance and functionality.

This chapter goes through the design considerations when deploying an Elastic Stack, taking into consideration the needs of each of the components as well as specific setup details. Throughout this chapter, we will describe how each component is affected by different resources, how we can handle resource constraints, and how to plan and size for different scenarios.

In this chapter, we will go through the following topics:

- Elasticsearch CPU sizing requirements
- How memory sizing affects Elasticsearch performance
- How data is stored within Elasticsearch and how to size for performance
- Requirements for Logstash and Kibana

Technical requirements

Although the documentation found at `https://www.elastic.co/guide/en/elasticsearch/guide/current/hardware.html` is outdated, the hardware requirements can be used as a starting point for CPU sizing. For more useful documentation, visit the following links:

- **Setup guide for indexing speed:** `https://www.elastic.co/guide/en/elasticsearch/reference/current/tune-for-indexing-speed.html`
- **Changing heap configuration for Elasticsearch:** `https://www.elastic.co/guide/en/elasticsearch/reference/current/heap-size.html`
- **Average system memory latency:** `http://www.crucial.com/usa/en/memory-performance-speed-latency`

- **Elasticsearch system paths:** `https://www.elastic.co/guide/en/elasticsearch/reference/master/path-settings.html`
- **Logstash persistent queues:** `https://www.elastic.co/guide/en/logstash/current/persistent-queues.html`
- **Logstash directory paths:** `https://www.elastic.co/guide/en/logstash/current/dir-layout.html`

Elasticsearch CPU requirements

As with any software, sizing for the right CPU requirements determines the overall application performance and processing time. Having the wrong CPU configuration can lead to an unusable application due to the processing taking too long to complete and making it frustrating for users, not to mention the fact that slow processing times can cause the application to fail altogether.

While Elasticsearch does not rely heavily on the CPU for indexing and searches, several things need to be taken into consideration when designing an Elastic Stack that performs well and returns results in a timely manner.

Although Elastic does not publish hard requirements for CPU, there are a couple of things that can be applied as a rule of thumb.

CPU count

Typically, having more cores is better, and this might be the case for most workloads. Elasticsearch leverages having multiple cores available on the system by scheduling tasks across multiple CPUs; however, it doesn't require large amounts of CPU processing power as most of the operations are performed on files that are already indexed.

Most cloud providers (if you are deploying on the cloud) have increased rates for high CPU count virtual machines, to avoid unnecessary cost, size for a VM type that balances more memory than CPU.

When sizing for sufficient CPU resources, you should allow for some growth without having to change settings midway. For a small setup, something with at least two CPUs should be sufficient. For testing purposes and a small number of indexes/sources, even one CPU should suffice, but performance will suffer, especially if all of the components—Elasticsearch, Logstash, and Kibana—are deployed on the same system.

CPU speed

While there is no hard documentation on the minimum CPU speed (clock speed) requirements, it is somewhat difficult to find a CPU with less than 2 GHz nowadays. This low watermark seems to be about the minimum required for Elasticsearch to avoid problems.

Anything above 2 GHz will perform acceptably, even with a single CPU; this is adequate for testing purposes. For production environments, look for CPU clock speeds above 2 GHz or 2.3 GHz to avoid problems.

CPU performance impact

If an incorrect sizing has been configured when it comes to the CPU, Elasticsearch will mostly suffer in the following three areas:

- Startup time
- Index per second
- Search latency

Startup

During startup, CPU usage might spike as the JVM starts and Elasticsearch reads the data from the cluster. Having a slower CPU configuration will cause Elasticsearch to take longer to start up.

If Elasticsearch nodes are to be constantly restarted, having the right CPU configuration will help to reduce the time it takes to reach an operational state.

Index per second

The CPU configuration directly affects the indexes per second that Elasticsearch is able to handle, as it will run out of cycles once more documents are indexed. Ideally, with multiple cores, Elasticsearch leverages indexing on multiple CPUs, allowing more clients to send data without any metric or event being lost.

Search latency

Performance will probably suffer the most regarding the amount of time it takes for searches to return results. Remember that one of the main features of Elasticsearch is how fast it can retrieve data and display it.

Having an undersized CPU configuration will lead to searches taking longer than expected, which can result in a frustrating user experience.

In the following screenshot, we can see that search latency spikes to almost 80 ms and hovers at around 20 ms:

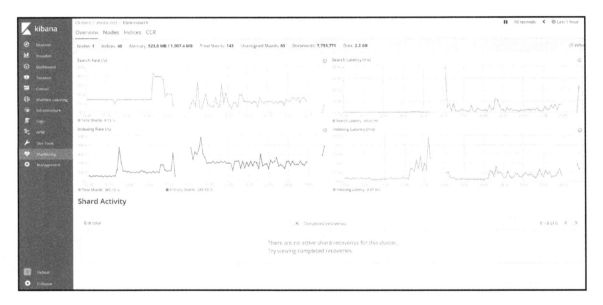

Monitoring latency in Kibana

 Note that the preceding screenshot was taken from an undersized system with just one CPU running at less than 2 GHz. The latency could be worse, but this was taken from a system running on a fast NVMe drive, which can have latency as low as 100 microseconds.

Recommendations

For optimal results, the correct CPU setup needs to be implemented. The following two main scenarios affect CPU sizing:

- Test/development
- Production

Test/dev

For testing, anything above one CPU and 2 GHz would be sufficient for a small test, with a couple of clients sending data to Elasticsearch. The search results might be a little slow to return, but it will work without any problems.

Production

For production, make sure that you use a CPU with at least 2.3 GHz or above. The CPU count does not greatly impact performance, but having at least two CPUs ensures optimal operation. Once more clients are added, the CPU count might need to be modified to meet the extra demand; more Elasticsearch nodes can be added if the CPU becomes a constraint.

Lastly, when choosing between the core count versus clock speeds, Elasticsearch leverages having multiple cores. The performance benefits of fewer but faster cores is not as impressive as having a larger number of slower cores.

> When deploying on Azure, you can use a DS2v3 VM type for a small setup, as it offers two CPUs and enough RAM for basic needs.

Once we correctly size the CPU, we can then focus on how the system memory (RAM) affects Elasticsearch performance and usability.

Memory sizing for Elasticsearch

Allocating enough RAM to Elasticsearch is probably the most important resource factor to consider to avoid problems and an underperforming setup.

Memory is one resource where having a lot of it is never a problem. As an architect, you need to bear in mind several things when sizing memory. Similar to the CPU resource, there is no hard documentation for minimum memory requirements.

Filesystem cache

Having a lot of RAM is always a good idea, because of the filesystem cache or Linux page cache.

The kernel uses free system memory to cache, read, or write requests by allocating some portion of RAM to I/O requests, considerably speeding up searches or indexes in the case of Elasticsearch.

As you can see in the following screenshot, the kernel has allocated about 1.2 GB as page cache:

```
[root@elastic ~]# free -m
              total        used        free      shared  buff/cache   available
Mem:           3790        2461         103           1        1224        1051
Swap:          2047          20        2027
```

Leveraging the use of the page cache can help to reduce the response time when doing searches or incoming indexes; be sure to size for as much RAM as possible. There is a point were cache usage will balance out, and no more RAM will be used for the page cache. At this point, it is worth monitoring the process to try and identify this threshold to avoid running into unnecessary charges. To put it into perspective, if a **Virtual Machine** (**VM**) is sized with 32 GB of RAM, but only uses about 10 GB for the cache and never goes above this number, then it might be worth resizing to a smaller VM, as the remaining RAM will be left unused.

As you can see in the Kibana dashboard in the following screenshot, you can monitor cache usage for Elasticsearch, which might help to identify whether resources are left unused:

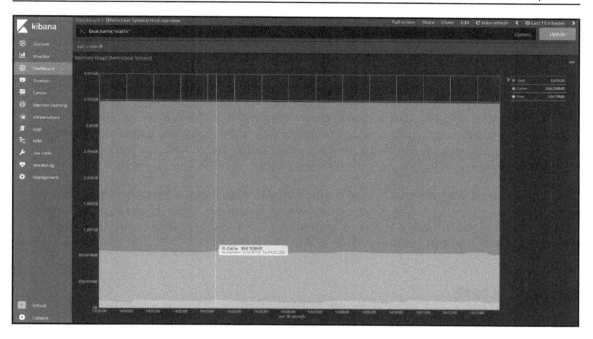

Monitoring cache usage for Elasticsearch

Disable swap

Swap is a mechanism that allows the kernel to move memory pages to disk in the event of infrequent access or when there's memory pressure (that is, when the system is running out of memory). One of the main problems of swapping is that, when a memory page is moved to disk, its access time becomes considerably slower than in RAM.

DDR4 memory has an average transfer rate of about 10 GB/s and, more impressively, an average response time (or latency) of just 13 ns (nanoseconds). Compare that to even the fastest NVMe SSD drives in the market, which can achieve just 3.5 GB/s and latencies of around 400 ūs (microseconds). You can quickly start seeing how this becomes a problem: not all cloud providers or on-premises setups use NVMe drives, and swapping to even slower spinning media can yield pretty bad results.

Because of this, Elasticsearch recommends disabling all forms of swapping and instead relying on the correct sizing for system memory.

Undersizing memory

Having the wrong memory configuration will result in different behaviors. It can be boiled down to two different situations: not having enough memory but having enough to run the system, and not having enough memory to the point that Elasticsearch can't even start.

For the first scenario, where there is a memory constraint, but there is just enough for Elasticsearch to start and run, the main problem would be that there is not enough memory for the page cache, which results in slow searches and reduced indexes per second. In this scenario, Elasticsearch is able to run, but with a reduced overall performance.

The other scenario can be split into two different situations: one where there's not enough memory to start Elasticsearch and the other where Elasticsearch is able to start, but as soon as some indexes are added, it runs out of memory. To avoid a system crash, Linux has a mechanism called **out-of-memory killer** (**OOM killer**).

Unable start

Elasticsearch uses the JVM and, by default, it is set to use a minimum of 1 GB of heap memory. This means that Java needs to allocate at least 1 GB of RAM to JVM, so for Elasticsearch to start with just the minimum, it requires about 2.5 GB of RAM.

The easiest way to tell when this problem is occurring is by verifying the status of the Elasticsearch service using `systemctl status elasticsearch`; it will return an error message similar to the following:

```
[root@elastic ~]# systemctl status elasticsearch -1
● elasticsearch.service - Elasticsearch
   Loaded: loaded (/usr/lib/systemd/system/elasticsearch.service; enabled; vendor preset: disabled)
   Active: failed (Result: exit-code) since Wed 2018-11-21 17:29:05 CST; 2min 42s ago
     Docs: http://www.elastic.co
  Process: 933 ExecStart=/usr/share/elasticsearch/bin/elasticsearch -p ${PID_DIR}/elasticsearch.pid --quiet (code=exited, status=1/FAILURE)
 Main PID: 933 (code=exited, status=1/FAILURE)

Nov 21 17:28:58 elastic systemd[1]: Starting Elasticsearch...
Nov 21 17:29:05 elastic elasticsearch[933]: OpenJDK 64-Bit Server VM warning: INFO: os::commit_memory(0x00000000ca660000, 899284992, 0) fail
ed; error='Cannot allocate memory' (errno=12)
Nov 21 17:29:05 elastic elasticsearch[933]: #
Nov 21 17:29:05 elastic elasticsearch[933]: # There is insufficient memory for the Java Runtime Environment to continue.
Nov 21 17:29:05 elastic elasticsearch[933]: # Native memory allocation (mmap) failed to map 899284992 bytes for committing reserved memory.
Nov 21 17:29:05 elastic elasticsearch[933]: # An error report file with more information is saved as:
Nov 21 17:29:05 elastic elasticsearch[933]: # /var/log/elasticsearch/hs_err_pid933.log
Nov 21 17:29:05 elastic systemd[1]: elasticsearch.service: main process exited, code=exited, status=1/FAILURE
Nov 21 17:29:05 elastic systemd[1]: Unit elasticsearch.service entered failed state.
Nov 21 17:29:05 elastic systemd[1]: elasticsearch.service failed.
```

Upon further inspection of the error log, we can clearly see how JVM failed to allocate the necessary memory, as shown in the following code:

```
# There is insufficient memory for the Java Runtime Environment to
continue.
# Native memory allocation (mmap) failed to map 899284992 bytes for
committing reserved memory.
# Possible reasons:
#    The system is out of physical RAM or swap space
#    In 32 bit mode, the process size limit was hit
# Possible solutions:
#    Reduce memory load on the system
#    Increase physical memory or swap space
#    Check if swap backing store is full
#    Use 64 bit Java on a 64 bit OS
#    Decrease Java heap size (-Xmx/-Xms)
#    Decrease number of Java threads
#    Decrease Java thread stack sizes (-Xss)
#    Set larger code cache with -XX:ReservedCodeCacheSize=
# This output file may be truncated or incomplete.
#
#  Out of Memory Error (os_linux.cpp:2760), pid=933, tid=0x00007f1471c0e700
```

 Testing using the default heap of 1 GB is sufficient. For production, make sure that you increase the heap to at least 2 GB and adjust as necessary.

To increase the heap, edit the /etc/elasticsearch/jvm.options file and find the following options:

```
-Xms1g
-Xmx1g
```

Change these two options to the following:

```
-Xms2g
-Xmx2g
```

 The -Xms2g phrase indicates that Java should have a minimum heap of 2 GB and -Xmx2g indicates the maximum heap of 2 GB.

OOM killer

The **out-of-memory killer** (**OOM killer**) mechanism's main purpose is to avoid a total system crash by killing processes that are running processes. Each process has an `oom_score` value. OOM killer decides which process to kill based on this score; the higher the score, the more likely it is that the process will be killed in the event of memory starvation. This score is calculated based on how much memory the process would free up if it were killed.

If we take the previous scenario as a starting point, were Elasticsearch is able to start with a minimum of 2.5 GB, once more indexes/sources are added to Elasticsearch it will start requiring more and more system memory, up to the point where there is no more memory, and the system is close to a total crash. At that moment, OOM killer jumps in and kills the process (or processes) that consumes the most memory—in our case, Elasticsearch.

When looking at the events under /var/log/messages, we can see how OOM killer kicks in and kills the Java process, and then the Elasticsearch service fails, as shown in the following screenshot:

```
[root@elastic ~]# grep -i "out of memory" /var/log/messages -A4
Nov 21 17:53:20 elastic kernel: Out of memory: Kill process 905 (java) score 576 or sacrifice child
Nov 21 17:53:20 elastic kernel: Killed process 1436 (controller) total-vm:72136kB, anon-rss:648kB, file-rss:0kB, shmem-rss:0kB
Nov 21 17:53:20 elastic kernel: metricbeat invoked oom-killer: gfp_mask=0x201da, order=0, oom_score_adj=0
Nov 21 17:53:20 elastic kernel: metricbeat cpuset=/ mems_allowed=0
Nov 21 17:53:20 elastic kernel: CPU: 1 PID: 917 Comm: metricbeat Kdump: loaded Not tainted 3.10.0-862.14.4.el7.x86_64 #1

Nov 21 17:53:20 elastic kernel: Out of memory: Kill process 905 (java) score 576 or sacrifice child
Nov 21 17:53:20 elastic kernel: Killed process 905 (java) total-vm:6944356kB, anon-rss:1376732kB, file-rss:0kB, shmem-rss:0kB
Nov 21 17:53:20 elastic systemd: elasticsearch.service: main process exited, code=killed, status=9/KILL
Nov 21 17:53:20 elastic systemd: Unit elasticsearch.service entered failed state.
Nov 21 17:53:20 elastic systemd: elasticsearch.service failed.
```

Recommendations

Ideally, enough memory should be allocated for Elasticsearch. The very minimum requirement for memory is about 2.5 GB, but that would lead to a situation where the system might run out of memory quickly.

For testing purposes, 2.5 GB might be enough for a couple of sources/indexes. Performance will undoubtedly suffer, but it will remain somewhat usable.

For production, make sure to have at least 4 GB or more for system memory. This should allow Elasticsearch to start without problems and normally run with multiple sources/indexes configured. Make sure the heap size for the JVM is increased accordingly, and consider allowing some RAM for the page cache for faster response times when interacting with the filesystem.

Next, we will look at the storage configuration required for Elasticsearch.

Storage configuration for Elasticsearch

Storage requirements for Elasticsearch are relatively straightforward, and can be divided into two main categories:

- Storage capacity
- Storage performance

Let's go through both of these and see how decisions made here can affect the overall performance.

Capacity

Storage capacity directly affects how much data Elasticsearch is able to store. As is the case in many other situations, this is a big and complex requirement to consider, as it depends upon so many other variables that affect the utilization of space.

The primary variable would be the size of the logs/metrics that are sent to Elasticsearch. This depends on the number of logs that are generated daily (or monthly). For example, if the daily log rate is 100 MB, then that means that, to be able to store a month's worth of logs, at least 3 GB of available space is needed (100 MB x 30 days = 3 GB).

Note that this is the minimum space required for a single source. Ideally, some overhead should be accounted for as data changes regularly and a figure of 100 MB/day might not be constant for all of the days in the month or other months might have a higher rate due to higher load. Additionally, once more sources (or clients) are added, data usage will grow accordingly.

 By default, Elasticsearch will store its data under the `/var/lib/elasticsearch` directory.

Performance

One of the main features of Elasticsearch is its ability to retrieve data really fast. While this is done using an enhanced mechanism of storing documents as JSON files, having the right performance setup definitely helps achieve the almost real-time search results.

There is no hard number provided by Elastic for storage requirements, but using a **Solid-State Drive** (**SSD**) for the `/var/lib/elasticsearch` directory helps in reducing latency when performing searches, as the SSD has a substantially lower latency when compared to HDD. An SSD also helps when ingesting data as writes get acknowledged faster, thereby allowing for more concurrent incoming indexes. This is reflected in the indexes per second that can be seen on the Kibana monitoring dashboard.

When sizing for the cloud, this really depends on the provider as some base the performance of the disks on their size, but others allow the performance to be manually configured (as is the case with IOPS and throughput).

Having a slower setup will result in searches taking longer than expected and a slower data ingestion, due to an unreliable, slower disk setup.

Considerations

For space, consider a sizing that will allow you enough space for unexpected data growth. If, for example, the expected data usage for an entire month would be 500 GB, consider sizing for at least 700 GB; doing this gives you a buffer and avoids situations where not enough space is left for Elasticsearch indexes. A good starting point is 500 GB, as it gives enough space for testing/production while the actual data usage and data change is calculated (if not previously known).

For performance, consider using faster storage solutions such as SSD to allow for low-latency searches and faster indexes/s. For the cloud, most providers have some sort of SSD offering that can be used with Elasticsearch. Make sure that at least 500 IOPS are provisioned for optimal performance.

 For Azure, you can use a P10 disk—which is an SSD that can provide up to 500 IOPS—or an E10 as a lower cost alternative that delivers the same result.

We will now look at what needs to be considered for Logstash and Kibana.

Logstash and Kibana requirements

There are no specific requirements for Logstash and Kibana, but keeping in mind a couple of things when designing an Elastic Stack is always a good approach.

Logstash

Logstash is not heavy on CPU nor RAM, but this depends entirely on how many sources are feeding Logstash data since, for each event that Logstash parses, there is some overhead required to complete the process. If Logstash is to be installed on its own (with no other components on the same system), anything above one vCPU and 2 GBs of RAM should suffice for small/testing deployments. Ideally, the actual usage should be monitored and the system tuned accordingly. Logstash by default has in-memory queues that are used to store events temporarily; this behavior can be changed to use persistent queues when processing events. This allows for persistent consistency and avoids data loss during an outage. Additionally, having persistent queues helps to absorb bursts of events by acting as a buffer between the clients and Logstash.

When using persistent queues for storage capacity, the `/var/lib/logstash` directory needs to be able to store events while being processed by Logstash. The amount of space depends on two factors: the egress speed when sending data to Elasticsearch and the number of events being sent to Logstash. The minimum would be 1 GB and the space needs to be increased accordingly when the number of sources is increased.

Kibana

The requirements for Kibana depend entirely on the number of users concurrently accessing the dashboard. The amount of resources allocated to Kibana needs to be based on the intended usage—for example, what is the expected user base? How many of those users will access Kibana at the same time?

For small deployments/testing, the minimum requirements are dictated by the JVM. One vCPU and 2 GB of RAM is enough for several users, but once more users start using the dashboard, RAM will be the first resource to become a bottleneck.

In general, an Elastic Stack has pretty loose requirements that are mostly dictated by the usage and the number of sources. Regarding software, the primary requirement is Java; since all of the components use the JVM, either the open JDK or the official JDK can be used.

Summary

In this chapter, we went through the requirements that are needed when designing an Elastic Stack using Elasticsearch, Logstash, and Kibana. For Elasticsearch, we determined that the minimum CPU requirement is two vCPUs for small setups, and the CPU speed should be kept above 2 GHz. If these minimum requirements are not met, Elasticsearch will take longer to start up and will perform more slowly. This manifests as a decrease in the number of indexes per second and an increased search latency, both of which are things that need to be avoided in order for us to be able to take full advantage of the near-instant searches that Elasticsearch provides.

Memory sizing is probably the most important specification when designing an Elasticsearch setup. Part of the system memory will be used for the filesystem cache (also known as the page cache), which helps with searches and indexes per second. Swapping is not recommended, as it is considered extremely slow when compared to actual RAM access, and so swapping should be disabled on Elasticsearch nodes. If the correct memory requirements are not met, Elasticsearch will fail to start altogether since there will not be enough memory for the JVM to start. If, on the other hand, enough memory is present to start the JVM, but the load increases over time and the system runs out of memory, the OOM or out-of-memory killer will be engaged to avoid a system crash that would lead to a failure of the application. The very minimum amount of RAM required is 2.5 GB, but resource constraints will be seen relatively quickly.

Storage capacity and performance play an important role when setting up Elasticsearch. The capacity depends on the amount of data that needs to be kept and the number of sources configured. Latency needs to be kept to a minimum in order for our searches to be fast. Ideally, SSD should be used.

Lastly, for Logstash and Kibana, the minimum requirements are one vCPU and 2 GB of RAM for each component. For Logstash, there is a space requirement for the persistent queues.

In the next chapter, we will jump into deploying an Elastic Stack using Elasticsearch, Logstash, and Kibana using the facts that learned in this chapter.

Questions

1. How many CPUs are recommended for Elasticsearch?
2. What is the recommended minimum CPU speed for Elasticsearch?
3. How does having the wrong CPU configuration impact Elasticsearch performance?
4. What is a page cache?
5. Why is it recommended that you disable swapping on Elasticsearch nodes?
6. How does undersizing memory affect Elasticsearch?
7. What is the minimum memory required for Elasticsearch?
8. Where does Elasticsearch store data by default?
9. Why is using an SSD recommended for Elasticsearch?
10. What are the minimum requirements for Logstash?
11. What are persistent queues?
12. What affects the resource usage in Kibana?

Further reading

For more information, you can read the following book:

- *Linux: Powerful Server Administration,* **by Uday R. Sawant, Et al.**: https://www.packtpub.com/networking-and-servers/linux-powerful-server-administration

12
Using Elasticsearch, Logstash, and Kibana to Manage Logs

Deploying **Elasticsearch**, **Logstash**, and **Kibana** (**ELK Stack**) is relatively straightforward, but there are several considerations that need to be taken into account when installing these components. While this will not be an in-depth guide for an Elastic Stack, the main takeaways will be the implementation aspects, the decisions that are made through the process, and how you, as an architect, should think when making these decisions.

This chapter will help you, as an architect, define the aspects that are needed to deploy an ELK Stack, and what configurations to use when working with the components that make up the Elastic Stack.

In this chapter, we will go through the following topics:

- Installing and configuring Elasticsearch
- Installing and configuring Logstash and Kibana
- Installing and explaining Beats
- Configuring Kibana dashboards

Technical requirements

The following tools and installations will be used in this chapter:

- **Elasticsearch installation guide**: https://www.elastic.co/guide/en/elasticsearch/reference/current/_installation.html
- **XFS stripe size and Stripe unit "how to"**: http://xfs.org/index.php/XFS_FAQ#Q:_How_to_calculate_the_correct_sunit.2Cswidth_values_for_optimal_performance

- **XFS write barriers**: https://access.redhat.com/documentation/en-us/red_hat_enterprise_linux/7/html/storage_administration_guide/writebarrieronoff
- **Elasticsearch configuration details**: https://www.elastic.co/guide/en/elasticsearch/reference/current/settings.html
- **Avoiding a split brain in Elasticsearch**: https://www.elastic.co/guide/en/elasticsearch/reference/current/modules-node.html#split-brain
- **Elasticsearch cluster state API**: https://www.elastic.co/guide/en/elasticsearch/reference/current/cluster-state.html
- **Logstash installation guide**: https://www.elastic.co/guide/en/logstash/current/installing-logstash.html
- **Kibana user guide and how to install**: https://www.elastic.co/guide/en/kibana/current/rpm.html
- **Logstash filter example for Beats modules**: https://www.elastic.co/guide/en/logstash/current/logstash-config-for-filebeat-modules.html
- **Structure of a Logstash config file**: https://www.elastic.co/guide/en/logstash/current/configuration-file-structure.html
- **Filebeat installation process**: https://www.elastic.co/guide/en/beats/filebeat/current/filebeat-installation.html
- **Metricbeat installation overview and details**: https://www.elastic.co/guide/en/beats/metricbeat/current/metricbeat-installation.html

Deployment overview

For this deployment, we will be using Elasticsearch version 6.5 (which is the latest version at the time of writing). This means that all subsequent components must be the same version. The base OS will be CentOS 7.6. While this specific deployment will be implemented on a local **virtual machine** (**VM**) setup, the concepts can still be applied to the cloud.

Elasticsearch will be deployed using 2 nodes on 2 vCPU VMs with 4 GB of RAM each (in Chapter 11, *Designing an ELK Stack*, we established that the minimum RAM required is about 2.5 GB). The underlying storage for the VMs is **non-volatile memory express** (**NVMe**), so some considerations need to be taken when replicating the setup somewhere else. In terms of space, the Elasticsearch nodes will have 64 GB of disk space each; the nodes will have the 64 GB disk mounted to the /var/lib/elasticsearch directory.

Logstash and Kibana will be deployed on the same VM using 2 vCPUs and 4 GB of RAM. As seen in `Chapter 11`, *Designing an ELK Stack*, Logstash has a requirement for persistent storage for queues. So, for this, we will be using a 32 GB dedicated disk. This disk will be mounted on the `/var/lib/logstash` directory for persistent queuing.

We can summarize what will be used for the deployment as follows:

- The base OS is CentOS 7.6
- Elasticsearch v6.5
- Logstash v6.5
- Kibana v6.5
- Elasticsearch using 2 nodes on 2 vCPU VMs with 4 GB of RAM
- Logstash and Kibana on a single VM using 2 vCPUs with 4 GB of RAM
- 64 GB disks for the Elasticsearch nodes
- 32 GB disk for the Logstash persistent queue

The following diagram illustrates the entire implementation and will give you an idea of how things are connected:

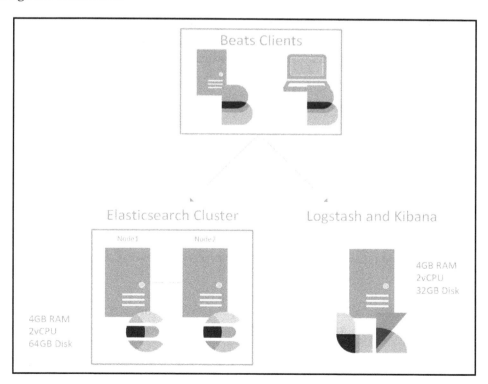

Installing Elasticsearch

Going from nothing to a functional Elasticsearch setup requires the software to be installed; this can be done in several ways and on different platforms. Some of these installation options are as follows:

- Installing from the source
- Installing `deb` for Debian-based Linux Distributions
- Installing `rpm` for **Red Hat Enterprise Linux** (**RHEL**), CentOS, **sound library for embedded systems** (**SLES**), OpenSLES, and RPM-based distributions
- Installing `msi` for Windows
- Deploying Docker images

For this setup, we will be using the RPM repository for consistency across versions, and for simplification purposes when updates are available.

The RPM repository

To install the RPM repository for RHEL and CentOS, we need to create a file in the `/etc/yum.repos.d` directory. Here, the name of the file doesn't matter but, in reality, it needs to be meaningful. The contents of the file indicate how `yum` will go and search for software.

Create a file named `/etc/yum.repos.d/elastic.repo` with the following code details:

```
[elasticsearch-6.x]
name=Elasticsearch repository for 6.x packages
baseurl=https://artifacts.elastic.co/packages/6.x/yum
gpgcheck=1
gpgkey=https://artifacts.elastic.co/GPG-KEY-elasticsearch
enabled=1
autorefresh=1
type=rpm-md
```

Once the repository file has been created, simply run the following command:

```
yum makecache
```

This will refresh the metadata of all of the configured repositories. Before installing Elasticsearch, we need to install the OpenJDK version, `1.8.0`; for this, we can run the following command:

```
yum install java-1.8.0-openjdk
```

Next, confirm that `java` is installed, as follows:

`java -version`

Then, you should see something similar to the following output:

```
[root@elastic1 ~]# java -version
openjdk version "1.8.0_191"
OpenJDK Runtime Environment (build 1.8.0_191-b12)
OpenJDK 64-Bit Server VM (build 25.191-b12, mixed mode)
```

We can then proceed to install `elasticsearch`, as follows:

`yum install elasticsearch`

 Before starting Elasticsearch, some configuration needs to be done.

The Elasticsearch data directory

The default configuration for Elasticsearch has the data directory set to the `/var/lib/elasticsearch` path. This is controlled through the `path.data` configuration option in the `/etc/elasticsearch/elasticsearch.yml` file:

```
# --------------------------------Paths--------------------------------
#
# Path to directory where to store the data (separate multiple locations by
comma):
#
path.data: /var/lib/elasticsearch
```

In this setup, a 64 GB disk will be mounted to this location.

 When deploying in Azure, make sure that the `path.data` option is configured to use a data disk rather than the OS disk.

Partitioning the disk

Before creating a filesystem, the disk needs to be partitioned. To do this, we can use the `parted` utility.

First, we need to initialize the disk as `gpt`; for this, we can use the following command:

```
sudo parted /dev/sdX mklabel gpt
```

Then, we create the partition:

```
sudo parted /dev/sdX mkpart xfs 0GB 64GB
```

Here, we're telling `parted` to create a partition from 0GB to 64GB, or from the beginning of the disk to the end. Additionally, we're using an `xfs` signature, since that is the filesystem that is going to be used for the data directory.

Finally, we verify that the partition has been successfully created with the correct boundaries by running the following command:

```
sudo parted /dev/sdX print
```

The output should be similar to the following code block:

```
[root@elastic1 ~]# parted /dev/sdb print
Model: ATA VBOX HARDDISK (scsi)
Disk /dev/sdb: 68.7GB
Sector size (logical/physical): 512B/512B
Partition Table: gpt
Disk Flags:
Number  Start End     Size    File system  Name Flags
1       1049kB  64.0GB 64.0GB               xfs
```

Formatting the filesystem

To be able to store data on the newly created partition, we first need to create a filesystem. For this setup, we will be using the XFS filesystem.

To format the disk, run the `mkfs.xfs` command, as follows:

```
[root@elastic1]# mkfs.xfs /dev/sdb1
meta-data=/dev/sdb1              isize=512    agcount=4, agsize=3906176
blks
         =                      sectsz=512   attr=2, projid32bit=1
         =                      crc=1        finobt=0, sparse=0
data     =                      bsize=4096   blocks=15624704, imaxpct=25
         =                      sunit=0      swidth=0 blks
naming   =version 2             bsize=4096   ascii-ci=0 ftype=1
log      =internal log          bsize=4096   blocks=7629, version=2
         =                      sectsz=512   sunit=0 blks, lazy-count=1
realtime =none                  extsz=4096   blocks=0, rtextents=0
```

By default, XFS uses a 4K block size that matches the memory page size; this is also ideal for relatively small files.

 Note that the partition of the device file is specified rather than the entire disk. While it is possible to use the disk itself, it is recommended that you create filesystems on partitions. Additionally, if the filesystem is going to be used on a RAID setup, then changing the stripe unit and stripe size generally helps with performance.

Persistent mounting using fstab

Now that the filesystem has been created, we need to make sure that it is mounted after every reboot at the correct location.

As a general rule, mounting the filesystem using the device file is not advised, especially in the cloud. This is because the disk order might change, causing the device file of the disks to be mixed up. To work around this problem, we can use the UUID of the disk, which is a unique identifier that will persist even when the disk is moved to another system.

To obtain the UUID of the disk, run the `blkid` command:

```
[root@elastic1 ~]# blkid
/dev/sda1: UUID="58c91edb-c361-470e-9805-a31efd85a472" TYPE="xfs"
/dev/sda2: UUID="H3KcJ3-gZOS-URMD-CD1J-8wIn-f7v9-mwkTWn" TYPE="LVM2_member"
/dev/sdb1: UUID="561fc663-0b63-4d2a-821e-12b6caf1115e" TYPE="xfs"
PARTLABEL="xfs" PARTUUID="7924e72d-15bd-447d-9104-388dd0ea4eb0"
```

In this case, `/dev/sdb1` is the 64 GB disk that we will be using for Elasticsearch. With the UUID, we can add it to the `/etc/fstab` file, which controls the filesystems that will be mounted during boot time. Simply edit the file and add the following entries:

```
UUID=561fc663-0b63-4d2a-821e-12b6caf1115e          /var/lib/elasticsearch  xfs
defaults,nobarrier,noatime,nofail       0  0
```

Here are some important details to take note of from the preceding command:

* `nobarrier`: This helps with write performance as it disables the mechanism used by XFS to acknowledge writes once they hit persistent storage. This is usually used on physical storage systems where there is no form of battery backup write cache.

- `noatime`: This disables the recording mechanism when a file is accessed or modified. When `atime` is enabled, every read will result in a small set of writes, since the access times will need to be updated. Disabling can help with reads as it doesn't generate any unnecessary writes.
- `nofail`: This allows the system to boot normally in the event of the disk that is backing the mount point going missing. This is particularly helpful when deploying on the cloud were no access to the console exists.

Next, verify that the disk has been mounted to the correct location before starting the Elasticsearch service:

```
[root@elastic1 /]# df -h
Filesystem                   Size  Used Avail Use% Mounted on
/dev/mapper/centos-root      14G   1.6G  12G   12% /
devtmpfs                     1.9G  0    1.9G  0%  /dev
tmpfs                        1.9G  0    1.9G  0%  /dev/shm
tmpfs                        1.9G  8.5M 1.9G  1%  /run
tmpfs                        1.9G  0    1.9G  0%  /sys/fs/cgroup
/dev/sdb1                    60G   33M   60G   1%  /var/lib/elasticsearch
/dev/sda1                    1014M 184M  831M  19% /boot
tmpfs                        379M  0    379M  0%  /run/user/0
```

Finally, make sure that the correct ownership of the `/var/lib/elasticsearch` directory is configured:

```
chown elasticsearch: /var/lib/elasticsearch
```

Configuring Elasticsearch

Before starting the Elasticsearch service, we need to define several parameters that control how Elasticsearch behaves. The configuration file is in the YAML format and is located on `/etc/elasticsearch/elasticsearch.yml`. Let's explore which main parameters need to be changed.

Elasticsearch YAML

The central control for Elasticsearch is done through the `/etc/elasticsearch/elasticsearch.yml` file, which is in the YAML format. The default configuration file is reasonably well-documented and explains what each parameter controls, but there are some entries that should be changed as part of the configuration process.

The main parameters to look for are as follows:

- Cluster name
- Discovery settings
- Node name
- Network host
- Path settings

Cluster name

Elasticsearch nodes will only be able to join a cluster when they have the same cluster name specified in their configuration. This is handled through the `cluster.name` parameter; for this setup, we will use `elastic-cluster`:

```
# -------------------------------Cluster---------------------------
#
# Use a descriptive name for your cluster:
#
cluster.name: elastic-cluster
#
```

This setting should be configured on both nodes so that they have the same value. Otherwise, the second node will not be able to join the cluster.

Discovery settings

The discovery parameters control how Elasticsearch manages intra-node communication that is used for clustering and master election.

The two main parameters regarding discovery are `discovery.zen.ping.unicast.hosts` and `discovery.zen.minimum_master_nodes`.

The `discovery.zen.ping.unicast.hosts` setting controls which nodes are going to be used for clustering. Since two nodes will be used in our setup, the configuration for `node1` should have the DNS name of `node2`, while `node2` should have the DNS of `node1`.

The `discovery.zen.minimum_master_nodes` setting controls the minimum number of master nodes in the cluster; this is used to avoid split-brain scenarios where there's more than one master node that is active in the cluster. The number for this parameter can be calculated based on a simple equation, as follows:

$$\left(\frac{N}{2}\right) + 1$$

Here, N is the number of nodes in the cluster. For this setup, since only 2 nodes are to be configured, the setting should be 2. Both parameters should be as follows:

```
# ---------------------------Discovery---------------------------
#
# Pass an initial list of hosts to perform discovery when new node is
started:
# The default list of hosts is ["127.0.0.1", "[::1]"]
#
discovery.zen.ping.unicast.hosts: ["elastic2"]
#
# Prevent the "split brain" by configuring the majority of nodes (total
number of master-eligible nodes / 2 + 1):
#
discovery.zen.minimum_master_nodes: 2
#
# For more information, consult the zen discovery module documentation.
```

For node2, change `discovery.zen.ping.unicast.hosts:` `["elastic2"]` to `discovery.zen.ping.unicast.hosts:` `["elastic1"]`.

Node name

By default, Elasticsearch uses a randomly-generated UUID for its node name, which is not very user-friendly. This parameter is relatively simple as it controls the name for the specific node. For this setup, we'll be using `elasticX`, where `X` is the node number; `node1` should be as follows:

```
#---------------------------Node---------------------------
#
# Use a descriptive name for the node:
#
node.name: elastic1
```

Change `node2` to match the naming convention, so it is `elastic2`.

Network host

This controls which IP address Elasticsearch will bind to and listen to requests. By default, it binds to the loopback IP address; this setting needs to be changed to allow other nodes from a cluster or allow Kibana and Logstash on other servers to send requests. This setting also accepts special parameters, such as the network interface. For this setup, we'll have Elasticsearch listen to all the addresses by setting the `network.host` parameter to `0.0.0.0`.

On both nodes, make sure that the setting is as follows:

```
#---------------------------Network---------------------------
#
# Set the bind address to a specific IP (IPv4 or IPv6):
#
network.host: 0.0.0.0
```

Path settings

Finally, the path parameters control where Elasticsearch stores its data and its logs.

By default, it is configured to store data under `/var/lib/elasticsearch`, and logs under `/var/log/elasticsearch`:

```
#----------------------------Paths----------------------------
#
# Path to directory where to store the data (separate multiple locations by
comma):
#
path.data: /var/lib/elasticsearch
#
# Path to log files:
#
path.logs: /var/log/elasticsearch
```

One crucial aspect of this parameter is that, under the `path.data` setting, multiple paths can be specified. Elasticsearch will use all the paths specified here to store data, thus increasing the overall performance and available space. For this setup, we'll leave the defaults as they were in the preceding steps, where we mounted a data disk under the `/var/lib/elasticsearch` directory.

Starting Elasticsearch

Now that we've configured Elasticsearch, we need to make sure that the service starts automatically and correctly during boot.

Start and enable the Elasticsearch service, as follows:

```
systemctl start elasticsearch && systemctl enable elasticsearch
```

Then, verify that Elasticsearch started correctly by running the following command:

```
curl -X GET "elastic1:9200"
```

The output should be similar to the following code block:

```
[root@elastic1 /]# curl -X GET "elastic1:9200"
{
  "name" : "elastic1",
  "cluster_name" : "elastic-cluster",
  "cluster_uuid" : "pIH5Z0yAQoeEGXcDuyEKQA",
  "version" : {
    "number" : "6.5.3",
    "build_flavor" : "default",
    "build_type" : "rpm",
    "build_hash" : "159a78a",
    "build_date" : "2018-12-06T20:11:28.826501Z",
    "build_snapshot" : false,
    "lucene_version" : "7.5.0",
    "minimum_wire_compatibility_version" : "5.6.0",
    "minimum_index_compatibility_version" : "5.0.0"
  },
  "tagline" : "You Know, for Search"
}
```

Adding an Elasticsearch node

At this point, we can add the second node to the Elasticsearch cluster.

The same configuration should be applied to the previous steps, making sure that the settings are changed to reflect the DNS name for node2.

To add the node to the cluster, all we need to do is simply start the Elasticsearch service.

When the service starts, messages are logged to /var/log/elasticsearch, which indicates that the node was successfully added to the cluster:

```
[2018-12-23T01:39:03,834][INFO ][o.e.c.s.ClusterApplierService] [elastic2]
detected_master
{elastic1}{XVaIWexSQROVVxYuSYIVXA}{fgpqeUmBRVuXzvlf0TM8sA}{192.168.1.150}{1
92.168.1.150:9300}{ml.machine_memory=3973599232, ml.max_open_jobs=20,
xpack.installed=true, ml.enabled=true}, added
{{elastic1}{XVaIWexSQROVVxYuSYIVXA}{fgpqeUmBRVuXzvlf0TM8sA}{192.168.1.150}{
192.168.1.150:9300}{ml.machine_memory=3973599232, ml.max_open_jobs=20,
xpack.installed=true, ml.enabled=true},}, reason: apply cluster state (from
master [master
{elastic1}{XVaIWexSQROVVxYuSYIVXA}{fgpqeUmBRVuXzvlf0TM8sA}{192.168.1.150}{1
92.168.1.150:9300}{ml.machine_memory=3973599232, ml.max_open_jobs=20,
xpack.installed=true, ml.enabled=true} committed version [1]])
```

You can use the following code to confirm that the cluster is up and running:

```
curl -X GET "elastic1:9200/_cluster/state?human&pretty"
```

The output should be similar to the following code block:

```
{
  "cluster_name" : "elastic-cluster",
  "compressed_size" : "10kb",
  "compressed_size_in_bytes" : 10271,
  "cluster_uuid" : "pIH5Z0yAQoeEGXcDuyEKQA",
  "version" : 24,
  "state_uuid" : "k6WuQsnKTECeRHFpHDPKVQ",
  "master_node" : "XVaIWexSQROVVxYuSYIVXA",
  "blocks" : { },
  "nodes" : {
    "XVaIWexSQROVVxYuSYIVXA" : {
      "name" : "elastic1",
      "ephemeral_id" : "fgpqeUmBRVuXzvlf0TM8sA",
      "transport_address" : "192.168.1.150:9300",
      "attributes" : {
        "ml.machine_memory" : "3973599232",
        "xpack.installed" : "true",
        "ml.max_open_jobs" : "20",
        "ml.enabled" : "true"
      }
    },
```

```
      "ncVAbF9kTnOB5K9pUhsvZQ" : {
        "name" : "elastic2",
        "ephemeral_id" : "GyAq8EkiQGqG9Ph-0RbSkg",
        "transport_address" : "192.168.1.151:9300",
        "attributes" : {
          "ml.machine_memory" : "3973599232",
          "ml.max_open_jobs" : "20",
          "xpack.installed" : "true",
          "ml.enabled" : "true"
        }
      }
    },
    "metadata" : {
...(truncated)
```

For any subsequent nodes that need to be added to the cluster, the previous steps should be followed, making sure that the `cluster.name` parameter is set to the correct value.

Installing Logstash and Kibana

With the Elasticsearch cluster up and running, we can now go ahead and install Logstash and Kibana.

The repository that was used in the previous steps is the same for the remaining components. So, the same process that was used before to add the repository should be applied to the Logstash and Kibana node.

This is a summary, the same process has been explored before:

1. Add the repository to `/etc/yum.repos.d/elastic.repo`
2. Update the `yum` cache to `sudo yum makecache`
3. Install Logstash and Kibana using `sudo yum install logstash kibana`
4. Initialize the disk for `/var/lib/logstash` and `sudo parted /dev/sdX mklabel gpt`
5. Create the `sudo parted /dev/sdX mkpart xfs 0GB 32GB` partition (note that this is a 32 GB disk)
6. Create the `sudo mkfs.xfs /dev/sdX1` filesystem
7. Update `fstab`
8. Update the `sudo chown logstash: /var/lib/logstash` directory permissions

The Logstash `systemd` unit is not added by default; to do so, run the script provided by Logstash:

```
sudo /usr/share/logstash/bin/system-install
```

Finally, one specific component that is required is a coordinating Elasticsearch node. This will serve as a load balancer for the Elasticsearch cluster that is used by Kibana to install Elasticsearch:

```
sudo yum install elasticsearch
```

More information on the coordinating node configuration is provided in the *Configuring Kibana* section.

Configuring Logstash

Similar to Elasticsearch, the main configuration file for Logstash is located under `/etc/logstash/logstash.yml`, and some settings will need to be changed to achieve the desired functionality.

Logstash YAML

First, the `node.name` parameter should be adjusted so that it identifies the Logstash node correctly. By default, it uses the machine's hostname as the `node.name` parameter. However, since we are running both Logstash and Kibana on the same system, it is worth changing this setting to avoid confusion.

Next, we need to consider the queuing settings; these control how Logstash manages the type of queues and where it stores queue data.

The first setting is `queue.type`, which defines the type of queue that is used by Logstash. For this setup, we are using persistent queuing:

```
# ------------ Queuing Settings --------------
#
# Internal queuing model, "memory" for legacy in-memory based queuing and
# "persisted" for disk-based acked queueing. Defaults is memory
#
queue.type: persisted
#
```

Since queuing is set to persistent, the events need to be stored in a temporary location before being sent to Elasticsearch; this is controlled by the `path.queue` parameter:

```
# If using queue.type: persisted, the directory path where the data files
will be stored.
# Default is path.data/queue
#
# path.queue:
#
```

If left by default, Logstash will use the `path.data/queue` directory to store events in the queue. The `path.data` directory defaults to `/var/lib/logstash`, which is where we configured the 32 GB disk; this is the desired configuration. If another location needs to be specified for queuing, this setting should be adjusted to match the correct path.

The last setting to be changed in the `logstash.yml` file is the `queue.max_bytes` setting, which controls the maximum space that is allowed for the queue. For this setup, since we added a dedicated 32 GB disk for only this purpose, the setting can be changed to 25 GB to allow for a buffer if more space is needed. The setting should look as follows:

```
# If using queue.type: persisted, the total capacity of the queue in number
of bytes.
# If you would like more unacked events to be buffered in Logstash, you can
increase the
# capacity using this setting. Please make sure your disk drive has
capacity greater than
# the size specified here. If both max_bytes and max_events are specified,
Logstash will pick
# whichever criteria is reached first
# Default is 1024mb or 1gb
#
queue.max_bytes: 25gb
```

As an option, the `xpack.monitoring.enabled` setting can be set to true to enable monitoring through Kibana.

 Make sure that the parameters in the `yaml` file don't have a space at the beginning of the line or it might fail to load the configuration.

Logstash pipelines

Logstash outputs are controlled by the pipelines that are configured through files placed under /etc/logstash/conf.d/; these files control how Logstash ingests data, processes it, and then returns it as an output for Elasticsearch. A pipeline configuration is similar to the following code:

```
# The # character at the beginning of a line indicates a comment. Use
 # comments to describe your configuration.
 input {
 }
 # The filter part of this file is commented out to indicate that it is
 # optional.
 # filter {
 #
 # }
 output {
 }
```

Here, the input section defines which data to accept and from which source; in this setup, we will be using beats as an input. The filter section controls how data is transformed before being sent to the output, and the output section defines where the data is sent. In this case, we will be sending data to the Elasticsearch nodes.

Let's create a configuration file for syslog messages to be filtered by Logstash, and then be sent to the Elasticsearch cluster. The file needs to be placed in /etc/logstash/conf.d, since the input will be from the beats module; let's call it the beats-syslog.conf file:

sudo vim /etc/logstash/conf.d/beats-syslog.conf

The file's contents is as follows:

```
input {
  beats {
    port => 5044
  }
}
filter {
  if [fileset][module] == "system" {
    if [fileset][name] == "auth" {
      grok {
        match => { "message" =>
["%{SYSLOGTIMESTAMP:[system][auth][timestamp]}
%{SYSLOGHOST:[system][auth][hostname]}
sshd(?:\[%{POSINT:[system][auth][pid]}\])?:
%{DATA:[system][auth][ssh][event]} %{DATA:[system][auth][ssh][method]} for
(invalid user )?%{DATA:[system][auth][user]} from
```

```
%{IPORHOST:[system][auth][ssh][ip]} port
%{NUMBER:[system][auth][ssh][port]} ssh2(:
%{GREEDYDATA:[system][auth][ssh][signature]})?",
                "%{SYSLOGTIMESTAMP:[system][auth][timestamp]}
%{SYSLOGHOST:[system][auth][hostname]}
sshd(?:\[%{POSINT:[system][auth][pid]}\])?:
%{DATA:[system][auth][ssh][event]} user %{DATA:[system][auth][user]} from
%{IPORHOST:[system][auth][ssh][ip]}",
                "%{SYSLOGTIMESTAMP:[system][auth][timestamp]}
%{SYSLOGHOST:[system][auth][hostname]}
sshd(?:\[%{POSINT:[system][auth][pid]}\])?: Did not receive identification
string from %{IPORHOST:[system][auth][ssh][dropped_ip]}",
                "%{SYSLOGTIMESTAMP:[system][auth][timestamp]}
%{SYSLOGHOST:[system][auth][hostname]}
sudo(?:\[%{POSINT:[system][auth][pid]}\])?: \s*%{DATA:[system][auth][user]}
:( %{DATA:[system][auth][sudo][error]} ;)?
TTY=%{DATA:[system][auth][sudo][tty]} ;
PWD=%{DATA:[system][auth][sudo][pwd]} ;
USER=%{DATA:[system][auth][sudo][user]} ;
COMMAND=%{GREEDYDATA:[system][auth][sudo][command]}",
                "%{SYSLOGTIMESTAMP:[system][auth][timestamp]}
%{SYSLOGHOST:[system][auth][hostname]}
groupadd(?:\[%{POSINT:[system][auth][pid]}\])?: new group:
name=%{DATA:system.auth.groupadd.name},
GID=%{NUMBER:system.auth.groupadd.gid}",
                "%{SYSLOGTIMESTAMP:[system][auth][timestamp]}
%{SYSLOGHOST:[system][auth][hostname]}
useradd(?:\[%{POSINT:[system][auth][pid]}\])?: new user:
name=%{DATA:[system][auth][user][add][name]},
UID=%{NUMBER:[system][auth][user][add][uid]},
GID=%{NUMBER:[system][auth][user][add][gid]},
home=%{DATA:[system][auth][user][add][home]},
shell=%{DATA:[system][auth][user][add][shell]}$",
                "%{SYSLOGTIMESTAMP:[system][auth][timestamp]}
%{SYSLOGHOST:[system][auth][hostname]}
%{DATA:[system][auth][program]}(?:\[%{POSINT:[system][auth][pid]}\])?:
%{GREEDYMULTILINE:[system][auth][message]}"] }
        pattern_definitions => {
           "GREEDYMULTILINE"=> "(.|\n)*"
         }
         remove_field => "message"
      }
      date {
        match => [ "[system][auth][timestamp]", "MMM  d HH:mm:ss", "MMM dd
HH:mm:ss" ]
       }
      geoip {
        source => "[system][auth][ssh][ip]"
```

```
            target => "[system][auth][ssh][geoip]"
        }
    }
    else if [fileset][name] == "syslog" {
        grok {
            match => { "message" =>
["%{SYSLOGTIMESTAMP:[system][syslog][timestamp]}
%{SYSLOGHOST:[system][syslog][hostname]}
%{DATA:[system][syslog][program]}(?:\[%{POSINT:[system][syslog][pid]}\])?:
%{GREEDYMULTILINE:[system][syslog][message]}"] }
            pattern_definitions => { "GREEDYMULTILINE" => "(.|\n)*" }
            remove_field => "message"
        }
        date {
            match => [ "[system][syslog][timestamp]", "MMM  d HH:mm:ss", "MMM
dd HH:mm:ss" ]
        }
    }
    }
}
output {
    elasticsearch {
        hosts => ["elastic1", "elastic2"]
        manage_template => false
        index => "%{[@metadata][beat]}-%{[@metadata][version]}-%{+YYYY.MM.dd}"
    }
}
```

Make sure that the output section has the DNS names or IPs of the Elasticsearch nodes:

```
output {
 elasticsearch {
    hosts => ["elastic1", "elastic2"]
    manage_template => false
    index => "%{[@metadata][beat]}-%{[@metadata][version]}-%{+YYYY.MM.dd}"
 }
}
```

In this pipeline configuration, the beats module sends logs to the Logstash node. Then Logstash will process the data and load balance the output between the Elasticsearch nodes. We can now go ahead and configure Kibana.

Configuring Kibana

The last piece of the Elastic Stack is Kibana; the configuration is handled by `/etc/kibana/kibana.yml` in a similar way to Elasticsearch and Logstash.

Kibana YAML

By default, Kibana listens on port `5601`; this is controlled by the `server.port` parameter, which can be changed if there's a need to access Kibana on a different port. For this setup, the default will be used.

The `server.host` setting controls which addresses Kibana will listen to for requests. Since access is needed from external sources (that is, other than `localhost`), we can use the following setting:

```
# Specifies the address to which the Kibana server will bind. IP addresses
and host names are both valid values.
 # The default is 'localhost', which usually means remote machines will not
be able to connect.
 # To allow connections from remote users, set this parameter to a non-
loopback address.
 server.host: "0.0.0.0"
```

The `server.name` parameter defaults to the hostname where Kibana runs, but since Logstash is running alongside Kibana, we can change this to identify the Kibana part:

```
# The Kibana server's name.  This is used for display purposes.
server.name: "kibana"
```

Finally, `elasticsearch.url` specifies which Elasticsearch node Kibana will connect to. As we mentioned previously, we will be using an Elasticsearch coordinate node to act as a load balancer between the other two nodes.

Here is the URL of the Elasticsearch instance to use for all your queries:

```
elasticsearch.url: "http://localhost:9200"
```

The coordinating node

A coordinating node is an Elasticsearch node that does not accept inputs, does not store data, nor does it take part in master or slave elections.

The goal of this node is to load balance requests for Kibana between the different Elasticsearch nodes on the cluster. The process of installing is the same as the one we used before, that is making sure that Java (open JDK) is also installed.

The configuration will be different as we want to achieve a number of things:

- Disable the master node role
- Disable the ingest node role
- Disable the data node role
- Disable cross-cluster search

To do this, we need the following settings on the `/etc/elasticsearch/elasticsearch.yml` file:

```
cluster.name: elastic-cluster
node.name: coordinate
network.host: 0.0.0.0
node.master: false
node.data: false
node.ingest: false
cluster.remote.connect: false
discovery.zen.ping.unicast.hosts: ["elastic1", "elastic2"]
```

Starting Logstash and Kibana

With all of the components already configured, we can start Logstash, Kibana, and the coordinating Elasticsearch node.

Logstash can be started first as it doesn't require any of the other components to be up:

```
sudo systemctl start logstash && sudo systemctl enable logstash
```

Then, we can start and enable the `elasticsearch` coordinating node:

```
sudo systemctl start elasticsearch && sudo systemctl enable elasticsearch
```

Last but not least, `kibana` can go through the same procedure:

```
sudo systemctl start kibana && sudo systemctl enable kibana
```

To verify it all started correctly, point your browser to the `kibana` address on port `5601` `http://kibana:5601`. Click on **Monitoring,** and then click on **Enable** monitoring; after a couple of seconds, you will see something similar to the following screenshot:

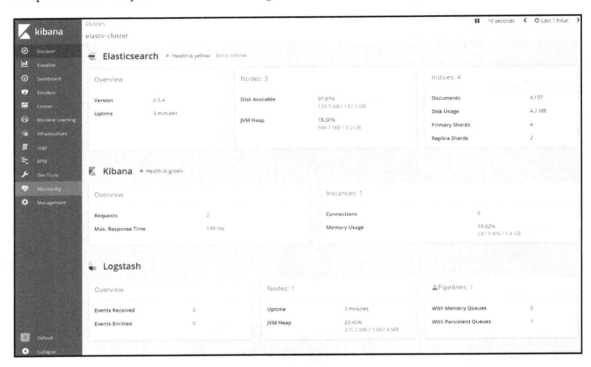

You should see all the components online; the **yellow** status is due to system indexes that are not replicated, but this is normal.

With this, the cluster is up and running and ready to accept incoming data from logs and metrics. We will be feeding data to the cluster using Beats, which we'll explore in the next section.

What are Beats?

Beats are the lightweight data shippers from Elastic.co (the company behind Elasticsearch). Beats are designed to be easy to configure and run.

Beats are the client part of the equation, living on the systems that are to be monitored. Beats capture metrics, logs, and more from servers across the environment and ship them to either Logstash for further processing or Elasticsearch for indexing and analysis.

There are multiple official Beats (which are developed and maintained by Elastic), and a multitude of open source Beats have been developed by the community.

The main Beats that we'll be using for this setup are **Filebeat** and **Metricbeat**.

Filebeat

The Filebeat function collects logs from sources (such as syslog, Apache, and Nginx), and then ships these to Elasticsearch or Logstash.

The Filebeat client needs to be installed in each of the servers that require data collection in order to be enabled. This component allows the logs to be sent to a centralized location for seamless search and indexing.

Metricbeat

Metricbeat collects metrics, such as CPU usage, memory usage, disk IO statistics, and network statistics, and then ships them to either Elasticsearch or Logstash.

There's really no need to transform metric data further, so feeding data directly to Elasticsearch makes more sense.

Metricbeat should be installed in all systems that require monitoring of resource usage; having Metricbeat installed on the Elasticsearch nodes allows you to keep a closer control on resource usage to avoid problems.

Other Beats exist, such as the following:

- **Packetbeat**: For network traffic monitoring
- **Journalbeat**: For `systemd` journal logs
- **Auditbeat**: For audit data such as logins

Additionally, Beats can be further adapted to suit a specific need through the use of modules. As an example, Metricbeat has a module to collect MySQL performance statistics.

Let's not skip a beat – installing Beats

The installation of the Beats provided by Elasticsearch can be done through the Elastic repository that was previously used to install Elasticsearch, Logstash, and Kibana.

First, let's install Filebeat on one of the Elasticsearch nodes:

```
sudo yum install -y filebeat
```

Once installed, confirm that it has completed by running the following code:

```
filebeat version
```

The output should be similar to the following command block:

```
[root@elastic1 ~]# filebeat version
filebeat version 6.5.4 (amd64), libbeat 6.5.4
[bd8922f1c7e93d12b07e0b3f7d349e17107f7826 built 2018-12-17 20:22:29 +0000
UTC]
```

To install `metricbeat`, the process is the same as it lives in the same repository:

```
sudo yum install metricbeat
```

To install Beats on other clients, simply add the Elastic repository as we previously explained and install it through `yum`. Beats are also provided as standalone packages in case there is no repository available for the distribution.

Configuring Beats clients

With both Filebeat and Metricbeat installed on one of the Elasticsearch nodes, we can go ahead and configure them to feed data to both Logstash and Elasticsearch.

Filebeat YAML

Now, it is no surprise that most of the Elastic components are configured through YAML files. Filebeat is no exception to that norm, and its configuration is handled by the `/etc/filebeat/filebeat.yml` file.

First, we need to tell `filebeat` where to look for the log files that are to be shipped to Logstash. In the `yaml` file, this is in the `filebeat.inputs` section; change `enabled: false` to `enabled: true`, as follows:

```
#========================= Filebeat inputs ===============================
filebeat.inputs:
# Each - is an input. Most options can be set at the input level, so
# you can use different inputs for various configurations.
# Below are the input specific configurations.
- type: log
  # Change to true to enable this input configuration.
  enabled: true
  # Paths that should be crawled and fetched. Glob based paths.
  paths:
    - /var/log/*.log
```

Filebeat comes embedded with Kibana dashboards for easy visualization of the data that's sent. This allows Filebeat to load the dashboards and then add the Kibana address to the `setup.kibana` section:

```
#==============================Kibana==================================
# Starting with Beats version 6.0.0, the dashboards are loaded via the
Kibana API.
# This requires a Kibana endpoint configuration.
setup.kibana:
  # Kibana Host
  # Scheme and port can be left out and will be set to the default (http and
5601)
  # In case you specify and additional path, the scheme is required:
http://localhost:5601/path
# IPv6 addresses should always be defined as: https://[2001:db8::1]:5601
  host: "kibana:5601"
```

Load the `dashboards`, as follows:

```
filebeat setup --dashboards
```

This configuration needs to be done only once for each new Beat installation; there is no need to change this setting on further Filebeat installations as the dashboards are already loaded.

Since we are going to be sending data to Logstash, comment out the `output.elasticsearch` section; then, uncomment the `output.logstash` section and add Logstash's details:

```
#---------------------- Elasticsearch output ----------------------------
#output.elasticsearch:
  # Array of hosts to connect to.
  # hosts: ["localhost:9200"]
  # Optional protocol and basic auth credentials.
  #protocol: "https"
  #username: "elastic"
  #password: "changeme"
#------------------------- Logstash output ------------------------------
output.logstash:
  # The Logstash hosts
  hosts: ["logstash:5044"]
```

Next, we'll be using the system module for Filebeat to send the output to Logstash; to enable this, simply run the following command:

```
filebeat modules enable system
```

Then, load the index template into `elasticsearch`, as follows:

```
filebeat setup --template -E output.logstash.enabled=false -E
'output.elasticsearch.hosts=["elastic1:9200", "elastic2"]'
```

Finally, start and enable `filebeat`, as follows:

```
sudo systemctl enable filebeat && sudo systemctl start filebeat
```

To verify that data is being sent, we can use one of the provided dashboards to visualize `syslog` events. On Kibana, go to **Dashboard** and type `Syslog Dashboard` into the search bar; you will see something similar to the following screenshot:

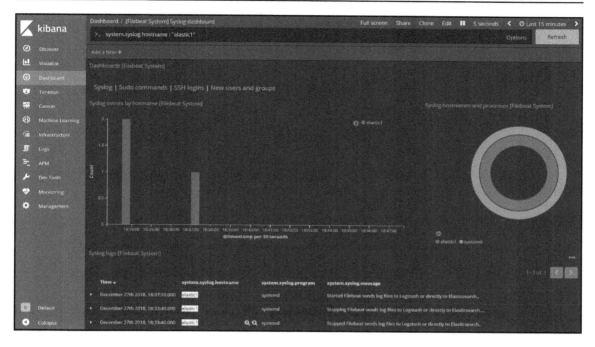

Kibana Dashboard showing search results for Syslog Dashboard

Metricbeat YAML

Metricbeat follows a similar process to Filebeat, where the `/etc/metricbeat/metricbeat.yml` file needs to edited to send output to Elasticsearch, and the Kibana dashboards need to be loaded (that is, they need to be run once).

To do this, edit the `metricbeat.yml` file to allow Metricbeat to load the Kibana dashboards:

```
setup.kibana:
  host: "kibana:5601"
```

Next, specify the `Elasticsearch` cluster:

```
#----------------------- Elasticsearch output ----------------------------
output.elasticsearch:
 # Array of hosts to connect to.
 hosts: ["elastic1:9200", "elastic2:9200"]
```

Load the Kibana `dashboards`, as follows:

```
metricbeat setup --dashboards
```

By default, `metricbeat` has the system module enabled, which will capture statistics for CPU, system load, memory, and network.

Start and enable the `metricbeat` service, as follows:

```
sudo systemctl enable metricbeat && sudo systemctl start metricbeat
```

To confirm that data is being sent to the cluster, go to **Discover** on the **kibana** screen; then, select the **metricbeat-*** index pattern and verify that events are being sent:

Events filtered with the metricbeat-* index pattern

Next steps

At this point, the cluster is now fully functional. All that is left is to install Metricbeat and Filebeat onto the other nodes of the cluster to ensure full visibility of the cluster's health and resource usage.

Adding more clients to the cluster is a matter of installing the appropriate Beat, depending on what needs to be monitored and which logs need to be indexed.

If load increases on the cluster, a number of options are available—either adding more nodes to the cluster to load balance requests or increasing the number of available resources for each of the nodes. In certain scenarios, simply adding more resources is a more cost-effective solution as it doesn't require a new node to be configured.

An implementation such as this one can be used to monitor the performance and events of a Kubernetes setup (such as the one described in `Chapter 11`, *Designing an ELK Stack*). Some of the Beats have specific modules that are used to extract data from Kubernetes clusters.

Finally, one enhancement that can be made to this setup to ease configuration and maintenance is to have the Beat clients point to the coordinating Elasticsearch node to act as a load balancer between the nodes; this avoids having to hardcode each of the Elasticsearch nodes in the output configuration for the Beats—only a single address is needed.

Summary

In this chapter, we went through many steps to configure an Elastic Stack, which is a collection of four main components—Elasticsearch, Logstash, Kibana, and Beats. For the setup, we used three VMs; we hosted two Elasticsearch nodes, and then, on a single system, we installed Logstash and Kibana, using version 6.5 for each of the components. We installed Elasticsearch using the RPM repository provided by Elastic Stack; `yum` was used to install the required packages. Elasticsearch configuration was done using the `elasticsearch.yml` file, which controls how `elasticsearch` behaves. We defined a number of settings that are required for a functional cluster, such as the `cluster.name` parameter and `discovery.zen.minimum_master_nodes`.

We added a new Elasticsearch node by configuring the cluster name and the discovery settings, which allows the node to join the cluster automatically. Then, we moved onto installing Kibana and Logstash, which are provided on the same RPM repository that was used for Elasticsearch; configuring Logstash and Kibana was done through their respective `.yml` files.

Once all three main components were up, and the operation was ready to accept incoming data, we moved onto installing Beats, which are the data shippers that are used by Elasticsearch and Logstash to ingest data. For logs and events, we used Filebeat, and for system metrics such as memory usage and CPU, we used Metricbeat.

In the next chapter, we will learn about the challenges of systems management and Salt's architecture.

Questions

1. How can Elasticsearch be installed?
2. How do you partition a disk?
3. How can you persistently mount a filesystem?
4. Which file controls Elasticsearch configuration?
5. What does the `cluster.name` setting do?
6. What is the recommended number of nodes in an Elasticsearch cluster?
7. How can an Elasticsearch node be added to an existing cluster?
8. What process is needed to install Logstash and Kibana?
9. What is persistent queuing?
10. What is a coordinating node?
11. What are Beats?
12. What is Filebeat used for?

Further reading

- *Fundamentals of Linux* **by Oliver Pelz**: `https://www.packtpub.com/networking-and-servers/fundamentals-linux`

Section 4: System Management Using Saltstack

4

In this section, the reader will be able to understand how **Infrastructure as Code (IaC)** works and the advantages of using Saltstack for systems management. Then an overview of some of the best practices for design.

The section contains the following chapters:

13
Solving Management Problems with Salty Solutions

In this chapter, we will discover and discuss why a business needs to have a centralized management utility for its infrastructure, including the high level of complexity that a heterogeneous environment brings to the table. We will be talking about solutions to this and things such as the following:

- How new technologies bring complexity to our business
- How we can centralize system management.
- How **infrastructure as code (IaC)** help us to maintain our system's state
- Tools that leverage IaC
- The SaltStack platform and its components

Let's begin our journey through system management.

Centralizing system management

Understanding the reason behind system management can be easily taken for granted. We often assume that just because a business has a big IT infrastructure, it needs a solution to manage its inventory. While this is obviously true, there is more to it than that. Our job as architects consists of listening to our customers' problems and understanding what exactly they are looking for.

New technologies and system management

In this ever-evolving IT world, changes come fast. New technologies come out almost every day. Technologies such as virtualization, IoT, and the cloud are shaping and changing the way we use IT by growing our infrastructures exponentially, which the bare-metal era never saw.

All these changes and exponential growth means that IT managers have a lot more to manage and far less time to train their staff to support these technologies, so many businesses can barely keep up with the pace. This can result in them becoming reluctant to adopt new technologies. But many have no choice but to adopt them for fear of becoming irrelevant and not being able to satisfy the demands of their customers. If their competitors have the advantage and deliver a better and faster service, they will likely go out of business.

Companies want to adopt these technologies as soon as possible, to gain an edge over their competitors, but new technologies often come with big learning curves. During this time, IT staff need to learn how to manage and maintain new systems, resulting in keeping critical systems and workloads available becoming a challenge. Not complying with our SLAs becomes a real threat; imagine a situation where a developer needs the operations team to apply a library patch to our dev environment systems in order to test a new release, and because our operations staff (or at least half of them) are in training, developers are tempted to bypass the standardized change-request process and apply the update themselves. Shadow IT in this type of situation is really common, and we need to avoid it at all costs. Shadow IT can make our company non-compliant with regulatory standards.

While IT leaders push to adopt new technologies, they are often left with very small and declining budgets to do this type of transformation. This also directly affects our critical systems and workloads because investment in system management declines and moves toward innovation. Moving toward innovation is not a bad thing, because it will eventually enable us to provide a better service, but it is important to understand that it also has consequences regarding the maintenance of our existing environments.

With new technology comes new infrastructure; mixed environments become more common every day, and it is crucial to understand how to manage these mixed environments in the best and most efficient way possible.

Recovering control of our own infrastructure

Having control of our infrastructure is the main goal of system management. But what does it mean to have control? Inventory listing, version control, automated patching, and software distribution are all part of system management. All of them are part of a bigger picture where IT regains control of its infrastructure and can ensure compliance and standardization across their systems no matter what Linux distribution they are running.

Often our systems are separated; this separation is because they might differ in their characteristics. We can have systems with Red Hat Enterprise Linux-based distributions or Debian-based distributions, systems that have different architectures such as x86, power servers, or even ARM. All these systems might not even talk to one another or serve the same purpose; all of them become silos that IT has to maintain and manage.

Imagine performing all the different tasks that systems' management is about on each separate silo by hand without a tool to centralize and automate the tasks. Human error is the most direct threat to this type of scenario, followed by the large complexity, time, and cost that an IT business has to incur to train its staff, hire staff, and buy specific administration tools for each different system type.

Centralized tools to disperse problems

Centralized configuration management can help us to control changes to systems in a controlled, consistent, and stable way. It is perfect for systems that are running a cluster or configured for high availability, as all the nodes across the cluster have to have the exact same configuration. With configuration management, we can also understand the reason behind permissions on certain files, a package installed on all the systems, or even a line of code in a configuration file.

These changes or configurations that we implement through a configuration management tool can also be rolled back, as most tools available in the market come with version control, and any typo, human error, or incompatible update can easily be rolled back.

As we slowly transition into cloud environments, virtual machines and resources become more and more a commodity and a service. Configuration management tools that can help us manage, provision, and maintain our cloud infrastructure become very valuable assets. With these types of tool, we can treat our infrastructure in a more elastic way, and define it in a descriptive way, in the sense that we can have templates that deploy the same infrastructure or implement changes based on a definition; this is what we call **infrastructure as code (IaC)**.

Coding for a desired state

The whole idea behind IaC is to have consistency and versioning within our environment. IaC seeks a more descriptive and standard way of provisioning resources, by avoiding unique and special deployments to prevent the situation in which recreating an environment is highly complex because of the uniqueness of each of its components.

IaC tools define configurations via a specific language or via existing languages such as YAML or JSON; in the following, we can see an example extract from a Terraform template that defines virtual machines in Microsoft Azure:

```
resource "azurerm_resource_group" "test" {
 name = "example"
 location = "East US 2"
}

resource "azurerm_kubernetes_cluster" "test" {
 name = "exampleaks"
 location = "${azurerm_resource_group.test.location}"
 resource_group_name = "${azurerm_resource_group.test.name}"
 dns_prefix = "acctestagent1"

 agent_pool_profile {
 name = "default"
 count = 1
 vm_size = "Standard_B1_ls"
 os_type = "Linux"
 os_disk_size_gb = 30
 }

 service_principal {
 client_id = "00000000-0000-0000-0000-000000000000"
 client_secret = "00000000000000000000000000000000"
 }

 tags = {
 Environment = "Production"
 }
}

output "client_certificate" {
 value = "${azurerm_kubernetes_cluster.test.kube_config}"
}

output "kube_config" {
 value = "${azurerm_kubernetes_cluster}"
}
```

In the world of cloud infrastructures, elasticity is key. Now we don't have existing resources provisioned on our datacenters waiting to be used. In the cloud, we pay for what we use and having VMs or storage sitting there increasing our monthly bill is not ideal. With IaC, we can scale up or scale down those environments on demand. For example, we know that we have an application that is at its peak consumption only during business hours and requires extra instances to support the load. But out of business hours, a single instance is enough to support the load. With IaC, we can have a script to create extra instances in the morning and lower the instances at the end of the day. Each instance is not unique and we can take advantage of configuration management tools that use descriptive files via IaC to achieve this.

There are several tools that can accomplish the afore mentioned example, but many tools don't just provision infrastructure in the cloud or in virtualized environments. Other configuration management tools do even more than that; they can push configuration files, install packages, create users, or even filesystems. There are several ways and methods in which these tools perform their configurations. Many tools require an agent, but a few others are agentless.

The way in which configuration management tools perform their changes is essentially via a **push** or a **pull**. This will depend (but not always) on whether the tool uses an agent or is agentless. Most agentless tools push the configuration changes you declare in IaC files and send the changes to either an API in the cloud or via SSH when you execute the tool via a command line or a script.

On the other hand, a pull is almost always through an agent. The agent is constantly consulting the configuration management server for definitions, verifying the desired state in case something was changed to pull those changes from the server and apply them to its host.

Pushes and pulls can be applied in two different ways: in a declarative way and in an imperative way. The declarative way specifies what the desired state is, and the changes are applied as they are defined in the IaC specification file. The imperative way consists of running a set of instructions or commands in a specific order to tell the system how to reach the desired state.

Some open source tools available for configuration management via IaC are as follows:

- Puppet
- Chef
- Ansible

- Terraform
- Salt
- Vagrant

We will be taking an in-depth look at Salt and its components in the `Chapter 14`, *Getting Your Hands Salty.*

Understanding NaCl

We learned about what IaC is, and the difficulties behind systems management. But as architects of future solutions, we need to know and understand which tools can help our customers face the challenges that configuration management brings to the table.

In this section, we will be talking about how we can use **Salt**, or **The SaltStack Platform** as it is also known, to help us achieve a centralized, agile, and elastic management infrastructure.

Introducing Salt

Salt is an open source project developed in Python and was created by Tomas S Hatch, back in 2011. Originally, it wasn't intended to be a configuration management tool, but rather a data collection tool and a remote command execution software that leveraged the `ZeroMQ` library. Later the same year, configuration management functionalities were added via states, which we will review later.

Due to the fact that Salt is written in Python, it is highly extensible and modular, and can easily write customized modules to extend its functionality even further.

It is crucial to understand that Salt is not just a configuration management tool, but in these chapters, we will be focusing on its configuration management capabilities due to the nature of the subject at hand. In the *Further reading* section, I will be adding several other book recommendations if you want to learn more about other Salt functionalities.

The ways you define desired states in Salt, or in other words the languages that Salt supports, are varied. The main and default language is YAML with support for `Jinja` templating.

An example of a YAML definition to create a new user can be as follows:

```
doge:
  user.present:
```

```
- fullname: much doge
- shell: /bin/bash
- home: /home/doge
```

YAML is a data-render language for Salt; data renders take definitions in the file and then transform them into Python data structures for Salt to consume.

The following are some other data-render languages that Salt supports:

- dson
- hjson
- json5
- json
- pydsl
- pyobjects
- py
- stateconf
- yamlex

Salt has two types of renders. The first one is the one we just talked about: data-renders. The second one is the text render, which is the category Jinja falls into. This **text renders** instead of returning a Python data structure, they return text instead, which is later translated for the data render.

Text renders are useful for setting up variables or loops if we need to repeat several definitions with different values but the same structure. For example, instead of creating a YAML for each user, we could create a Jinja template and create several users with the same file, as follows:

```
{% for user in [dsala, eflores, elilu] %}
{{ user }}:
user.present:
    - home: /home/{{ user }}
    - shell: /bin/bash
```

The preceding example will create three users instead of creating one user by file or definition. This way is more efficient because we not only save time and work by not typing the same definition over and over again, we can also easily add more users if needed in the array, without having to create an entirely new file or definition for the extra user.

Besides `Jinja`, Salt text-renders support other templating engines, such as the following :

- Cheetah
- Genshi
- GPG
- Jinja
- Mako
- NaCl
- Pass
- Py
- Wempy

We will be focusing on `Jinja` and YAML for the rest of the chapters.

The SaltStack platform

We previously talked about the different methods and approaches that IaC has. Salt is perfect for us to understand all of them because Salt uses both push and pull methods and also both **declarative** and **imperative** approaches.

Let's take an overview of Salt's basic functionality:

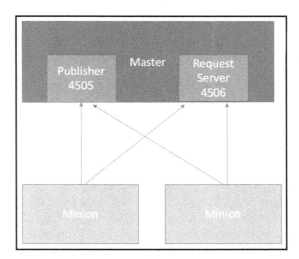

Like any other client/server cluster, Salt consists of two basic types of node:

- **Master**: This server, or group of servers, is in charge of coordinating the minions and where they query for their desired states. Masters are also the ones that send the commands to be executed on minions.
- **Minion**: Servers managed by the master.

The master server listens from two TCP ports: `4505` and `4506`. Both ports have very different roles and very different connection types.

The `4505` port or **Publisher** is where all minions listen for messages from the master. The `4506` port or the **Request Server** is where minions request specific files or data directed directly through them through a secure way. Salt's network transport utilizes the ZeroMQ messaging queuing system, which uses **Elliptic Curve Cryptography** with 4,096-bit RSA keys that are generated in both the master and minions, as we will see later in this chapter.

Salt is an agent-based tool and all communication between masters and minions is possible through the agent that is installed on the minions. Minions are in charge of initiating communications with the masters.

This matters because, in a segmented network that might or might not have the internet in between, you will have many security boundaries between your masters and minions, and every minion may not have a unique address defined to it. In a scenario where the masters initiate the communications, all your minions in the stack might have to have a public IP address, or a lot of networking configuration and **network address translation** (**NAT**) has to be implemented every time you add a minion to be managed.

Because of the way Salt communications work, you can have your masters in a DMZ zone with publicly addressable IP addresses, and all your minions connecting to those IPs. You will always have fewer masters than minions, and therefore the network configuration that needs to be implemented will decrease significantly. Salt is a highly scalable platform, where some stacks contain thousands of minions; imagine having to configure the network so that three or four masters can reach thousands of minions.

Having masters with public IPs can be scary, but remember that as long as you verify the RSA key fingerprints, you can be certain that all communications between the nodes are secured thanks to ZeroMQ's cryptography mechanisms.

Salt capabilities

After a brief overview of Salt's architecture, it is time to go through its different functionalities and capabilities.

Remote command execution modules

Remember that we said that Salt uses both push and pull methods alongside declarative and imperative approaches. The remote command execution feature is how we leverage Salt's push method in an imperative way.

If you need to run a command in multiple minions or specific minions remotely, you will be using **execution modules**. Let's take a look at a simple example:

```
dsala@master1:~$ salt '*'  cmd.run 'ls /home'
minion-1:
    jdoe
    dev1
master:
    dsala
    eflores
```

The previous command pushed an `ls` to the minions that are registered to the master. Let's take a closer look at the commands:

- `salt`: This is Salt's most basic command to execute commands in parallel on remote minions.
- `'*'`: Indicates that we will be running the command on all servers that are managed by our masters; you can also define specific targets.
- `cmd.run`: The execution module to be invoked.
- `'ls /home'`: The parameters of the execution module.
- **Output**: Ordered by the minion's name followed by the output of that server.

Execution modules are the most basic form in which Salt uses its remote execution framework. Do you remember that Salt is written in Python? Well, execution modules are actually Python modules with a set of functions that serve a common purpose. Salt comes with several prebuilt modules that you can use, and you can even write your own modules and add them to your SaltStack platform. All execution modules are supposed to be distribution agnostic, but you can run into some that are not available in some distributions. Windows-specific modules are mostly defined by a starting `win_` at the beginning of the function.

In our previous example, we used the `cmd` module with the `run` function. The format in which we work with a function from a module involves defining the module to import followed by a period and the function. Whenever a function is called, Salt proceeds in the following way:

1. The Publisher port (4505) from the master in which the command was executed sends the command to the specified targets.
2. The targeted minions evaluate the command and decide whether they have to run the command.
3. Minions that ran the command format the output and send it to the master's request server port (4506).

Knowing what execution modules are will not be enough for us to know what we have at our disposal. Many predefined modules are the ones most commonly used, and it's worth taking a look at them and what their main functions are.

The sys module

This module is the equivalent of the `man` command. With `sys`, we can consult, list, and even check which argument accepts each function. You will find yourself using mostly the following functions of the `sys` module:

- `list_modules`: This function will list the modules available to the target minion. It is important to note that execution modules are executed on the minions themselves and not in the master from where the command was executed.
- `list_functions`: With `list_functions`, you can list the available functions for a certain module.
- `argspec`: Lists available arguments and default values for the desired function.

Now we can run one of the preceding functions of the `sys` module to see a real example:

```
dsala@master1:~$ sudo salt 'minion1' sys.argspec pkg.install
minion1:
    ----------
    pkg.install:
        ----------
        args:
            - name
            - refresh
            - fromrepo
            - skip_verify
            - debconf
            - pkgs
```

```
            - sources
            - reinstall
            - ignore_epoch
        defaults:
            - None
            - False
            - None
            - False
            - None
            - None
            - None
            - False
            - False
        kwargs:
            True
        varargs:
            None
```

The pkg module

Now that we have used a `pkg` function as an example for the `sys` module, I want to talk about the `pkg` module. This is another of the most common and used modules that Salt offers. This module handles all related package tasks, from installing and upgrading to deleting packages. As Salt tries to be as distro-agnostic as possible, the `pkg` module actually invokes a set of different modules and functions under the hood, specific to the distribution in which the module was invoked. For example, if a `pkg.install` was targeting Ubuntu-based systems when the minions receive the message, in reality the `aptpkg` module is the one that is going to be called in the minion. This is why `pkg` is called a **virtual module**.

Some different modules invoked by `pkg` are the following:

- `aptpkg`: For Debian distributions with `apt-get` package management.
- `brew`: For macOS with Homebrew package management.
- `yumpkg`: Red Hat-based distributions with `yum` or `dnf` as package managers.
- `zypper`: For SUSE-based distributions with `zypper` as the package manager.

The following is an example of installing the `nginx` web server with `pkg`:

```
dsala@master1:~$ sudo salt 'minion1' pkg.install nginx
minion1:
        ----------
        nginx:
        ----------
    new:
```

```
        1.15.10
old:
```

The test module

Last, but not least, I want to talk to you about the **test module**. The test module will allow us to test our SaltStack platform. Things such as checking the health status of minions, the Salt version that they are running, and even just making them send an echo, are possible with the test module.

Different functions of the test module can be found with the `sys.list_functions` function, but it is worth mentioning some of the most common ones that you might use very frequently:

- **ping**: The ping function tests for a response from the minions; this is not an ICMP ping command.
- **version**: Returns Salt's version of your minions.
- **versions_information**: Returns a full list of all of Salt's dependencies, kernel version, distribution version, and Salt version.

Salt states

Now that we know about the remote execution framework, we can start exploring the rest of the systems that Salt has to offer. The remote execution framework is the basis of something called the **state system**. The state system is a declarative and idempotent way that leverages IaC files to configure a minion's desired state. The state system utilizes state modules that are much like execution modules but with the difference that Salt states actually check whether the desired configuration is already present in the minion. For example, let's take a look at the following state definition:

```
dsala@master:/srv/salt/httpd $ cat httpd.sls
    httpd_package:
        pkg.installed:
            - name: httpd
```

The preceding state will install the `httpd` (Apache) package in targeted servers at runtime but only if the package is not present. If the package is not present, the state module will invoke the local `pkg.install` execution function and install the package in the minion(s).

Take a look at the fact that we `cat` that file from a `/srv/salt` directory. This directory is the default location of Salt's state directory tree where state definitions are placed. This directory is where you will be creating folders containing formulas, which are a set of Salt states that contain all the necessary configurations to deploy an application. For example, we can not only install `httpd`, we can also configure the virtual hosts and download the Git repos containing the actual websites that will be running on that Apache web server.

There is a set of rules that the directory tree follows for you to invoke state modules and run formulas, but this will be a subject for the `Chapter 14`, *Getting Your Hands Salty*, where we will delve into configurations and actual usage.

Grains of Salt

We have learned that you can run execution modules by defining the minion name or via * when running on all minions. But running Salt states and execution modules on all the minions in the stack, or on individual minions, is less than ideal when you have hundreds or even thousands of minions being managed by your masters.

Here is where Salt introduces the `grains` interface, which allows us to identify minions by specific characteristics or even set our own type of label or role to a group of minions that share a same purpose or characteristics, so we can perform more targeted configuration management.

We can leverage the `grains` interface with the same syntax in which we would execute any command in Salt:

```
dsala@master:~$ salt "minion1" grains.items
```

With the preceding command, we list all the different hardware and software characteristics of the system that we targeted. In the output, we can see things such as the operating system family, the system architecture, and even the hypervisor that we are using to run the VM.

This will help us to create state definitions targeting specific systems via something called a `top` file, which we will discuss in the `Chapter 14`, *Getting Your Hands Salty*. An example of a Salt state top file definition using `grains` and targeting all `Debian` family VMs will look like this:

```
base:
    'os_family:Debian:
        - match: grain
      - httpd
```

As mentioned before, we can also create custom `grains` in our minions to define roles and tag our minions with unique value pairs. This is useful for grouping minions in specific tasks; for example, all the VMs of the QA team can be tagged with a key value pair, `departement: qa`, for example. Another way of grouping could be by role, such as `appfoo: frontend`, and so on. There are many ways to use grain targeting, and all will depend on how we want to administer or push and maintain the desired states.

Salt pillars

With **grains**, we can target specific minions, but at the end, we defined those targeting policies that are in the top files, which form part of a formula. Formulas are usually stored in Git repositories and sometimes even in public ones. That's why we can't, or rather we shouldn't, declare sensitive information in Salt states. The same happens with Dockerfiles as we saw in our previous chapters, and Kubernetes solves this with the **Secrets** API object. Salt has its own version of secrets and it's called **Pillars**.

Unlike grains, pillars are stored in the masters instead of the minions. Only minions that are targeted by the pillar will have access to the information in the pillar. This, again, makes it perfect for sensitive information. When storing sensitive information, pillars can also be encrypted at rest, and thanks to Salt's render system, pillars will be decrypted during pillar compilation.

Pillars decreases the surface area of sensitive data by only storing it in the master:

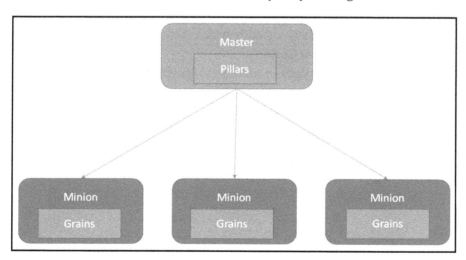

With Salt pillars, we finish our brief overview of the basic components that the SaltStack platform has to offer. We will be discussing them in more depth and working with real-life examples in Chapter 14, *Getting Your Hands Salty*, so you can get hands-on and start managing systems through Salt.

Summary

In this chapter, we covered the different problems that businesses face when it comes to maintaining their infrastructures. We went through different technologies such as IaC and centralized system management. We went through the different methods whereby IaC **pushes** or **pulls** changes into managed systems and learned about several applications that leverage IaC.

We also discussed what Salt is and its different components that help us achieve a centralized managed infrastructure.

In the next chapter, we will learn how to design a Salt solution and install the software.

Questions

1. What is systems management?
2. What are the challenges behind systems' management?
3. What applications can help us with system management?
4. What is Infrastructure as Code?
5. What are the different types of method with which we can manage our systems?
6. What is Salt?
7. What are Salt's different components?

Further reading

- **Gartner**: 'Every budget is an IT budget'
- **Forrester:** https://www.forrester.com/report/Cloud+Investments+Will+Reconfigure+Future+IT+Budgets/-/E-RES83041#
- **Declarative vs. Imperative Models for Configuration Management**: https://www.upguard.com/blog/articles/declarative-vs.-imperative-models-for-configuration-management
- **SALTSTACK**: https://s.saltstack.com/beyond-configuration-management/
- **Salt Configuration Management**: https://red45.wordpress.com/2011/05/29/salt-configuration-management/
- **Renderers**: https://docs.saltstack.com/en/latest/ref/renderers/
- **Remote Execution**: https://docs.saltstack.com/en/getstarted/system/execution.html
- **Targeting using grains**: https://docs.saltstack.com/en/latest/topics/targeting/grains.html
- **Grains**: https://docs.saltstack.com/en/latest/topics/grains/
- **Functions**: https://docs.saltstack.com/en/getstarted/config/functions.html

Getting Your Hands Salty

14

After going through the basic concepts of **Salt**, we will finally in this chapter get hands-on with Salt. We will have the chance to work on a real-life scenario and to design and install proof-of-concept infrastructure for our potential customer. We will do such things as the following:

- Provisioning cloud infrastructure via Terraform
- Installing and configuring Salt masters
- Installing and configuring minions
- Creating states and formulas for minions
- Provisioning a load balancer via Salt

After performing these tasks, you should have the basic knowledge and hands-on experience to start learning Salt more in depth.

Hands-on with Salt

We have learned about the different Salt components and capabilities that the software has, and how it can help us to achieve control of our infrastructure. But we haven't used any of the components to actually maintain any system or even install Salt. So, let's get our hands dirty with Salt and start making use of our newly acquired knowledge.

Before starting, we are going to set up a scenario to make more sense of what we will be doing in this chapter, and it will be related to a real-life scenario.

Scenario

You have been hired by Mr. Don High to design the system's management platform for his company. He wants to run his web server workloads on Azure **Virtual Machines (VMs)**, with an **Infrastructure as a Service (IaaS)** model.

His setup is fairly simple: he wants to have two virtual machines running a website written in Node.js in front of an nginx load balancer to route the traffic into the website's VMs. All of his infrastructure has to be managed via a configuration management solution, in a way that, every time they provision a new VM, the application is loaded alongside any configuration that might be needed for their website to run.

One more thing that he mentioned to you is that the company's staff haven't deployed any resources in Azure, and that they would like to see how **Infrastructure as Code** (**IaC**) works for deployments in the cloud, so that their developers are able to use it in the future.

Terraforming our initial infrastructure

We mentioned **Terraform** in the previous chapter, and we want to take advantage of the fact that our client is asking us to deploy his infrastructure via an IaC software, so this is the perfect chance to use this great tool.

We will briefly explain each step before executing it, but if you would like to find out more, we will suggest more books in the *Further reading* section that talk more in depth about Terraform.

Setting up Terraform

We will assume that you will be executing the following steps from a Unix-like workstation. Installing Terraform is fairly simple. Terraform is only a binary that can be downloaded from the terraform.io website.

> https://www.terraform.io/downloads.html

In my case, I will be using a macOS Terminal to install Terraform:

```
                                              ✔  2481   K8sAzureCNI/default  ⚙  18:40:15 ⊘
└ wget https://releases.hashicorp.com/terraform/0.11.13/terraform_0.11.13_darwin_amd64.zip -O terraform.zip
--2019-04-07 18:42:46--  https://releases.hashicorp.com/terraform/0.11.13/terraform_0.11.13_darwin_amd64.zip
Resolving releases.hashicorp.com (releases.hashicorp.com)... 151.101.5.183
Connecting to releases.hashicorp.com (releases.hashicorp.com)|151.101.5.183|:443... connected.
HTTP request sent, awaiting response... 200 OK
Length: 22547753 (22M) [application/zip]
Saving to: 'terraform.zip'

terraform.zip         100%[===================================================>]  21.50M   763KB/s    in 24s

2019-04-07 18:43:11 (902 KB/s) - 'terraform.zip' saved [22547753/22547753]
```

Once downloaded, you can go ahead and unzip the binary in a directory part of your path:

Check the Terraform version by running `terraform version`:

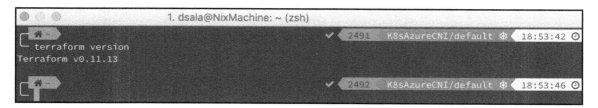

Once Terraform has been installed, we require the Azure CLI to be installed to configure access to the customer's Azure subscription. You can find the steps to install the Azure CLI and set up the subscription in our *Installing Kubernetes* chapters.

With the Azure CLI installed and your default account set, we can configure Terraform to use the appropriate credentials in order for it to be able to deploy infrastructure.

First, we will create a directory to store our Terraform files:

```
dsala@NixMachine: ~ $ mkdir terrafiles
```

Next, we will create a service principal ID via the Azure CLI, which will be used to authenticate Terraform with our subscription.

Save the subscription ID from the output of this command into a `$SUB_ID` variable:

```
dsala@NixMachine: ~ $ az account show --query "{subscriptionId:id}"

dsala@NixMachine: ~ $ SUB_ID=<subscription id>
```

Now, run the following command to create the service principal:

```
dsala@NixMachine: ~ $ az ad sp create-for-rbac \
--role="Contributor" \
--scopes="/subscriptions/${SUB_ID}"
```

Take note of the returned values of `appId`, `password`, and `tenant` returned from the previous command.

Now, inside the `terrafiles` directory, create a file called `terraform.tfvars`.

 This file is special because Terraform will automatically load by default any file with this name if any is present in the directory when we execute Terraform.

This file should contain the following information:

```
subscription_id = "azure-subscription-id"
tenant_id = "tenant-from-service-principal"
client_id = "appId-from-service-principal"
client_secret = "password-from-service-principal"
```

When you have the file ready, create another file called `az_creds.tf` with the following:

```
variable subscription_id {}
variable tenant_id {}
variable client_id {}
variable client_secret {}

provider "azurerm" {
  subscription_id = "${var.subscription_id}"
  tenant_id = "${var.tenant_id}"
  client_id = "${var.client_id}"
  client_secret = "${var.client_secret}"
}
```

 This file will be our variables file, and it will load the credential variables into the Azure Resource Manager Terraform provider.

Creating IaC

Now we are ready to start creating our IaC declaration files. Terraform uses its own language called **Hashicorp Configuration Language** (**HCL**). You can find out more about it in the following link: `https://www.terraform.io/docs/configuration/index.html`.

Let's begin defining our resources. Create a file called `main.tf`. This will be our main modules file. A module is a set of resources that share a common goal or are all part of the same application.

 The name `main.tf` is the recommended name by Hashicorp, the company owner of the Terraform Open Source project, for a minimal module.
You can find out more about modules in the Terraform documentation here:
`https://www.terraform.io/docs/modules/index.html`.

Our file should contain all of the following resources that we will be declaring next.

Here is the resource group that will contain our Azure resources:

```
resource "azurerm_resource_group" "salt" {
name     = "Salt"
location = "East US"
}
```

Here is the virtual network for our subnets:

```
resource "azurerm_virtual_network" "salt" {
name                = "saltnet"
address_space       = ["10.0.0.0/16"]
location            = "${azurerm_resource_group.salt.location}"
resource_group_name = "${azurerm_resource_group.salt.name}"
}
```

Note that we are getting values from our previous resources, by calling them with the following syntax:

```
"resource_type.local_name.value".
```

Here is the subnet(s) with the address space for our VMs:

```
resource "azurerm_subnet" "salt" {
name                 = "saltsubnet"
resource_group_name  = "${azurerm_resource_group.salt.name}"
virtual_network_name = "${azurerm_virtual_network.salt.name}"
address_prefix       = "10.0.0.0/24"
}
```

Here, we are creating only one subnet that will contain our masters and minions, but you can always create separate subnets, as long as they are inside the VNET address space, for the masters and minions to have network separation.

With our virtual network and subnet created, we need to create the firewall rules for our virtual machines. Firewalls in Azure are called **network security groups**, and we will go ahead and use the network security group provider to create the firewall and its rules.

Here is the network security group for the load balancer:

```
resource "azurerm_network_security_group" "saltlb" {
  name                = "lb-nsg"
  location            = "${azurerm_resource_group.salt.location}"
  resource_group_name = "${azurerm_resource_group.salt.name}"
}
```

The following are the network security group rules for access to the load balancer VM.

Ports for `https`:

```
resource "azurerm_network_security_rule" "httpslb" {
  name = "https"
  priority = 100
  direction = "inbound"
  access = "Allow"
  protocol = "Tcp"
  source_port_range = "*"
  destination_port_range = "8443"
  source_address_prefix = "*"
  destination_address_prefix = "*"
  resource_group_name = "${azurerm_resource_group.salt.name}"
  network_security_group_name =
  "${azurerm_network_security_group.saltlb.name}"
}
```

Port for `http`:

```
resource "azurerm_network_security_rule" "httplb" {
  name                       = "http"
  priority                   = 101
  direction                  = "inbound"
  access                     = "Allow"
  protocol                   = "Tcp"
  source_port_range          = "*"
  destination_port_range     = "8080"
  source_address_prefix      = "*"
  destination_address_prefix = "*"
  resource_group_name        = "${azurerm_resource_group.salt.name}"
  network_security_group_name =
  "${azurerm_network_security_group.saltlb.name}"
}
```

Port for SSH `access`:

```
resource "azurerm_network_security_rule" "sshlb" {
  name                        = "sshlb"
  priority                    = 103 direction                     = "inbound"
  access                      = "Allow"
  protocol                    = "Tcp"
  source_port_range           = "*" destination_port_range = "22"
  source_address_prefix       = "*"
  destination_address_prefix  = "*"
  resource_group_name         = "${azurerm_resource_group.salt.name}"
  network_security_group_name =
"${azurerm_network_security_group.saltlb.name}"
}
```

The second network security group for the master VM is as follows:

```
resource "azurerm_network_security_group" "saltMaster" {
  name                = "masternsg"
  location            = "${azurerm_resource_group.salt.location}"
  resource_group_name = "${azurerm_resource_group.salt.name}"
}
```

The following are the network security group rules for the master VM.

The following is the Salt `publisher` port:

```
resource "azurerm_network_security_rule" "publisher" {
  name                        = "publisher"
  priority                    = 100
  direction                   = "inbound"
  access                      = "Allow"
  protocol                    = "Tcp"
  source_port_range           = "*"
  destination_port_range      = "4505"
  source_address_prefix       = "*"
  destination_address_prefix  = "*"
  resource_group_name         = "${azurerm_resource_group.salt.name}"
  network_security_group_name =
"${azurerm_network_security_group.saltMaster.name}"
}
```

The following is the request server port for Salt:

```
resource "azurerm_network_security_rule" "requestsrv" {
  name                        = "requestsrv"
  priority                    = 101
  direction                   = "inbound"
```

```
access                     = "Allow"
protocol                   = "Tcp"
source_port_range          = "*"
destination_port_range     = "4506"
source_address_prefix      = "*"
destination_address_prefix = "*"
resource_group_name        = "${azurerm_resource_group.salt.name}"
network_security_group_name =
"${azurerm_network_security_group.saltMaster.name}"
}
```

The `ssh` port for the master is as follows:

```
resource "azurerm_network_security_rule" "sshmaster" {
  name                     = "ssh"
  priority                 = 103
  direction                = "inbound"
  access                   = "Allow"
  protocol                 = "Tcp"
  source_port_range        = "*"
  destination_port_range   = "22"
  source_address_prefix    = "*"
  destination_address_prefix = "*"
  resource_group_name      = "${azurerm_resource_group.salt.name}"
  network_security_group_name =
"${azurerm_network_security_group.saltMaster.name}"
}
```

The network security group for the minions is as follows:

```
resource "azurerm_network_security_group" "saltMinions" {
  name                = "saltminions"
  location            = "${azurerm_resource_group.salt.location}"
  resource_group_name = "${azurerm_resource_group.salt.name}"
}
```

This last network security group is special because we will not create any rules for it. The default rules that Azure provides only allow VMs to talk with Azure resources, which is exactly what we want for these VMs.

A public IP address for our Nginx load balancer VM is as follows:

```
resource "azurerm_public_ip" "saltnginxpip" {
  name                         = "lbpip"
  location                     = "${azurerm_resource_group.salt.location}"
  resource_group_name          = "${azurerm_resource_group.salt.name}"
  public_ip_address_allocation = "static"
}
```

The virtual network interface for our load balancer is as follows:

```
resource "azurerm_network_interface" "saltlb" {
  name                      = "lbnic"
  location                  = "${azurerm_resource_group.salt.location}"
  resource_group_name       = "${azurerm_resource_group.salt.name}"
  network_security_group_id = "${azurerm_network_security_group.saltlb.id}"

  ip_configuration {
    name                          = "lbip"
    subnet_id                     = "${azurerm_subnet.salt.id}"
    private_ip_address_allocation = "dynamic"
    public_ip_address_id          = "${azurerm_public_ip.saltnginxpip.id}"
  }
}
```

The virtual network interfaces for our web server VMs are as follows:

```
resource "azurerm_network_interface" "saltminions" {
  count                 = 2
  name                  = "webnic${count.index}"
  location              = "${azurerm_resource_group.salt.location}"
  resource_group_name   = "${azurerm_resource_group.salt.name}"
  network_security_group_id =
"${azurerm_network_security_group.saltMinions.id}"

  ip_configuration {
    name                          = "web${count.index}"
    subnet_id                     = "${azurerm_subnet.salt.id}"
    private_ip_address_allocation = "dynamic"
  }
}
```

Following is the public IP address for our master VM:

```
resource "azurerm_public_ip" "saltmasterpip" {
  name                = "masterpip"
  location            = "${azurerm_resource_group.salt.location}"
  resource_group_name = "${azurerm_resource_group.salt.name}"
  allocation_method   = "Dynamic"
}
```

This public IP address will be used for us to SSH into the master VM; that's why we are allocating it dynamically.

The virtual network interface for the master VM is as follows:

```
resource "azurerm_network_interface" "saltmaster" {
 name                = "masternic"
 location            = "${azurerm_resource_group.salt.location}"
 resource_group_name = "${azurerm_resource_group.salt.name}"
 network_security_group_id     =
"${azurerm_network_security_group.saltMaster.id}"

 ip_configuration {
   name                        = "masterip"
   subnet_id                   = "${azurerm_subnet.salt.id}"
   private_ip_address_allocation = "static"
   private_ip_address          = "10.0.0.10"
   public_ip_address_id        = "${azurerm_public_ip.saltmasterpip.id}"
 }
}
```

Following are the web server VMs:

```
resource "azurerm_virtual_machine" "saltminions" {
count               = 2
name                = "web-0${count.index}"
location            = "${azurerm_resource_group.salt.location}"
resource_group_name = "${azurerm_resource_group.salt.name}"
network_interface_ids =
["${element(azurerm_network_interface.saltminions.*.id, count.index)}"]
vm_size             = "Standard_B1s"
storage_image_reference {
  publisher = "Canonical"
  offer     = "UbuntuServer"
  sku       = "16.04-LTS"
  version   = "latest"
}
storage_os_disk {
  name              = "webosdisk${count.index}"
  caching           = "ReadWrite"
  create_option     = "FromImage"
  managed_disk_type = "Standard_LRS"
}
os_profile {
  computer_name  = "web-0${count.index}"
  admin_username = "dsala"
}
os_profile_linux_config {
  disable_password_authentication = true
    ssh_keys = {
      path     = "/home/dsala/.ssh/authorized_keys"
```

```
        key_data = "${file("~/.ssh/id_rsa.pub")}"
    }
  }
}
```

Replace os_profile.admin_username and os_profile_linux_config.key_data with your own information.

The master VM is as follows:

```
resource "azurerm_virtual_machine" "saltmaster" {
name                 = "salt"
location             = "${azurerm_resource_group.salt.location}"
resource_group_name  = "${azurerm_resource_group.salt.name}"
network_interface_ids = ["${azurerm_network_interface.saltmaster.id}"]
vm_size              = "Standard_B1ms"

storage_image_reference {
  publisher = "OpenLogic"
  offer     = "CentOS"
  sku       = "7.5"
  version   = "latest"
}

storage_os_disk {
  name              = "saltos"
  caching           = "ReadWrite"
  create_option     = "FromImage"
  managed_disk_type = "Standard_LRS"
}

os_profile {
  computer_name  = "salt"
  admin_username = "dsala"
}

os_profile_linux_config {
  disable_password_authentication = true
    ssh_keys = {
      path     = "/home/dsala/.ssh/authorized_keys"
      key_data = "${file("~/.ssh/id_rsa.pub")}"
    }
  }
}
```

Following is the Nginx load balancer VM:

```
resource "azurerm_virtual_machine" "saltlb" {
name                  = "lb-vm"
location              = "${azurerm_resource_group.salt.location}"
resource_group_name   = "${azurerm_resource_group.salt.name}"
network_interface_ids = ["${azurerm_network_interface.saltlb.id}"]
vm_size               = "Standard_B1ms"

storage_image_reference {
  publisher = "OpenLogic"
  offer     = "CentOS"
  sku       = "7.5"
  version   = "latest"
}

storage_os_disk {
  name              = "lbos"
  caching           = "ReadWrite"
  create_option     = "FromImage"
  managed_disk_type = "Standard_LRS"
}

os_profile {
  computer_name  = "lb-vm"
  admin_username = "dsala"
}

os_profile_linux_config {
  disable_password_authentication = true
    ssh_keys = {
    path     = "/home/dsala/.ssh/authorized_keys"
    key_data = "${file("~/.ssh/id_rsa.pub")}"
  }
 }
}
```

Once you have saved the file with all of the previously created resources, run the `terraform init` command; this will initialize the current directory with the Terraform files and download the Azure Resource Manager plugin:

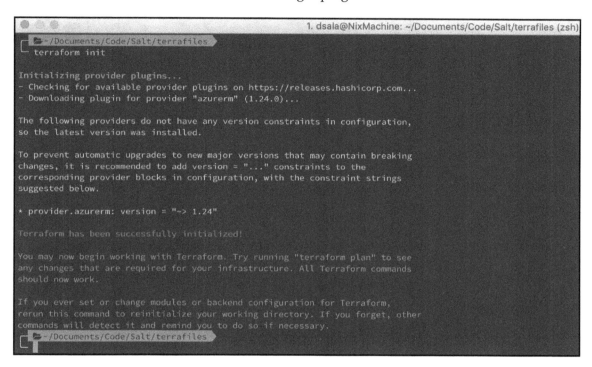

 If you want to learn more about the `init` command, you can go to `https://www.terraform.io/docs/commands/init.html`.

After running the `init` command, we will proceed to run the `terraform plan` command, which will calculate all of the changes necessary to achieve the desired state that we defined in our `tf` file.

This will not make any changes to the existing infrastructure until we run
the `terraformapply` command:

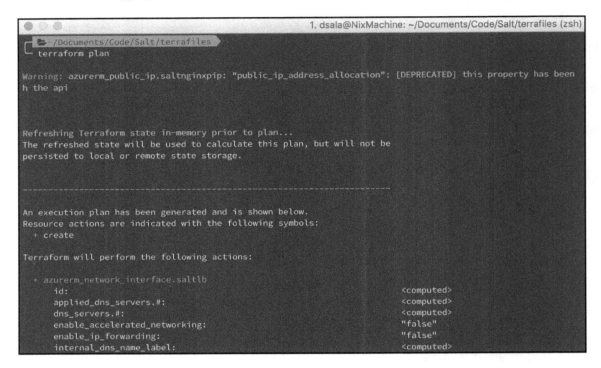

```
1. dsala@NixMachine: ~/Documents/Code/Salt/terrafiles (zsh)
 ~/Documents/Code/Salt/terrafiles
  terraform plan

Warning: azurerm_public_ip.saltnginxpip: "public_ip_address_allocation": [DEPRECATED] this property has been
h the api




Refreshing Terraform state in-memory prior to plan...
The refreshed state will be used to calculate this plan, but will not be
persisted to local or remote state storage.



- - - - - - - - - - - - - - - - - - - - - - - - - - - - - - - - - - - - - - -


An execution plan has been generated and is shown below.
Resource actions are indicated with the following symbols:
  + create

Terraform will perform the following actions:

  + azurerm_network_interface.saltlb
      id:                                              <computed>
      applied_dns_servers.#:                           <computed>
      dns_servers.#:                                   <computed>
      enable_accelerated_networking:                   "false"
      enable_ip_forwarding:                            "false"
      internal_dns_name_label:                         <computed>
```

For more information about the `plan` command, visit `https://www.`
`terraform.io/docs/commands/plan.html`.

Immediately after you have finished the `plan` command, you can go ahead and run `terraform apply` and you will be prompted with a confirmation to apply the changes:

```
                                                    1. terraform apply (terraform-provid)
    storage_os_disk.0.caching:                          "ReadWrite"
    storage_os_disk.0.create_option:                    "FromImage"
    storage_os_disk.0.disk_size_gb:                     <computed>
    storage_os_disk.0.managed_disk_id:                  <computed>
    storage_os_disk.0.managed_disk_type:                "Standard_LRS"
    storage_os_disk.0.name:                             "webosdisk1"
    storage_os_disk.0.write_accelerator_enabled:        "false"
    tags.%:                                             <computed>
    vm_size:                                            "Standard_B1s"

  + azurerm_virtual_network.salt
    id:                                                 <computed>
    address_space.#:                                    "1"
    address_space.0:                                    "10.0.0.0/16"
    location:                                           "eastus"
    name:                                               "saltnet"
    resource_group_name:                                "Salt"
    subnet.#:                                           <computed>
    tags.%:                                             <computed>


Plan: 13 to add, 0 to change, 0 to destroy.

Do you want to perform these actions?
  Terraform will perform the actions described above.
  Only 'yes' will be accepted to approve.

  Enter a value: █
```

Once it is finished, you should be able to see the following message:

```
Apply complete! Resources: 18 added, 0 changed, 0 destroyed.
  Installing, Configuring and Managing Salt
```

There are two ways of installing Salt: you can either use a bootstrap script to install the masters and minions, or you can install and configure them manually via the Salt repositories.

We will be covering both ways in order to familiarize ourselves with the install process.

Installing Salt with package managers

In our current infrastructure, we have one master and three minions. Our master and one minion are running CentOS 7.5 and the rest of the VMs are on Ubuntu 16.04. The process will be sort of different on both distros but some steps will be the same on both.

Installing CentOS yum

Previously, Salt was only available through the EPEL repositories. But now SaltStack has its own repository that we can import and perform the install from there.

First, install SSH into the master VM and run the following command to import the SaltStack repository:

```
[dsala@salt ~]$ sudo yum install \
https://repo.saltstack.com/yum/redhat/salt-repo-latest.el7.noarch.rpm
```

Optionally, you can run yum clean expire-cache, but as this is a new VM, this is not necessary.

Once finished, we will go ahead and install the salt-master package:

```
[dsala@salt ~]$ sudo yum install salt-master -y
```

Go ahead and enable the systemd salt-master service unit:

```
[dsala@salt ~]$ sudo systemctl enable salt-master --now
```

Check whether the service is running:

```
1. dsala@salt:~ (ssh)
[dsala@salt ~]$ systemctl status salt-master
● salt-master.service - The Salt Master Server
   Loaded: loaded (/usr/lib/systemd/system/salt-master.service; enabled; vendor preset: disabled)
   Active: active (running) since Mon 2019-04-08 17:19:02 UTC; 8s ago
     Docs: man:salt-master(1)
           file:///usr/share/doc/salt/html/contents.html
           https://docs.saltstack.com/en/latest/contents.html
 Main PID: 66418 (salt-master)
   CGroup: /system.slice/salt-master.service
           ├─66418 /usr/bin/python /usr/bin/salt-master
           ├─66432 /usr/bin/python /usr/bin/salt-master
           ├─66437 /usr/bin/python /usr/bin/salt-master
           ├─66438 /usr/bin/python /usr/bin/salt-master
           ├─66441 /usr/bin/python /usr/bin/salt-master
           ├─66442 /usr/bin/python /usr/bin/salt-master
           ├─66443 /usr/bin/python /usr/bin/salt-master
           ├─66444 /usr/bin/python /usr/bin/salt-master
           ├─66445 /usr/bin/python /usr/bin/salt-master
           ├─66446 /usr/bin/python /usr/bin/salt-master
           ├─66453 /usr/bin/python /usr/bin/salt-master
           ├─66454 /usr/bin/python /usr/bin/salt-master
           ├─66455 /usr/bin/python /usr/bin/salt-master
           ├─66544 /usr/bin/python /usr/bin/salt-master
           ├─66545 /usr/bin/python /usr/bin/salt-master
           ├─66546 /usr/bin/python /usr/bin/salt-master
           ├─66547 /usr/bin/python /usr/bin/salt-master
           └─66549 /usr/bin/python /usr/bin/salt-master
[dsala@salt ~]$
```

Once the service is up and running, check whether the private IP of the VM is the one that we configured in our Terraform definitions by running the following:

```
[dsala@salt ~]$ ifconfig eth0 | grep inet | head -1 | awk '{print $2}'
```

Once you have the IP address confirmed, open another terminal and SSH into the load balancer minion. Repeat the process of adding the repository as we did in the master VM.

Once the repository is added, run the following command to install the salt-minion package:

```
[dsala@lb-vm ~]$ sudo yum install salt-minion -y
```

Enable and start the `systemd` service unit by running this:

```
[dsala@lb-vm ~]$ sudo systemctl enable salt-minion --now
```

Let's check whether the service started successfully before we implement any changes to it:

```
                              1. dsala@lb-vm:~ (ssh)
 ✕   dsala@salt:~ (ssh)  ⌘1    ✕  dsala@lb-vm:~ (ssh)  ⌘2
[dsala@lb-vm ~]$ sudo systemctl status salt-minion
● salt-minion.service - The Salt Minion
   Loaded: loaded (/usr/lib/systemd/system/salt-minion.service; enabled; vendor preset: disabled)
   Active: active (running) since Mon 2019-04-08 19:08:43 UTC; 4min 49s ago
     Docs: man:salt-minion(1)
           file:///usr/share/doc/salt/html/contents.html
           https://docs.saltstack.com/en/latest/contents.html
 Main PID: 71779 (salt-minion)
   CGroup: /system.slice/salt-minion.service
           ├─71779 /usr/bin/python /usr/bin/salt-minion
           ├─71782 /usr/bin/python /usr/bin/salt-minion
           └─71790 /usr/bin/python /usr/bin/salt-minion

Apr 08 19:11:55 lb-vm salt-minion[71779]: [ERROR   ] The Salt Master has cached the public key for thi...cate
Apr 08 19:12:05 lb-vm salt-minion[71779]: [ERROR   ] The Salt Master has cached the public key for thi...cate
Apr 08 19:12:15 lb-vm salt-minion[71779]: [ERROR   ] The Salt Master has cached the public key for thi...cate
Apr 08 19:12:25 lb-vm salt-minion[71779]: [ERROR   ] The Salt Master has cached the public key for thi...cate
Apr 08 19:12:35 lb-vm salt-minion[71779]: [ERROR   ] The Salt Master has cached the public key for thi...cate
Apr 08 19:12:45 lb-vm salt-minion[71779]: [ERROR   ] The Salt Master has cached the public key for thi...cate
Apr 08 19:12:55 lb-vm salt-minion[71779]: [ERROR   ] The Salt Master has cached the public key for thi...cate
Apr 08 19:13:05 lb-vm salt-minion[71779]: [ERROR   ] The Salt Master has cached the public key for thi...cate
Apr 08 19:13:15 lb-vm salt-minion[71779]: [ERROR   ] The Salt Master has cached the public key for thi...cate
Apr 08 19:13:25 lb-vm salt-minion[71779]: [ERROR   ] The Salt Master has cached the public key for thi...cate
Hint: Some lines were ellipsized, use -l to show in full.
[dsala@lb-vm ~]$ 
```

We can see that we are getting errors on the service saying that the master has changed the public key and we are not unable to connect to the Salt master. We now need to configure the minion to talk to the master. But first, let's install the remaining two Ubuntu minions, because the process of registering the minions is the same on both distributions.

Ubuntu apt-getting Salt

The only complicated part of this is that, due to the fact that our web servers do not have a public IP address assigned to them, you have to SSH to them from either the master VM or the load balancer VM. To do this, you can set up SSH key authentication to the minions from either of these two VMs. If you are reading this book, you will be familiar with how to perform such a task.

When you log in to the web server VMs, perform the following task in both VMs.

Import the gpg key for the Salt repository:

Run the following to create the repository:

```
dsala@web-00:~$ echo "deb
http://repo.saltstack.com/apt/ubuntu/16.04/amd64/latest xenial main" \
| sudo tee /etc/apt/sources.list.d/saltstack.list
```

Once the repository has been added, run `apt update`, and you should be able to see the repository listed:

Proceed to install the `salt-minion` package:

```
dsala@web-00:~$ sudo apt install salt-minion -y
```

Enable and check the status of the `salt-minion` service by running the following:

```
dsala@web-00:~$ sudo systemctl enable salt-minion --now && systemctl status
salt-minion
```

You should see the same messages we saw in the CentOS LB virtual machine.

Installing Salt via the bootstrap script

The second way of installing Salt is via a **bootstrap script**. This script automatically detects our distribution and downloads the defined packages. The script also provides us with the -A flag, which will add the address of the master to our minions.

To get the script, you can either use `wget` or `curl`; the official SaltStack uses `curl`:

```
user@master:~$ curl -L https://bootstrap.saltstack.com -o install_salt.sh
```

This script applies for both masters and minions; the difference is which flags you use when running the script.

To install the master components, run the script with the -M flag for master and -P to allow any Python `pip` packages to be installed. We can also specify the master address with -A and tell the script not to install the minion service in the master with the -N flag:

```
user@master:~$ sudo sh install_salt.sh -P -M
```

To install the minion, just run this:

```
user@master:~$ sudo sh install_salt.sh -P -A <salt master IP>
```

Master and minion handshake

On this stage of the install, we will go ahead and allow our minions to talk to the master, verify their fingerprints, and set up configuration files.

First, we will SSH into the master VM and edit the master's configuration file to tell the salt-master daemon to which IP we want it to bind.

Edit the `/etc/salt/master` file, look for the `interface:` line, and add the master's IP address:

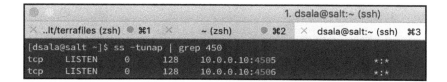

After modifying the file, run the `daemon-reload` and `restart` commands so that the service acknowledges the changes:

```
[dsala@salt ~]$ sudo systemctl daemon-reload && sudo systemctl restart
salt-master
```

You can verify whether the Salt master is listening on the correct IP address by running an `ss` command:

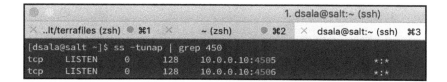

Now that our master is listening on the IP address that we require, it's time to configure our minions.

Let's start by modifying the minion's configuration file. Remember that these steps are to be performed on all of the minions regardless of their distribution.

Look for the `/etc/salt/minion` file and edit it by adding the noted IP address of the master under `master:`. We will find an already-configured value: `master: salt`; this is because Salt, by default, looks for the master via a DNS query to the hostname, `salt`, but as we intend in the future to have more than one master, we will be setting this file with the static IP address of our master VM:

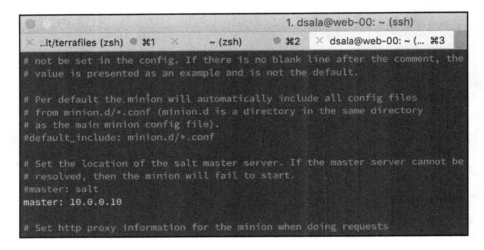

Before our minions can exchange keys, we need to add the master's fingerprint into our minions' configuration file.

SSH back to the master and run the following command to obtain your master's public fingerprint:

Copy the value of `master.pub` and go back to editing the minion's configuration file. In the minion's configuration file, edit the `master_finger: ' '` line with the master's public key, obtained in the preceding step:

```
                                    1. dsala@web-00: ~ (ssh)
  dsala@salt:~ (ssh)  ⌘1    ...a@web-00: ~ (ssh)  ⌘2
# The state_output_diff setting changes whether or not the output from
# successful states is returned. Useful when even the terse output of these
# states is cluttering the logs. Set it to True to ignore them.
#state_output_diff: False

# The state_output_profile setting changes whether profile information
# will be shown for each state run.
#state_output_profile: True

# Fingerprint of the master public key to validate the identity of your Salt master
# before the initial key exchange. The master fingerprint can be found by running
# "salt-key -f master.pub" on the Salt master.
master_finger: '29:2d:15:09:ab:e0:7d:dc:09:d7:9b:d6:a8:04:50:48:b9:11:ee:3b:a0:3c:b0:68:0b:37:f4:9e:92:a7:8a:55'
```

Reload and restart the minion daemon, once you have completed this last task:

```
[dsala@web-00 ~]$ sudo systemctl daemon-reload && sudo systemctl restart
salt-master
```

Before exiting each minion, run the following command and take note of the minion's fingerprint:

```
[dsala@web-00 ~]$ sudo salt-call --local key.finger
```

Once you have taken note of all of the minions' fingerprints, go ahead and log in to the master.

In the master, we will compare the fingerprints that the master sees to the fingerprint that we saw locally on each minion. In this way, we will identify that the minions that we will be accepting are indeed our minions.

To do this, run the following command in the master: `salt-key -F`. This will print all of the keys, so you don't have to print each key individually:

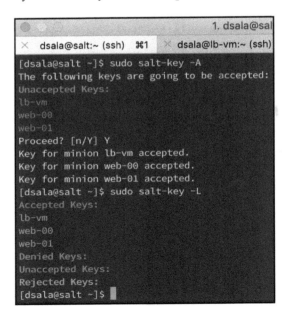

Make sure the keys are the same, and then we will proceed to accept the keys.

Under the `salt-key -F` command, we saw that we have unaccepted keys to accept after verifying them; we will run `salt-key -A` to accept all of the pending keys and you can run `salt-key -L` to verify that the keys were accepted:

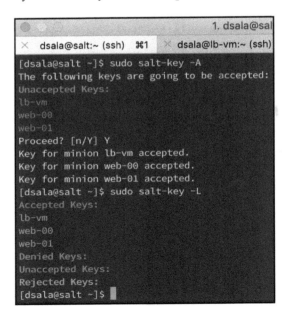

Now that our minions have been authenticated, we can go ahead and issue commands from our master.

To test our minions, we will invoke the `ping` function from the test module:

```
1. dsala@sal
✕   dsala@salt:~ (ssh)   ⌘1    ✕  dsala@lb-vm:~ (ssh)
[dsala@salt ~]$ sudo salt '*' test.ping
web-00:
    True
lb-vm:
    True
web-01:
    True
[dsala@salt ~]$
```

All minions should respond `True`, meaning that the Salt minion daemon is responding and we are ready to begin managing our infrastructure.

Working with Salt

With our SaltStack up and running, we are ready to start creating the formulas and customized configurations for our VMs.

Creating WebServer formulas

We will now be creating the necessary state files to create the formula that will install and configure our webservers.

Before we begin, we need to create our state tree first, which will contain all of our state files:

```
[dsala@salt ~]$ sudo mkdir /srv/salt
```

Inside this directory, we will be creating something called the `top.sls` file. This file is what tells Salt which states are applied to which minions. As for every definition in Salt, `top.sls` is a YAML- based file that will contain the minions to target and the state files that should be applied to those minions.

Create a file called `top.sls` in the `/srv/salt` directory with the following content:

```
base:
    'web*':
        - webserver.nodejs
```

`base:` means the environment in which we are working on; as this is a simple environment, we only need the base environment; for working with multiple environments, you can consult one of the books we will suggest in the *Further reading* section.

Next, we have the `web*` entry; this entry tells Salt which minion IDs are going to be the states applied to. As you can see, you are able to use globbing to target minion IDs.

Finally, `- webserver.nodejs` is where we indicate which states to apply; `webserver` indicates the folder in which the `nodejs.sls` file is in. As the YAML is read by the Python interpreter, we need to define the paths with periods (.) instead of slashes (/). The last word would be the name of the `.sls` file to load.

Because we defined the `Node.js` file to be in a directory called `webserver`, which is the directory that we will be storing all of our web server state files, we need to create such a directory:

```
[dsala@salt ~]$ sudo mkdir /srv/salt/webserver
```

Now that we have the directory where we will store our state definitions, let's create our first state definition that will install the `node.js` package and `npm`. Create a file called `nodejs.sls` in the `/srv/salt/webserver/` directory with the following content:

```
nodejs:
    pkg.installed

npm:
    pkg.installed
```

The `nodejs` field is the package to be installed, followed by the `pkg.installed` function to invoke.

With the `state` file created, apply the `state` files to the web server minions:

```
[dsala@salt ~]$ sudo salt 'web*' state.apply
```

After a while, you will receive output with the applied changes and the duration:

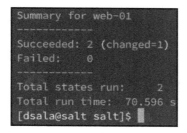

 The output of the following example has been truncated for readability.

With Node.JS installed, we need to create now the user for the Node.JS website to run on.

We will create another state file that will define the user configuration.

Create another file called `webuser.sls` under the `/srv/salt/webserver/` directory, with the following declaration:

```
webuser:
  user.present:
    - name: webuser
    - uid: 4000
    - home: /home/webuser
```

Before executing the state, modify the `top.sls` file to reflect the newly added state file:

```
base:
  'web*':
    - webserver.nodejs
    - webserver.webuser
```

Execute the `salt '*' state.apply` command again, and you should receive the output of the user creation:

```
          ID: webuser
    Function: user.present
      Result: True
     Comment: New user webuser created
     Started: 05:44:54.292257
    Duration: 506.713 ms
     Changes:
              ----------
              fullname:
              gid:
                  4000
              groups:
                  - webuser
              home:
                  /home/webuser
              homephone:
              name:
                  webuser
              other:
              passwd:
                  x
              roomnumber:
              shell:
              uid:
                  4000
              workphone:

Summary for web-01
------------
Succeeded: 3 (changed=1)
Failed:    0
------------
Total states run:     3
Total run time: 586.187 ms
[dsala@salt salt]$
```

Now that we have the user that will be running the website, it's time to copy the website files into our website servers. For this, we will be creating another state file, which will use Git to download the website files and load them into the VM.

Modify your `top.sls` file and add another state called `gitfetch` under the same web server directory, like this:

```
base:
    'web*':
        - webserver.nodejs
        - webserver.webuser
        - webserver.gitfetch
```

Now, proceed to create the `gitfetch.sls` file using the `git.latest` function to download the code from a Git repository and install the `Node.js` dependencies every time the repository is downloaded:

```
node-app:
    git.latest:
        - name: https://github.com/dsalamancaMS/SaltChap.git
        - target: /home/webuser/app
        - user: webuser

dep-install:
    cmd.wait:
        - cwd: /home/webuser/app
        - runas: webuser
        - name: npm install
        - watch:
            - git: node-app
```

Go ahead and run the `state.apply` function again to download the application on both web servers. You should be able to see output similar to this after running the command:

```
          ID: node-app
    Function: git.latest
        Name: https://github.com/dsalamancaMS/SaltChap.git
      Result: True
     Comment: https://github.com/dsalamancaMS/SaltChap.git cloned to /home/webuser/app
     Started: 06:12:50.037084
    Duration: 2557.135 ms
     Changes:
              ----------
              new:
                  https://github.com/dsalamancaMS/SaltChap.git => /home/webuser/app
              revision:
                  ----------
                  new:
                      7726a5c4b30e20fc26448884079f760d833a0611
                  old:
                      None

Summary for web-01
------------
Succeeded: 4 (changed=1)
Failed:    0
------------
Total states run:     4
Total run time:    2.642 s
[dsala@salt salt]$
```

With the code in our web servers, we are almost done with the configuration of our Ubuntu minions.

We now require our Node.JS application to run as a daemon.

 For this, we will be using the Supervisor Open Source Project: `https://github.com/Supervisor/supervisor`.

Now, let's configure Salt, to make `Supervisor` watch our Node.JS web application. Edit the `top.sls` file with the following line, as we have done before:

```
- webserver.suppkg
```

Before creating the `supervisor` state file, we first need to create the configuration file for `supervisor` that we are going to push to our minions. Create a file called `supervisor.conf` in the web server directory, with the following content:

```
[program:node-app]
command=nodejs .
directory=/home/webuser/app
user=webuser
```

Now create the `suppkg.sls` state file, which will be in charge of managing the previous configuration file, under the web server folder:

```
supervisor:
  pkg.installed:
    - only_upgrade: False
  service.running:
    - watch:
      - file: /etc/supervisor/conf.d/node-app.conf

/etc/supervisor/conf.d/node-app.conf:
  file.managed:
    - source: salt://webserver/supervisor.conf
```

Once the file is created, go ahead and run the `salt 'web*' state.apply` command to apply the latest states.

With this last state applied, our web application should be up and running. You can try accessing it via the `curl` command:

Now that our web servers are ready, we shall tag them as such. Remember in the previous chapter when we talked about grains. This is what we will be doing next.

Let's go ahead and tag our `web-00` and `web-01` servers with the appropriate role tags.

To do this, run the following command for each server:

```
1. dsala@salt:/srv/salt (ssh)
× ...alt (ssh) ⌘1    × ...lt (zsh) ⌘2    × ...p (ssh) ⌘3    × ...:~ (ssh) ⌘4
[dsala@salt salt]$ sudo salt 'web-00' grains.set roles frontend
web-00:
    ----------
    changes:
        ----------
        roles:
            frontend
    comment:
    result:
        True
[dsala@salt salt]$
```

You can check whether the roles were successfully applied by running the following `grep`:

```
[dsala@salt salt]$ sudo salt 'web-01' grains.items | grep roles -A1
    roles:
        frontend
```

Creating load-balancing formulas

Now that both our web servers are correctly set up, we can configure our last minion. This minion will be running Nginx in order to balance and proxy requests to our web servers behind the load balancer.

Let's create a directory where we will store all of the states for our load balancer:

```
[dsala@salt ~]$ sudo mkdir /srv/salt/nginxlb
```

With the directory created, let's proceed to edit our `top.sls` file one last time to include the `load balancer` state file. The `top.sls` file should look like this:

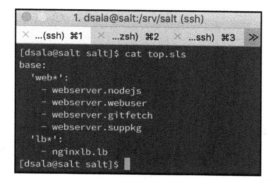

Before we create our `load balancer` state file, we will create the Nginx configuration file that we will be pushing to our `load balancer` VM. Create a file called `nginx.conf` with the following content:

```
events { }
http {
 upstream webapp {
   server web-00:8080;
   server web-01:8080;
 }
 server {
   listen 8080;
   location / {
     proxy_pass http://webapp;
   }
 }
}
```

Now, let's proceed to create our final state file. Create a file named `lb.sls` under the `nginxlb` directory in `/srv/salt/`, with the following content:

```
epel-release:
 pkg.installed

nginx:
 pkg.installed:
 - only_upgrade: False
 service.running:
 - watch:
     - file: /etc/nginx/nginx.conf
```

```
/etc/nginx/nginx.conf:
  file.managed:
    - source: salt://nginxlb/nginx.conf
```

To apply the final changes, you can run the `state.apply` command.

Once it's done, you can go ahead and test the load balancer running a cURL to its public IP address:

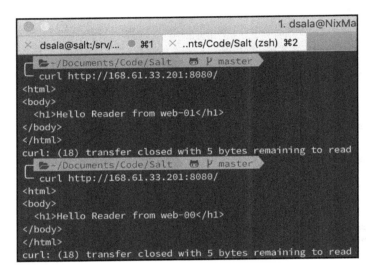

With this final configuration, we have concluded the proof of concept for Mr. Don High. One very important fact to note is that this example is nowhere near ready for be put into production; this is just an example to show you the basic functionalities and what is possible with Salt Stack.

Summary

In this chapter, we finally got hands-on interaction with Salt by deploying an infrastructure through IaC. We used Terraform to set up our initial environment and to start using Terraform, we simply downloaded the binary from `terraform.io`. The version of Terraform can be checked through the `terraform version` command. With Terraform installed, we obtained the correct details to connect to our Azure subscription using the AZ CLI.

Once Terraform was able to connect to Azure, we proceeded to create the IaC declaration file, which contained the necessary information to correctly deploy the resources we wanted in Azure, the way we wanted it.

With the deployment up and running through Terraform, we then moved into installing Salt. This can be done in two different ways, through the package manager of the OS (`yum` and `apt`) or through a bootstrap script.

When installing through the package manager, we needed to add the Salt repository, as it was not available in the base repos; we did this by downloading the `rpm` from the `saltstack` site.

To install the master, we ran `sudo yum install salt-master`, and to install the minions, we ran `sudo yum install salt-minion -y`. For Ubuntu, the process was similar, except the `apt` package manager was used.

After Salt completed the installation, we enabled the `systemctl` units. Once Salt was running, we needed to allow the minions to talk to the master; this was done through SSH fingerprints.

At this point, Salt was running and the minions were communicating to the master, so we then moved into creating the web server formulas, which ran the definitions necessary to deploy the application.

In the next chapter, the last of this book, we will go through some of the best practices when designing solutions.

15
Design Best Practices

To wrap up this book, our final chapter will talk about the different best practices that you will have to follow in order to design a resilient and failure-proof solution. Even though this is the last chapter of this book, it will help you as a starting point for what things to consider when, for example, migrating to the cloud.

We will be covering the basics of subjects such the following:

- Moving to the cloud
- Container design
- Continuous integration pipelines
- Continuous deployment pipelines
- Automated testing

The topics and practices that we will be covering in this chapter are no where near extensive and we will be giving a 10,000 feet overview. With these basics, you can start to reinforce your knowledge in each area to make the ultimate design decisions for your customers.

Designing for the occasion

In our previous chapters, we learned everything we needed for very specific solutions. Here, we will be talking about generalities, the basic rules or recommendations you need to follow or at least try to adhere to for every design you create. But don't be confused by what I'm going to say next; best practices per se do not exist. Every solution will have its own identity, its own goals, and its own unique characteristics. Always try to satisfy the situation you are in and the business needs of your customer.

Many solutions, though, will have to comply with certain industry standards, as they may handle sensitive information. In these types of scenarios, we already have a very well-defined set of rules and policies that our designs have to satisfy. This breaks our statement that all designs are different, but again, these are very specific scenarios for very specific industries. Some of the standards that we need to comply with when dealing with sensitive data are the following:

- **Health Insurance Portability and Accountability Act (HIPAA)**
- **Payment Card Industry Data Security Standards (PCI-DSS)**
- **The General Data Protection Regulation (GDPR)**

These standards are fixed no matter what, locally and internationally, and regulated by their respective authorities. But not all design patterns or ways to comply with certain solution requirements are as clear as these ones.

As a solutions architect, you will find yourself in many scenarios that will help you expand your portfolio and apply it in different solutions. Every design you create is only as strong as its weakest link. When you are designing, always try to see how you can break your design:

- Where does it have points of failure?
- Where does it have bottlenecks?
- Will my servers be able to handle the load?

These are a few examples of some questions you need to ask yourself. We need to shape our way of thinking and ask ourselves the question *why?* more often. Why are we doing what we are doing this way, or that way? It is crucial to question ourselves about every decision we make.

Changing our way of thinking is the best thing we can do, as nowadays technologies are evolving faster than ever before. Technologies might change over the years, and what we implemented today might be totally unusable tomorrow, but our way of thinking will allow us to adapt and analyze from all the points necessary for us to be successful.

Every situation and environment will be different, but at the time of writing we can say that you will be dealing with two major types of environments:

- On-premises/bare metal environments
- Cloud environments

In this chapter, we will be going through the basic considerations that you will need to deal with when you're working in these environments.

On-premises environments

Linux is adaptable; it can run pretty much anywhere. It wouldn't surprise me if I found the Linux kernel on a lawn mower in the next few years. In a world where IT is becoming more and more relevant for our daily lives, alongside the rise of the Internet of Things, the presence of Linux has spiked like never before. Therefore, as Linux architects, we need to be prepared to design with almost everything.

In an on-premises environment, we are most probably facing two scenarios:

- Bare metal server
- **Virtual machines** (**VMs**)

Both of them will be very different, as the options that we will have to make our solution more resilient will vary.

Bare metal server

Bare metal servers are perfect for workloads that require a considerable amount of resources to run. Small workloads will not be efficiently placed on a single server; for instance, a small web application that will not be serving a lot of user requests has no place on a 64-core 1 TB of RAM physical server. It's a waste of resources and a terrible economic decision. Most of the time, 90% of this server would be totally idle, wasting precious resources that could be used for something else. These types of applications should be put into a VM or containerized altogether.

The first thing that we should understand before moving or creating an infrastructure on bare metal are the resource requirements of the application for which you are building the infrastructure for.

Systems that require lots of resources for data processing and high-performance computing will take full advantage of the resources available. Solutions such as the following ones are examples of what to run on bare metal servers:

- Type 1/ Type 2 Hypervisors (**Kernel-based Virtual Machine** (**KVM**), **Linux containers** (**LXC**), XEN)
- Linux for SAP HANA
- Apache Hadoop
- Linux for Oracle DB
- Large MongoDB deployments for memory caching
- **High-performance computing** (**HPC**)

In-house applications that specify that their memory requirements exceed the hundreds of GB or hundreds of CPU cores are all better served on a bare metal server where RAM/CPU will not be consumed on any other overhead process that is not part of the workload that you design that server for.

Virtual machines

Hypervisors are also better on bare metal servers; since they are going to be sharing their resources across multiple hosted VMs, they require large quantities of resources. One thing to note is that some of the resources of the hypervisor will be consumed by the hypervisor itself, which creates a resource overhead on hardware interrupts and other operations.

Sometimes, when building physical servers, we focus a lot on the CPU cores that our application will need. With hypervisors, CPU time is served to VMs on priority or a first-come-first-served basis to the available core; depending on how it is configured, the CPU resource is shared across the running VMs. On the contrary, RAM memory is not shared across the VMs, and we need to be careful in the resource balancing that we are implementing. Deploying a server with the necessary CPU cores but with enough RAM that can satisfy any period of contention that we can face is something to take into account. With hundreds of VMs running on a single host, we can run out of memory really quickly and start swapping, and this is a situation that we want to avoid.

With resource provisioning, we also need to take into account that if we are running a cluster of hypervisors, there can be situations when one of the cluster nodes needs to go into maintenance or go down because of an unexpected failure. Scenarios such as this are the reason we should always leave some resources to be able to manage additional unexpected workloads from VMs that might failover due to the aforementioned reasons.

When dealing with hypervisors, you have to be careful, as you will not be running just a single workload per physical host. The number and the VMs themselves will always vary, unless you have some type of affinity rule configured. Things such as how much network bandwidth your network interface cards support are of utmost relevance. Depending on the amount of resources of the host hypervisor, tens or hundreds of VMs will be sharing the same network hardware to perform their I/O. Here is where deciding, for example, whether a 10 GbE network card instead of a 1 GbE network card is required.

One more thing to take into consideration when picking the network interfaces of your physical host is the type of storage you will be using; for example, if you are considering a **network filesystem** (**NFS**) solution or an iSCSI solution, you have to keep in mind that, many times, they will be sharing the same interfaces such as the ones for the regular network traffic. If you know the infrastructure you are designing will have a very congested network and require a good storage performance, it is better to have another approach, such as choosing a fibre channel storage area network, with its own dedicated hardware just for storage I/O.

Network segmentation is crucial for virtualized environments, management traffic, application network traffic, and storage network traffic, which should always be segmented. You can achieve this in several ways, such as by provisioning dedicated network interface cards for each purpose or via VLAN tagging. Each hypervisor will have its own set of tools to achieve segmentation, but the idea behind it is the same.

Cloud environments

Working with **cloud environments** creates a wide number of options for designing IT solutions. Independently from the cloud provider, you will be able to select from services such as these:

- **Infrastructure as a Service (IaaS)**
- **Platform as a Service (PaaS)**
- **Software as a Service (SaaS)**

Your choice will depend on the maturity of your customer in cloud architecture models. But before we can even talk about design patterns or best practices for cloud environments, we need to talk about how you perform the migration of your on-premises environment to the cloud or how you can start adopting the cloud as the infrastructure for your customer.

The journey to the cloud

These migration strategies are adopted from Gartner research. Gartner also calls out a fifth strategy called **replace** with SaaS.

The following research paper is discussed in this section:

Devise an Effective Cloud Computing Strategy by Answering Five Key Questions, Gartner, David W Cearley, November 2015, refreshed June 23, 2017.

When migrating to the cloud, we don't have to see the cloud as a destination, but rather as a journey. As cheesy as it sounds, it is like that. Every customer's path to the cloud will be different; some paths will be easy and others will be painfully hard. It will all depend on what led the customer to take the decision to move and how they are deciding to move their infrastructure. Some customers might decide not only to move their infrastructure to an IaaS model but also take advantage of the move and modernize some of the workloads into a PaaS or even a serverless model. Each path will require a different level of preparation, regardless of which one they choose. A typical transition can look as follows:

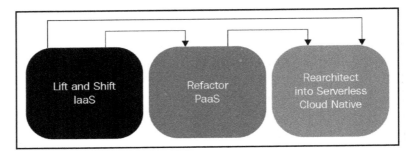

Each step will require a higher degree of changes to be implemented on the applications or infrastructure to migrate.

We can see the aforementioned steps as part of a greater journey that begins with the assessment of the assets to migrate.

Let's explore each step of the migration in more detail.

Assessing

In this step, we will evaluate which workloads we want to migrate. After identifying the candidates for migration, we should always run an inventory of our VMs or physical servers and calculate what the **total cost of ownership** (**TCO**) of maintaining the infrastructure is. Things such as hardware cost, support maintenance contracts, electricity bills, and even space rental come into play here. This will help us to understand how much we will be saving in an eventual migration to the cloud. This data is crucial to convince management and any C-level decision makers that may have any doubts about the benefits in cost of migrating infrastructure to a cloud provider.

The ideal scenario to begin a migration is to look for smaller applications that don't require an entire infrastructure to be migrated in order for them to be put into production. Applications with few dependencies are perfect to begin your assessment. Dependencies such as which servers we need to migrate together, and network requirements for our application such as ports and IP operational ranges are to be taken into consideration. Questions such as the following will help us to prepare for a successful migration:

- Is my Linux distribution endorsed by the cloud provider I am migrating to?
- Am I running the Kernel version that's supported by my cloud provider?
- Do I have to install any additional kernel modules?
- Does my cloud provider require any type of agent running on my OS?

With these questions answered, we can start performing the actual migration.

Migrating

When migrating our infrastructure to the cloud, there are four basic ways of doing it:

- **Lift and shift**
- **Refactor**
- **Rearchitect**
- **Rebuild**

Each of these methods will take advantage of different services and different features of the cloud. Choosing which method to use will depend on many things, such as how quickly you need to migrate, how much effort you are willing to undergo to migrate, and whether you want to take advantage of the migration and modernize your workloads as you migrate.

Lift and shift

This method is literally a rehost, as you will be moving your on-premises physical servers or VMs into VMs in your cloud provider. This method is the easiest and quickest of all the methods, because you will be moving your environment and your applications as you have them on-premises. No code changes or re-architecture of your applications is required for this method. Here, you will only be taking advantage of the IaaS advantages of the cloud provider of your choice.

Things such as the agility of having resources at your disposal if you need to increment storage or compute on demand and the lack of hardware maintenance and administration will be things to take advantage of in this model.

Refactor

With **refactor**, your applications require minimal to no code changes. With this method, we can exploit a mix of IaaS and PaaS features. Migrating a three-tier web application into a managed middleware and into a managed database is a perfect example of this migration model.

With a managed database or managed middleware, we don't have to worry about things such as OS management, database engine installation and administration, framework updates, security patches, and even configuring additional instances for load balancing, as it is all taken care of for us. We just need to upload our code and select the framework that we need for it to run. We still can run monolithic applications, and very little code changes are required; the main purpose of this method is to migrate by taking things such as management and configuration off our shoulders, thus increasing the agility of our workloads.

Rearchitecting

Rearchitecting while migrating does involve heavy changes in our applications, but this stage is where we modernize our business.

We can find ourselves taking apart a monolithic application and breaking it into microservices by taking advantage of technologies such as containers and Kubernetes. We will be making our applications more portable, scalable, agile, and ready to be delivered via methodologies such as DevOps. With microservices, containers, and the automation that DevOps brings to the table, you will not only have a faster delivery of your applications to production, but you will also be using the compute resources on which your application will run more efficiently.

Rearchitecting might not be easy, nor is it the quickest way to migrate your workloads to the cloud, but it will give you a substantial advantage and cost savings in the long run.

Rebuild

Rearchitecting requires major code changes, but this last migration model is all about taking advantage of the movement to the cloud and create what are called **cloud-native applications**.

Cloud-native applications are those that take advantage of cloud services such as PaaS and SaaS applications that are designed to be run on the cloud. Some of them can even be entirely run on serverless computing. Serverless computing is to run code directly on a cloud service, or consume an API or a service that is already provided by the cloud provider. Combining several services that consume one another and work on a common goal or result are what we call cloud-native applications.

The whole idea behind moving to the cloud is to save: save economically, save in maintenance, save time to recovery by moving into a more resilient and elastic platform. But we will not always automatically take advantage of all the benefits of it. After moving, we still have some terrain to cover in order to have our new cloud workloads completely optimized.

Optimizing

Maybe if you had moved your infrastructure via a lift and shift, the move might have been easy, and whatever workload was running on that VM is probably already in production with not many changes, if any at all. The problem is that your VMs are still the same size as they were on your on-premises environment. You are still having that VM use a small percentage of its actual total compute resources. In the cloud, this is wasting money, as you are paying for the hours that the VM is running, but the price that you pay for those hours is based on the total amount of resources of that VM, whether you are using 100% of them or not.

This stage is where we actually start performing appropriate sizings and optimizing our infrastructure to actually use what we really need to actually take advantage of the elasticity of the cloud. All cloud providers have tools and services that you can use to monitor the resource consumption of your VM and other services. With these tools, we can easily identify and address our sizing requirements in a way that is cost-efficient.

The elasticity of the cloud not only allows us to size our resources on demand, without having to wait for the IT operations team to allocate or buy new hardware in the case that we run out resources in our hypervisors or dedicated physical servers.

We can also provision extra VMs or instances of the service that we are consuming on demand, based on resource thresholds that we establish. Requests to these resources are automatically load balanced to our extra instances so that we only have to pay for those extra resources on periods of resource contention.

Optimizing is not all about reducing VM sizes for a better price. Other areas that we can optimize are management and time to market. Adopting things such as PaaS and SaaS can help us achieve this.

Once our applications are running on VMs on the cloud, we can easily start transitioning to these more managed services. Managed services help us forget about OS maintenance or middleware configurations, and our developers can spend more time actually developing and deploying applications rather than fighting with the operations team about an update that a library requires to be able to run the latest version of the production app, which eventually takes us a faster time to market and less money and time spent in management or operating system support contracts.

Faster time to market, less management, and fewer conflicts between operations and development are the things that DevOps is all about. We have mentioned DevOps in several stages of the migrate phase, but let's take a deeper look into what DevOps is and what it's trying to accomplish on a closer level.

DevOps

In synthesis, DevOps is the combination of development and operations. It is the union and collaboration between these two IT groups—developers and system administrators—that make DevOps possible. Notice that we said collaboration; it is important to understand that collaboration is the core of DevOps. There is not authority behind DevOps, like there is for the scrum framework, for example. On the contrary, it has no standard, but it follows a set practices born from a cultural exchange between these two groups, to achieve shorter development cycles and increased deployment frequency with agile methodologies.

You will frequently see the term DevOps misused in different ways, for example:

- **Position (DevOps Engineer)**: The nature of DevOps is collaboration across the operations and developer teams, and therefore DevOps is not a position or a specific team that does DevOps.
- **Set of tools**: The tools that are used to help achieve the goals behind DevOps are also confused. Kubernetes, Docker, and Jenkins are all often confused with DevOps, but they are only the means to an end.

- **Standard**: As we mentioned previously, the DevOps movement does not have any authority regulating its practices and flow; it is the people who are implementing and following a basic set of practices and adapting it to suit its own business needs.

We now know that DevOps is a cultural movement, and that brings us more frequent development cycles, frequency, and integration between operations and development. Now, let's understand the problems behind the benefits of adopting DevOps.

Monolithic waterfalls

The traditional method of developing software applications is called a **waterfall**. A waterfall is a linear sequential way of doing software; basically, you go only in one direction. It was adopted by software engineering from manufacturing and construction industries. The waterfall model steps are as follows:

1. Requirements
2. Design
3. Implementation
4. Verification
5. Maintenance

The main problem is that due to the fact that this methodology was invented for manufacturing and construction, it is not agile at all. In these industries, every change or every problem that you face might cost you a lot, so all the precautions before moving on to the next stage have to be taken into consideration. Because of this, each stage takes quite a while, and therefore the time to market is reduced significantly.

With this methodology, before even starting to create the application, developers have to design all the features, and time is spent talking and planning before even a line of code is written. These type of scenarios make a lot of sense for the origins of this methodology, because if you are building a skyscraper or a residential home, you want to know how it will be designed and structured before even starting the construction itself. In software development, the quicker you get feedback, the quicker you can adapt and make the changes that are necessary to fit the needs of your customer. With waterfall, feedback isn't provided until the very end, when the product is almost ready and changes are more difficult to implement.

Waterfall in its own nature is monolithic and bulky, even though we have different teams working on different features of the product, and in the end all these features are compiled together to deliver a single big instance of a release. With this type of monolith, if there's a **quality assurance** (**QA**) team, they have to test all the features of that release. This takes a lot of time and increases the time to market the product even more. The worst case would be that a change is needed or a bug gets through QA into production. A rollback will imply the full release with all its features together instead of just the one with the bug, bringing a lot of risk to the table when it comes to big releases.

Agile solutions to monolithic problems

With waterfall, we realize too late that things that we thought that are going to work didn't work as planned in the installation stage, or even later in the production stage. Performing those changes implied a whole lot of steps, and course correction was slow and painful.

Software evolves quickly, and the needs of our clients might change in the middle of the design. That's why we need a more agile and flexible methodology other than waterfall. The quicker we get feedback, the quicker we can adapt and deliver the exact expectations of our customers.

This is exactly what the **Agile** methodology is for. Agile seeks to deliver the software in multiple releases, each one going through a set of tests and feedback in order to obtain it more quickly and make changes and course correction in a quicker and more agile way.

Agile was a game changer, but it generated conflicts between **operations** and **developers**.

Deploying releases more frequently can be unstandardized and different every time, if a different engineer performs the deployment. Let's say you have a deployment at night. If the person who is deploying in the morning is a different engineer than the one that performed the last deployment, they could have a completely different way of deploying the code to production. These types of things generate discrepancy and can cause problem. For example, if something happens and it needs to be rolled back, a different person rolling it back might not know what the steps that were taken in deployment were in order to roll back the changes.

With these releases, system availability can be affected unpredictably. Operations engineers are measured by the stability of the systems that they are managing, and it's in their interest to keep it that way. Deploying unpredictable changes to production is something that they want to avoid. Developers, on the other hand, are measured by how quickly they can put their new changes, features, and releases into production. You can see how these two teams have completely opposite goals, and they almost have to fight each other to fulfil them.

Different goals across teams isolates each team from another. This creates silos, and throws the problem or app over the fence. This develops into a non-collaborative working environment, where everybody blames one another and things move at an even slower pace, instead of solving the problem.

Continuous culture for CI/CD

So far, I feel that you have noticed that we haven't talked about any tools to make DevOps possible. This is because tools will not solve all these types of problems. They will help you and your customers enforce the DevOps culture, but they are not what makes DevOps possible.

Standardization and testing before we deliver our product is essential to Agile and DevOps, and tools will help us achieve these two goals. Let's take a look into the Agile workflow and the DevOps workflow:

Here is a look at the Agile workflow:

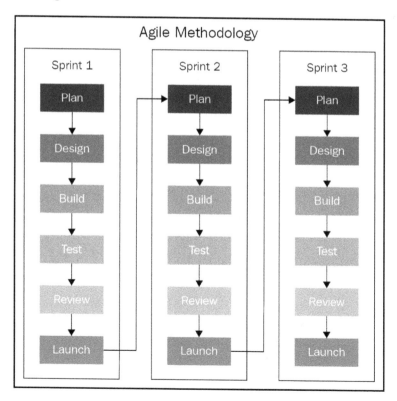

Here is how it compares to DevOps:

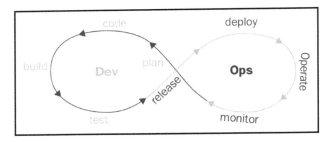

It is very clear that both go hand in hand and that they overlap each other, as they seek the same goals. DevOps has extra steps, such as operate and monitor, which take place after the deployment of the code. These steps are very self-explanatory; monitor consists of monitoring our application in production, checking its behavior regarding whether it presents any bugs, of whether it is using all the resources that were allocated to it. Operate the hardware, VM, or PaaS where it was deployed.

The idea behind **continuous deployment (CD)** and **continuous integration (CI)** is to bring us standardization and the means for us to make sure that changes and releases make it into production as quickly as possible with the least possible failures. If a failure happens, we can revert quickly and easily as well. The whole point of CI/CD is to automate manual processes, and many companies still compile releases manually and still send emails to operations with the binaries and instructions on how to deploy their code. To achieve CI/CD, we have tools that will help us automate the whole build, test, deploy, and release cycle.

A typical pipeline of CI/CD is triggered by a commit to a Git repository, which then triggers an automated build process that usually generates an artifact or a drop, which triggers automated testing and automated deployment of the application.

Let's take a look at some of the different open source tools, with a brief explanation of each and to which stage of the DevOps cycle it belongs to.

This is nowhere near an extensive list, and the explanations are a brief summary of their purpose:

- **Code:**
    - **Git**: A version control system that allows developers to have a distributed repository of their code and track changes across the development cycle.

- **GitHub, GitLab, Bitbucket**: These three are Git type repositories instead of tools. However, they are worth the mentioning, as they are the most used public and private repositories of Git that are used in the industry.
- **Apache subversion** (**SVN**): This is another versioning system. Although it is no longer as popular as it was since the release of Git, it is worth mentioning that it exists, as you might run into it in legacy environments.

- **Build**:

  - **Docker**: Docker, as we discussed in the `Chapter 14`, *Getting Your Hands Salty*, is a tool you can use to build your container images, independent of which language your application is written in. Docker uses **Buildkit** under the hood, which can also be used as a standalone product to build the docker images.
  - **Apache ant**: This tool was the first one to replace the famous Unix build binary that was made for Java applications. It uses `xml` to define the steps of the build. This tool is mainly for Java applications.
  - **Apache Maven**: Apache Maven is also another Java build tool, but it came to fix problems such as dependency management that Apache Ant lacked.
  - **Gradle**: Grade was built on the basis of Apache Ant and Apache Maven, but Gradle uses it's own specific language based on Groovy for defining the steps that are required. Gradle is the most modular of all, and mostly all functionalities are added through plugins.
  - **Grunt**: This is the Ant or Maven equivalent of JavaScript; it automates and runs tasks such as linting, unit testing, minification, and compilation. Grunt is highly modular, as there are thousands of plugins available.

- **Test**:

  - **Selenium**: This is mainly a web application tester that can be run against of most modern-day web browsers. With Selenium, you don't necessarily need to know a test programming language as it offers an IDE and the option to use several of the most popular programming languages.

- **Apache JMeter**: This is basically a load performance tool that generates a heavy load on servers to test static and dynamic content so that you can analyse its performance on different load types.
- **Appium**: On the other hand, Appium not only tests web applications, but it can also perform tests on mobile and desktop apps.

- **Release, Deploy, Manage, Orchestrate, Operate**:
    - **Jenkins**: This is probably the most used tool in the DevOps culture. Jenkins is an automation server that makes all the steps possible via triggers that call the automation of the build and the release process, as well as any automated testing that is configured in the pipelines.
    - **Ansible**: This is mostly a configuration management tool, but it can also help us release our applications via its modularity and provides an easy way of developing your own playbooks to run against a set of servers.
    - **Puppet**: This is another configuration management tool that helps us maintain configurations and manage package patch installations on our environment servers.
    - **Helm**: Look at Helm as the `yum` or the `apt` of Kubernetes: on its own, it is unable to automate any deployment process, but with the help of tools such as Jenkins, you can use it to deploy your own custom charts to Kubernetes, as well as keep a release history if a rollback is needed.

- **Monitor**:
    - **Nagios**: This is the classical monitoring centralized tool that monitors everything from system performance to the status of services and much more.
    - **Prometheus**: A project under the umbrella of the cloud native computing foundation. It allows us to create our own metrics and alerting.
    - **Fluentbit**: This allows you to collect multiple logs and/or data and send it to multiple destinations for log gathering or processing.

Summary

This being the last chapter, we wrapped up with some considerations when designing solutions. In this chapter, we went through what we should have in mind when dealing with different scenarios.

Knowing where and how we'll be deploying our solutions helps us have an idea of what sort of requirements might be in place; for example, certain industries will have hard requirements that can't be ignored, such as HIPAA, PCI, and GDPR.

Then, we spoke about deploying on-premises solutions and how different workloads are better for bare metal and what considerations to have when implementing in VMs.

We touched on how moving to the cloud is not as simple as clicking on a portal and waiting, but rather how it is a journey, since it allows for the modernization of workloads given the plethora of options available in the cloud.

Also, we mentioned that there are different methods for migrating existing workloads, such as lift and shift, refactor, rearchitect, and rebuild.

Lastly, we described how DevOps is helping shape the industry by unifying the development and operations aspects and how this ties with how CI/CD has changed how software is deployed and used.

Questions

1. What is HIPAA?
2. What workloads are preferred to run on bare metal?
3. Should hypervisors run on bare metal?
4. Do VMs share resources?
5. What is network segmentation?
6. What is lift and shift?
7. What is refactor?
8. What is Rearchitect?

Further reading

Production of Large Computer Programs: http://sunset.usc.edu/csse/TECHRPTS/1983/usccse83-501/usccse83-501.pdf

Managing the development of large software systems: http://www-scf.usc.edu/~csci201/lectures/Lecture11/royce1970.pdf

Azure Migration Center: https://azure.microsoft.com/en-gb/migration/get-started/

3 Journeys for Migrating a Data Center to Cloud IaaS: https://www.gartner.com/smarterwithgartner/3-journeys-for-migrating-a-data-center-to-cloud-iaas/

Assessments

Chapter 1: Introduction to Design Methodology

1. Problem Statement → Information Gathering → Solution Proposal → Implementation.
2. Because it allows for the correct requirements to be established.
3. To allow room for the customer to choose the right solution.
4. Explored in the section *Analyzing the problem and asking the right questions.*
5. Proof of Concept.
6. The actual solution is delivered and tested.
7. It allows us to explore the different concepts of the solution of an actual working environment.

Chapter 2: Defining GlusterFS Storage

1. `Chapter 5`, *Analyzing Performance in a Gluster System* further analyzes this.
2. File storage is better suited for how GlusterFS works.
3. Almost all cloud providers offer object storage these days.
4. File storage, block storage (through iSCSI Initiator), and object storage (through a plugin).
5. No, but it does contribute to the project.
6. GlusterFS is free, open source software; simply download it from your favorite package manager.
7. It does through the Geo-replication function.

Chapter 3: Architecting a Storage Cluster

1. It depends on the volume type used, but 2 CPUs and 4+GB of RAM is a good starting point.
2. GlusterFS would use the brick's filesystem cache mechanism.
3. It is a fast storage layer where I/Os will be served instead of going to slower storage. Cache can be RAM or faster storage media, such as SSDs.
4. As more concurrency is achieved, the software will require more CPU cycles to server the requests.
5. Distributed will aggregate space, Replicated will mirror data, hence "halving" space, Dispersed will aggregate space but will consume 1 node for parity. Think of it as a RAID5.
6. Depends on many variables such as retention periods, data ingress, etc...
7. The expected amount of data growth.
8. Throughput is a function of a given amount of data over a given amount of time, normally displayed as MB/s or Megabytes per second
   Input output operations per second (IOPS) is a function of certain amount of operations per second
   I/O size refers to the request size done by the appliance
9. The layout of the storage locations used by GlusterFS.
10. GlusterFS's process of replicating data from a cluster to another, normally located in a different Geo-location..

Chapter 4: Using GlusterFS on Cloud Infrastructure

1. The storage locations used by GlusterFS to store actual data.
2. The Z FileSytem, an advanced filesystem created by Sun Microsystems and later made open source.
3. A ZFS storage pool.
4. A disk used for read request, typically faster and lower latency than the disks used in the zpool.
5. Normally through the Operating System's package manager, such as yum.
6. A pool of GlusterFS nodes that will participate in the same cluster.
7. Gluster volume creates <Volume name> <Volume Type> <Number of nodes> <node and brick paths>.

8. This setting controls how much memory will be used for caching.
9. Adaptive Replacement Cache, this is ZFSs caching algorithm.

Chapter 5: Analyzing Performance in a Gluster System

1. Megabytes per second, a throughput measurement.
2. Shows ZFS's I/O statistics.
3. Part of the sysstat package, used for block devices I/O statistics.
4. This is the read latency, measured in milliseconds.
5. The amount of time the CPU is waiting for outstanding I/O to complete.
6. Flexible I/O Tested, a tool used for I/O benchmarking.
7. Either through a configuration file or by passing the parameters to the command directly.
8. A file that tells FIO how to run a test.
9. By purposely killing one of the nodes.
10. By increasing resources on the nodes or increasing disk size.

Chapter 6: Creating a Highly Available Self-Healing Architecture

1. The main Kubernetes components are divided into the control plane and the API objects.
2. The three of them are managed Kubernetes solutions, provided by the three mayor public Cloud providers, Google, Amazon, and Microsoft respectively.
3. Containers have a smaller attack surface, but that doesn't exempt them from exploits, but the mayor container runtime projects are well maintained and if an exploit is detected it is rapidly addressed.
4. That will depend on the type of application you are trying to run and your familiarity with the technology. To migrate an application to containers is generally easy, but to do it in the most efficient way is what requires work.
5. No, you can find the Docker Engine for Windows and, at the time of writing, Kubernetes Windows Nodes are in beta.

Chapter 7: Understanding the Core Components of a Kubernetes Cluster

1. Kubernetes, at the time of writing, is the mayor Container orchestrator in the market.
2. Kubernetes is composed of the binaries that make up the cluster, and the logical objects called API objects.
3. Kubernetes API objects are the logical objects managed by the orchestrator.
4. We can run orchestrated containarized workloads.
5. A container orchestrator is a tool in charge of managing our running containers and different tasks related to keeping our workloads highly available.
6. A Pod is the smallest logical object of Kubernetes that encapsulates one or more containers in shared namespaces.
7. A Deployment is a set of replicated Pods that are managed by the Kubernetes replication controllers.

Chapter 8: Architecting Kubernetes on Azure

1. Due to the majority mechanisms of ETCD odd numbers are preferred in order to be able to reach a majority of votes all the times.
2. Yes, but it can also run in a separate set of notes.
3. Lower latency is recommended because of the heartbeat and leader election frequencies.
4. The worker nodes or Nodes, are the cluster members in charge of running the container workloads.
5. Types of Workloads and the amount of containers that each is going to run.
6. All storage providers or provisionares can be found here: `https://kubernetes.io/docs/concepts/storage/storage-classes/#provisioner`
7. A load balancer is needed to send requests across all our replicated Pods.
8. Namespaces can be used to logically partition our cluster and assign roles and resources to each logical partition.

Chapter 9: Deploying and Configuring Kubernetes

1. There are several ways to install Kubernetes, from auto provisioning tools like `kubeadm` and `kubespray`, to a totally manual installation. You can find more about the installation methods going to the following link: `https://kubernetes.io/docs/setup/`

2. A `kubeconfig` file contains all the necessary information to communicate and authenticate with the API server.

3. You can create SSL certificates with several tools, in this book we used `cffssl`. But you can also use `openssl` and `easyrsa`.

4. **Azure Kubernetes Services** (**AKS**) is the managed Kubernetes solution provided by Microsoft for their public cloud Azure.

5. Azure CLI can be used in either operating system as it is a Python-based command line interface.

6. You can either create a resource group via Azure CLI, PowerShell, or the Azure GUI.

7. You can find the different ways of installing etcd in the following link: `http://play.etcd.io/install`

Chapter 10: Monitoring with ELK stack

1. The process of actively gathering data.

2. By knowing usage trends, decisions such as buying more resources can be made with actual data.

3. By having data in a single place, events can be proactively detected before they can occur.

4. By knowing what is the normal behavior of a storage system, hence providing a baseline for performance.

5. When spikes are seen where they're not supposed to be, this can mean erratic behavior.

6. Instead of going through each of the hosts in an environment, they can be checked through a single centralized location.

7. A software for data indexing and analysis.

8. Elasticsearch stores data in json format.

9. Logstash is a data processing parser that allows for data to be manipulated before being sent to Elasticsearch.

10. Kibana provides the visualisation interface for Elasticsearch, allowing for data to be easily visualized.

Chapter 11: Designing an ELK Stack

1. At least 2 CPU cores are needed for optimal functionality on smaller deployments.
2. At least 2Ghz.
3. Slower or less than 2 CPUs impact mostly Elasticsearch startup time, indexing rate and latency.
4. The kernel uses available RAM for caching requests to the filesystem.
5. If swapping occurs, search latency will be greatly impacted.
6. Elasticsearch will fail to start if there's not enough memory, once running if there's not sufficient memory OOM will kill Elasticsearch.
7. The minimum is 2.5GB but 4GB is recommended.
8. `/var/lib/elasticsearch`
9. Lower latency helps with the indexing/ search latency.
10. 2GB RAM and 1 CPU.
11. This is a storage location where logstash will persistently store queues in the scenario of a crash.
12. How many users will access concurrently the dashboard.

Chapter 12: Using Elasticsearch, Logstash, and Kibana to Manage Logs

1. Elasticsearch can be installed through the package manager.
2. This is done through parted.
3. Adding the UUID of the disks to `/etc/fstab`.
4. `/etc/elasticsearch/elasticsearch.yml`
5. This gives the name to the cluster, the name should be consistent across nodes so each join the same cluster.

6. The number is dictated by `(N/2)+1`.

7. By using the same cluster.name setting, the second node will join to the same cluster.

8. Add the repo, install through `yum`, partition the disk for logstash.

9. This is a storage location where logstash will persistently store queues in the scenario of a crash.

10. A coordinating node is an Elasticsearch node that does not accept inputs, does not store data or takes part in master/slave elections.

11. Beats are the lightweight data shippers from Elastic.co.

12. Filebeat function is to collect logs from sources like `syslog`, apache and others to later ship it to Elasticsearch or Logstash.

Chapter 13: Solving Management Problems with Salty Solutions

1. Is the task of maintaining existing IT infrastructure.

2. Centralize all infrastructure regardless of its operating system or architecture.

3. Puppet, Chef, Ansible, Spacewalk, SaltStack and many others.

4. Writing desired states on a specific language that can describe the state of an IT infrastructure.

5. Push and Pull.

6. Salt is an open source project/software that comes to solve many of the challenges of systems' management.

7. Master and Minions.

Chapter 14: Designing a Salt Solution and Installing the Software

1. Any Linux distribution.

2. One self-managed node is the minimum.

3. Provide High availability and Balancing to our SaltStack.

4. Manually installing the binaries, and through the bootstrap script.

5. Via their keys.
6. Through the `test.ping` function.
7. Grains contain minion specific information (metadata) or labels. Pillars contain configuration and sensitive information.

Chapter 15: Design Best Practices

1. HIPAA stands for Health Insurance Portability and Accountability Act which is a standard for handling health and medical data.
2. Type 1/ Type 2 Hypervisors (**Kernel-based Virtual Machine (KVM)**, **Linux containers (LXC)**, XEN)
   Linux for SAP HANA
   Apache Hadoop
   Linux for Oracle DB
   Large MongoDB deployments for memory caching
   High-performance computing (HPC)
3. Yes, ideally hypervisors need access to the resources to more effectively provide them to virtual machines.
4. Yes, CPU is the major resource being shared as the physical CPU has to serve cycles for all of the VMs in the same node.
5. Allowing for different network traffic to go through different NICs/ Subnets.
6. This is a method of migration which literally moves existing workloads from on-premises to the cloud.
7. This is a method of migration which leverages some changes to the architecture to take advantage of solutions provided on the cloud.
8. This is a method of migration which involves re-architecting the solution into the cloud.

Other Books You May Enjoy

If you enjoyed this book, you may be interested in these other books by Packt:

Hands-On Linux Administration on Azure
Frederik Vos

ISBN: 9781789130966

- Understand why Azure is the ideal solution for your open source workloads
- Master essential Linux skills and learn to find your way around the Linux environment
- Deploy Linux in an Azure environment
- Use configuration management to manage Linux in Azure
- Manage containers in an Azure environment
- Enhance Linux security and use Azure's identity management systems
- Automate deployment with Azure Resource Manager (ARM) and Powershell
- Employ Ansible to manage Linux instances in an Azure cloud environment

Linux Administration Cookbook
Adam K. Dean

ISBN: 9781789342529

- Install and manage a Linux server, both locally and in the cloud
- Understand how to perform administration across all Linux distros
- Work through evolving concepts such as IaaS versus PaaS, containers, and automation
- Explore security and configuration best practices
- Troubleshoot your system if something goes wrong
- Discover and mitigate hardware issues, such as faulty memory and failing drives

Leave a review - let other readers know what you think

Please share your thoughts on this book with others by leaving a review on the site that you bought it from. If you purchased the book from Amazon, please leave us an honest review on this book's Amazon page. This is vital so that other potential readers can see and use your unbiased opinion to make purchasing decisions, we can understand what our customers think about our products, and our authors can see your feedback on the title that they have worked with Packt to create. It will only take a few minutes of your time, but is valuable to other potential customers, our authors, and Packt. Thank you!

Index

www.ingramcontent.com/pod-product-compliance
Lightning Source LLC
Chambersburg PA
CBHW080612060326
40690CB00021B/4664